W9-BKI-190

DOCTOR STRANGE

The Choice

WRITER
Mark Waid

ARTISTS
Jesús Saiz (#18-19)
& Javier Pina (#20)

COLOR ARTISTS
Jesús Saiz (#18-19)
& Brian Reber (#20)

COVER ART
Jesús Saiz

Doctor Strange Annual #1

"A Hallowed Evening"

WRITER
Tini Howard

ARTIST
Andy MacDonald

COLOR ARTIST
Triona Farrell

"Treat"

WRITER
Pornsak Pichetshote

PENCILER
Lalit Kumar Sharma

INKER
Sean Parsons

COLOR ARTIST
José Villarrubia

COVER ART
Ariel Olivetti

LETTERER
VC's Cory Petit

ASSISTANT EDITORS
**Danny Khazem
& Lauren Amaro**

EDITORS
**Nick Lowe &
Darren Shan**

18

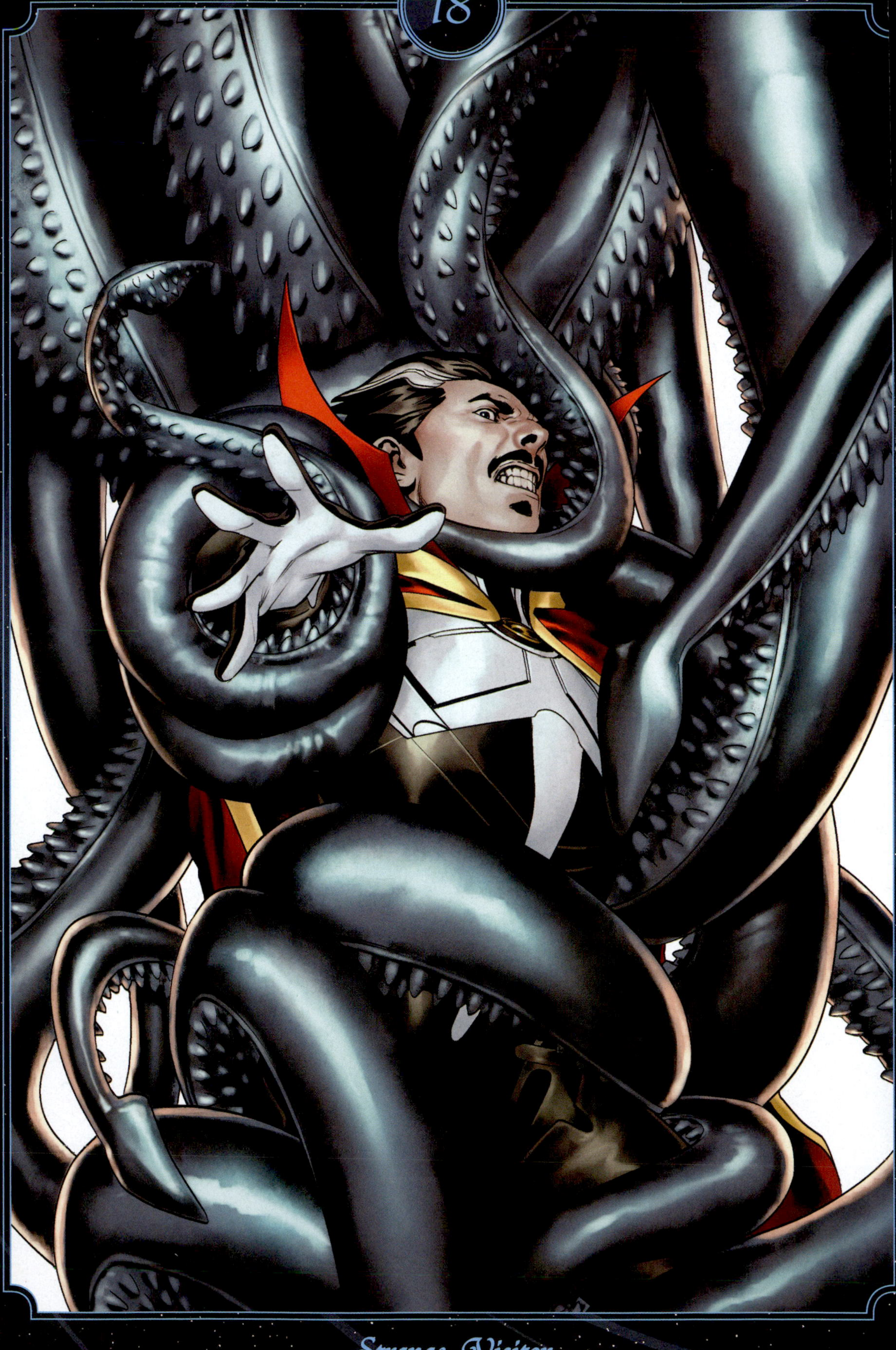

Strange, Visitor

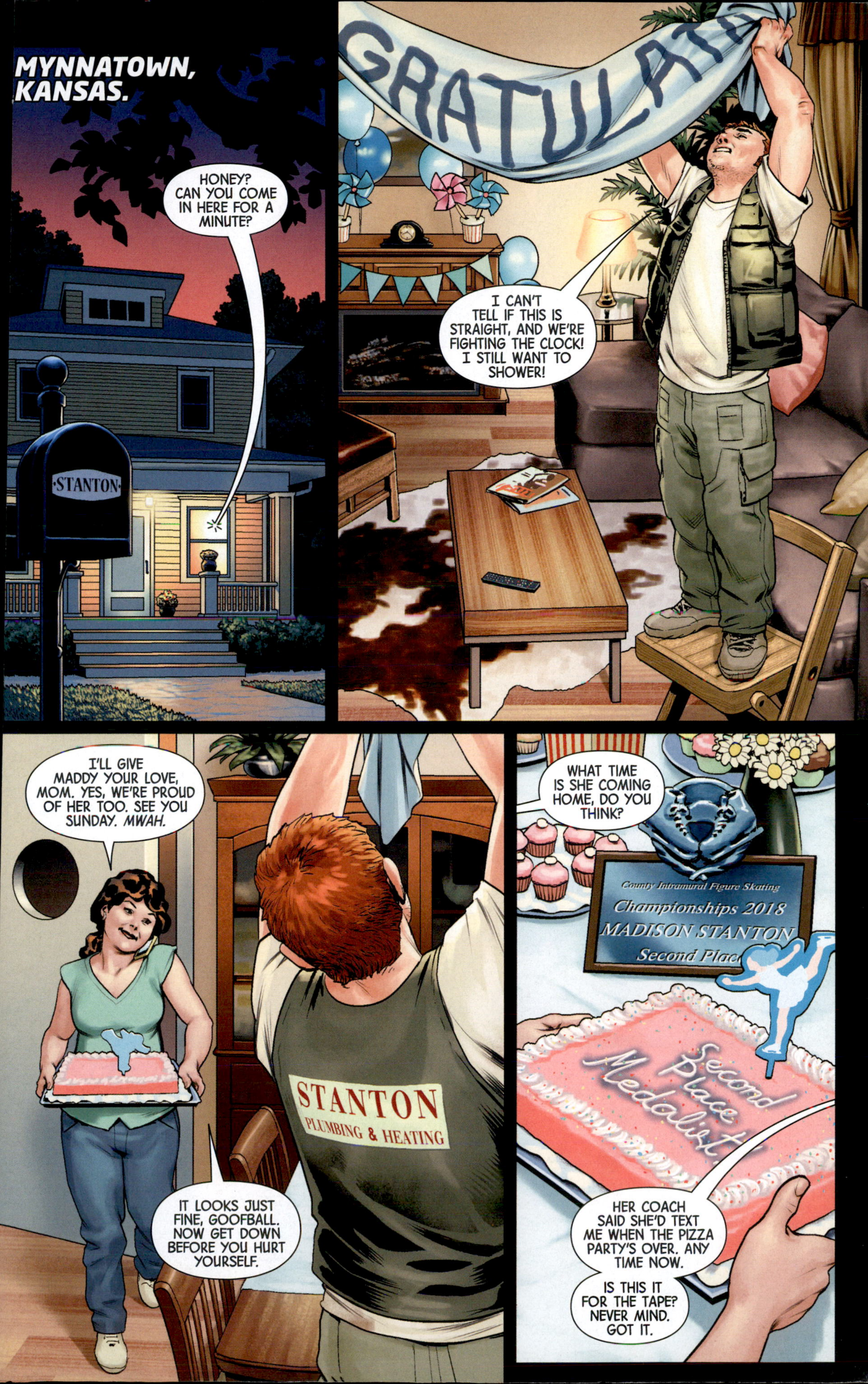
MYNNATOWN, KANSAS.
HONEY? CAN YOU COME IN HERE FOR A MINUTE?
STANTON
GRATULAT
I CAN'T TELL IF THIS IS STRAIGHT, AND WE'RE FIGHTING THE CLOCK! I STILL WANT TO SHOWER!
I'LL GIVE MADDY YOUR LOVE, MOM. YES, WE'RE PROUD OF HER TOO. SEE YOU SUNDAY. *MWAH.*
STANTON PLUMBING & HEATING
IT LOOKS JUST FINE, GOOFBALL. NOW GET DOWN BEFORE YOU HURT YOURSELF.
WHAT TIME IS SHE COMING HOME, DO YOU THINK?
County Intramural Figure Skating
Championships 2018
MADISON STANTON
Second Plac
Second Place Medalist
HER COACH SAID SHE'D TEXT ME WHEN THE PIZZA PARTY'S OVER. ANY TIME NOW.
IS THIS IT FOR THE TAPE? NEVER MIND. GOT IT.

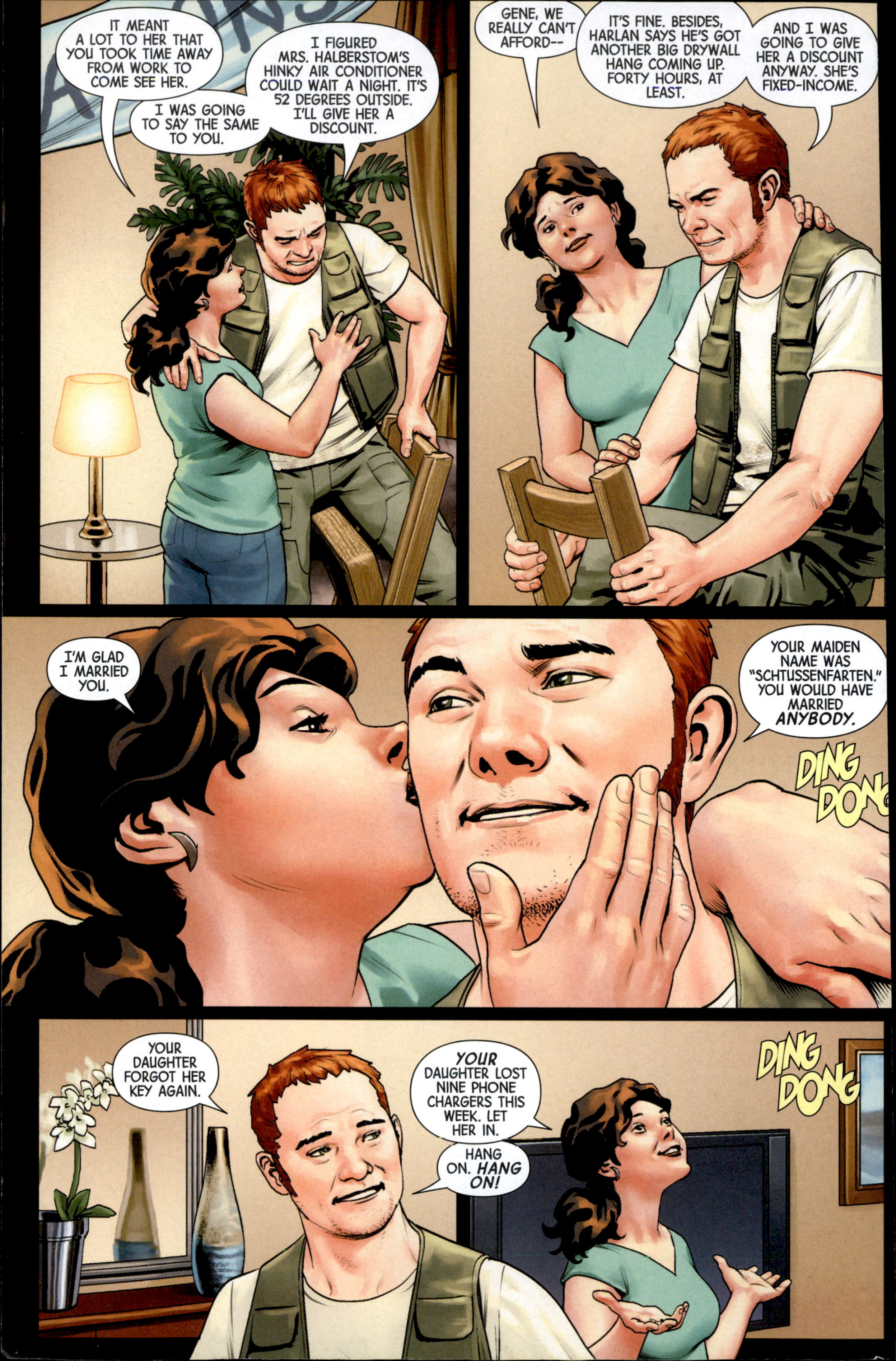
IT MEANT A LOT TO HER THAT YOU TOOK TIME AWAY FROM WORK TO COME SEE HER.
I WAS GOING TO SAY THE SAME TO YOU.
I FIGURED MRS. HALBERSTOM'S HINKY AIR CONDITIONER COULD WAIT A NIGHT. IT'S 52 DEGREES OUTSIDE. I'LL GIVE HER A DISCOUNT.
GENE, WE REALLY CAN'T AFFORD--
IT'S FINE. BESIDES, HARLAN SAYS HE'S GOT ANOTHER BIG DRYWALL HANG COMING UP. FORTY HOURS, AT LEAST.
AND I WAS GOING TO GIVE HER A DISCOUNT ANYWAY. SHE'S FIXED-INCOME.
I'M GLAD I MARRIED YOU.
YOUR MAIDEN NAME WAS "SCHTUSSENFARTEN." YOU WOULD HAVE MARRIED ANYBODY.
DING DONG
YOUR DAUGHTER FORGOT HER KEY AGAIN.
YOUR DAUGHTER LOST NINE PHONE CHARGERS THIS WEEK. LET HER IN.
HANG ON. HANG ON!
DING DONG

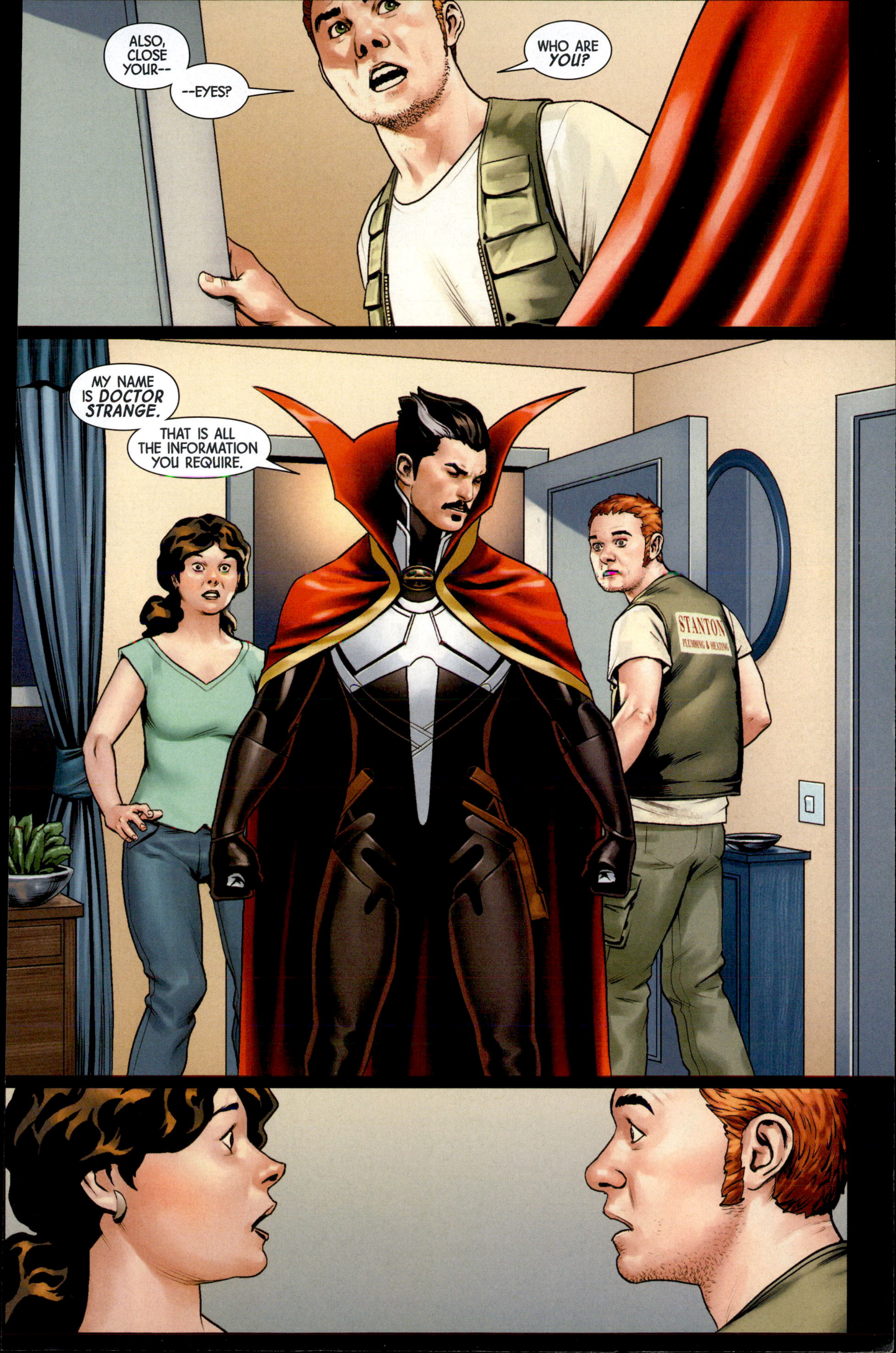
ALSO, CLOSE YOUR--
--EYES?
WHO ARE YOU?
MY NAME IS DOCTOR STRANGE.
THAT IS ALL THE INFORMATION YOU REQUIRE.
STANTON PLUMBING & HEATING

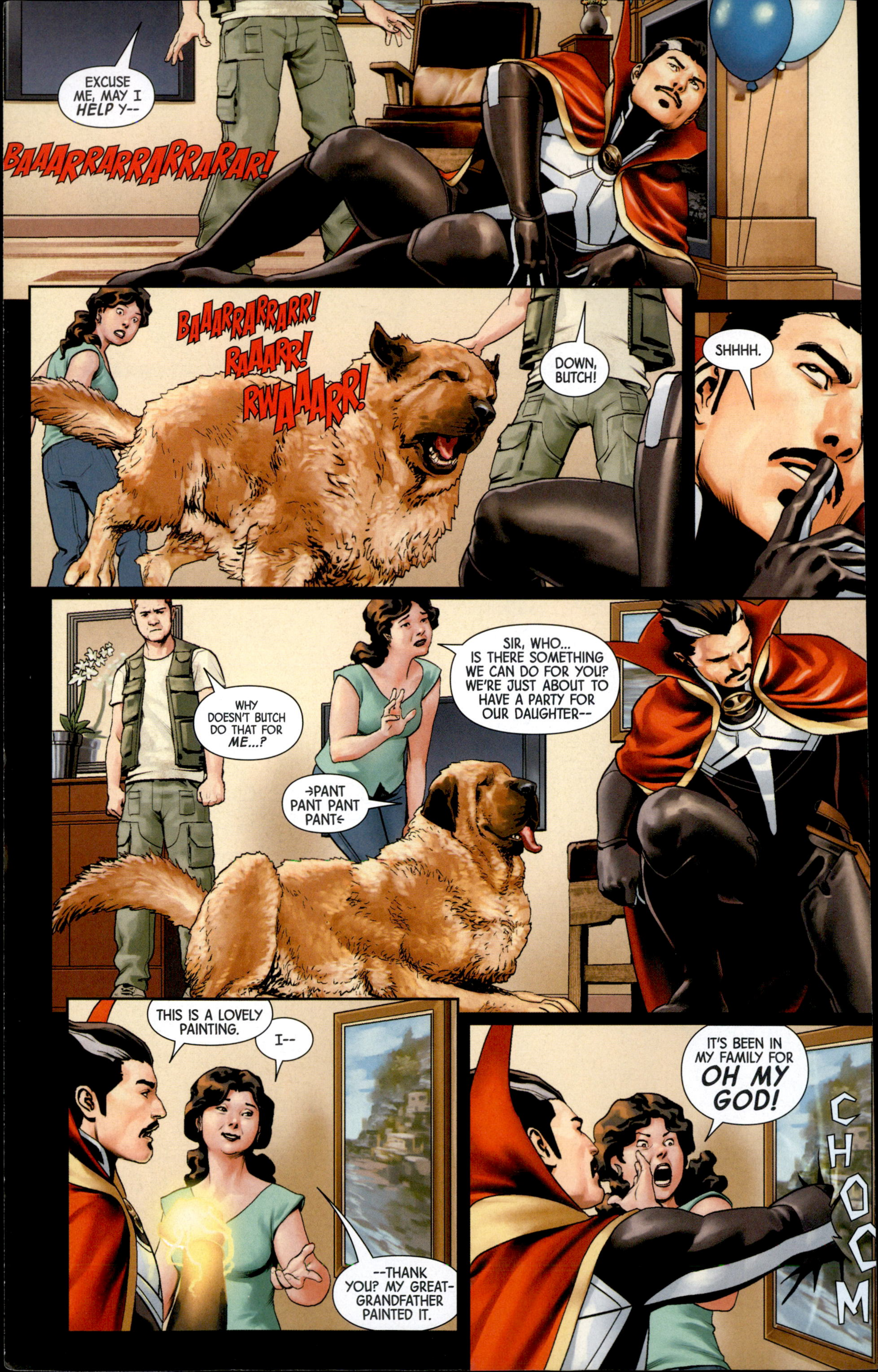
EXCUSE ME, MAY I *HELP* Y--
BAAARRARRARRARAR!
BAAARRARRARR! RAAARR! RWAAARR!
DOWN, BUTCH!
SHHHH.
WHY DOESN'T BUTCH DO THAT FOR *ME...?*
SIR, WHO... IS THERE SOMETHING WE CAN DO FOR YOU? WE'RE JUST ABOUT TO HAVE A PARTY FOR OUR DAUGHTER--
PANT PANT PANT PANT
THIS IS A LOVELY PAINTING.
I--
--THANK YOU? MY GREAT-GRANDFATHER PAINTED IT.
IT'S BEEN IN MY FAMILY FOR **OH MY GOD!**
CHOOM

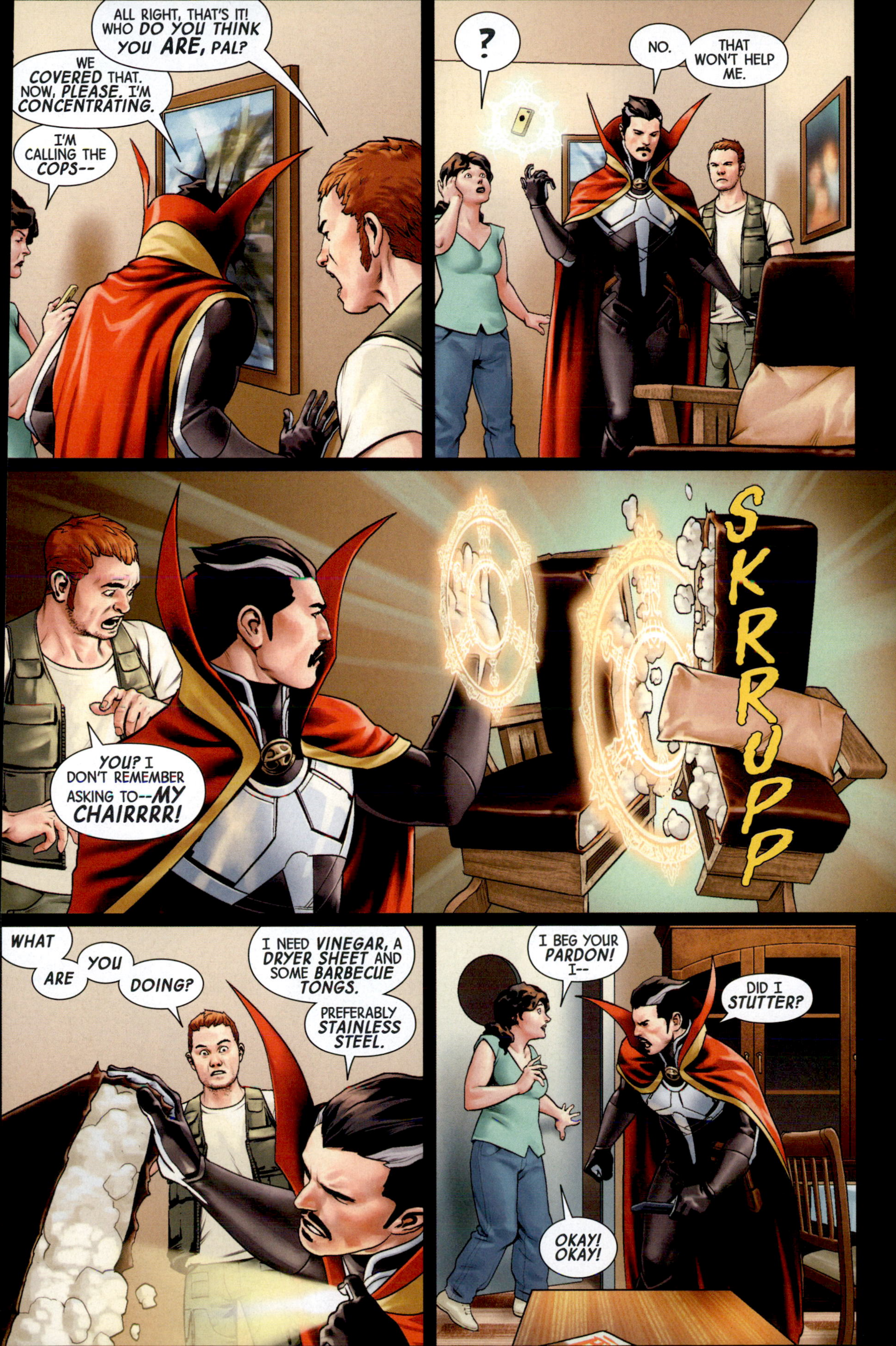
ALL RIGHT, THAT'S IT! WHO DO YOU THINK YOU ARE, PAL?
WE COVERED THAT. NOW, PLEASE. I'M CONCENTRATING.
I'M CALLING THE COPS--
?
NO.
THAT WON'T HELP ME.
YOU? I DON'T REMEMBER ASKING TO--MY CHAIRRRR!
SKRRUPP
WHAT ARE YOU DOING?
I NEED VINEGAR, A DRYER SHEET AND SOME BARBECUE TONGS.
PREFERABLY STAINLESS STEEL.
I BEG YOUR PARDON! I--
DID I STUTTER?
OKAY! OKAY!

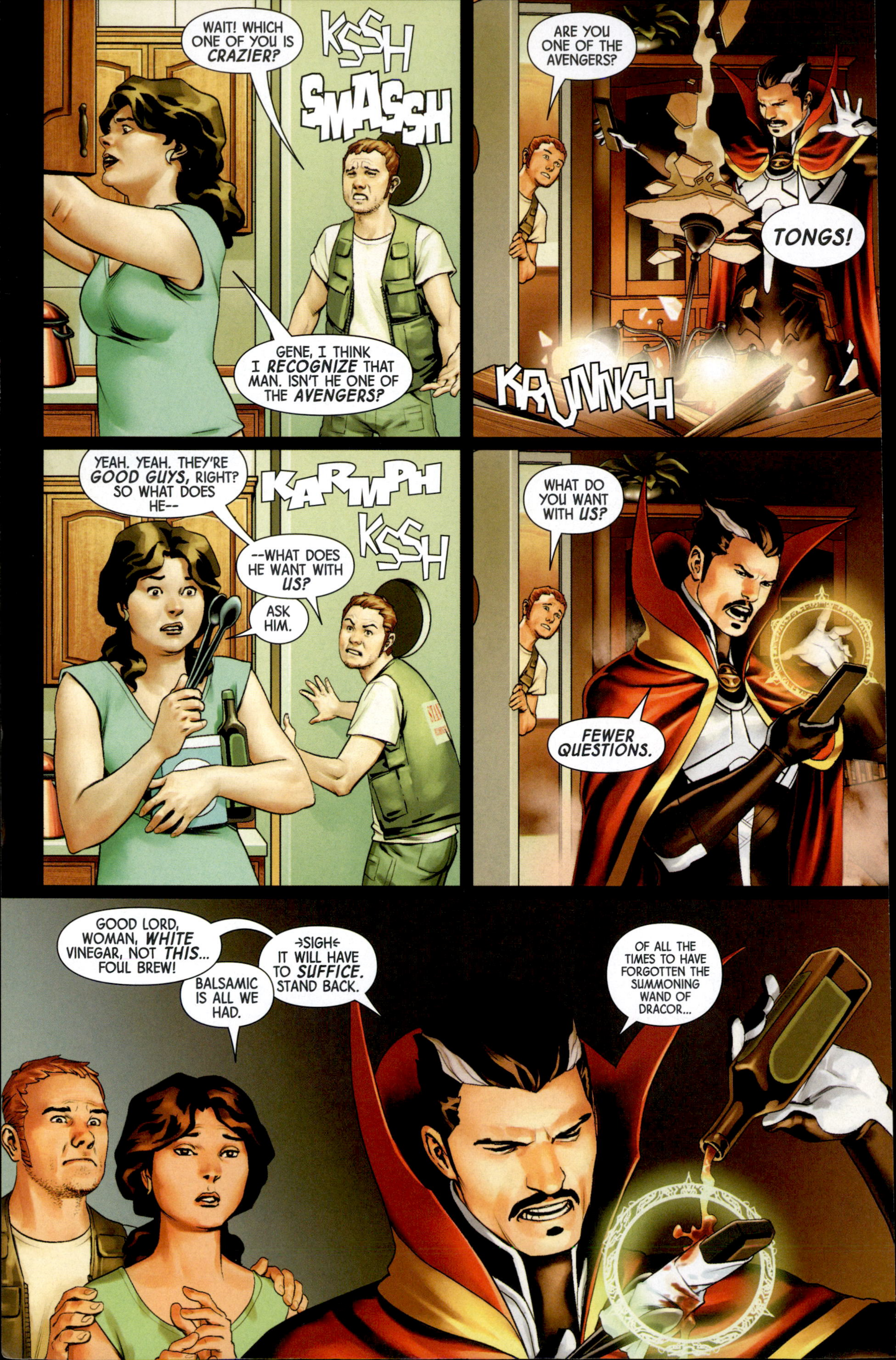
WAIT! WHICH ONE OF YOU IS CRAZIER?
KSSH
SMASSH
GENE, I THINK I RECOGNIZE THAT MAN. ISN'T HE ONE OF THE AVENGERS?
ARE YOU ONE OF THE AVENGERS?
TONGS!
KRUNNCH
YEAH. YEAH. THEY'RE GOOD GUYS, RIGHT? SO WHAT DOES HE--
KARMPH
KSSH
--WHAT DOES HE WANT WITH US?
ASK HIM.
WHAT DO YOU WANT WITH US?
FEWER QUESTIONS.
GOOD LORD, WOMAN, WHITE VINEGAR, NOT THIS... FOUL BREW!
BALSAMIC IS ALL WE HAD.
→SIGH← IT WILL HAVE TO SUFFICE. STAND BACK.
OF ALL THE TIMES TO HAVE FORGOTTEN THE SUMMONING WAND OF DRACOR...

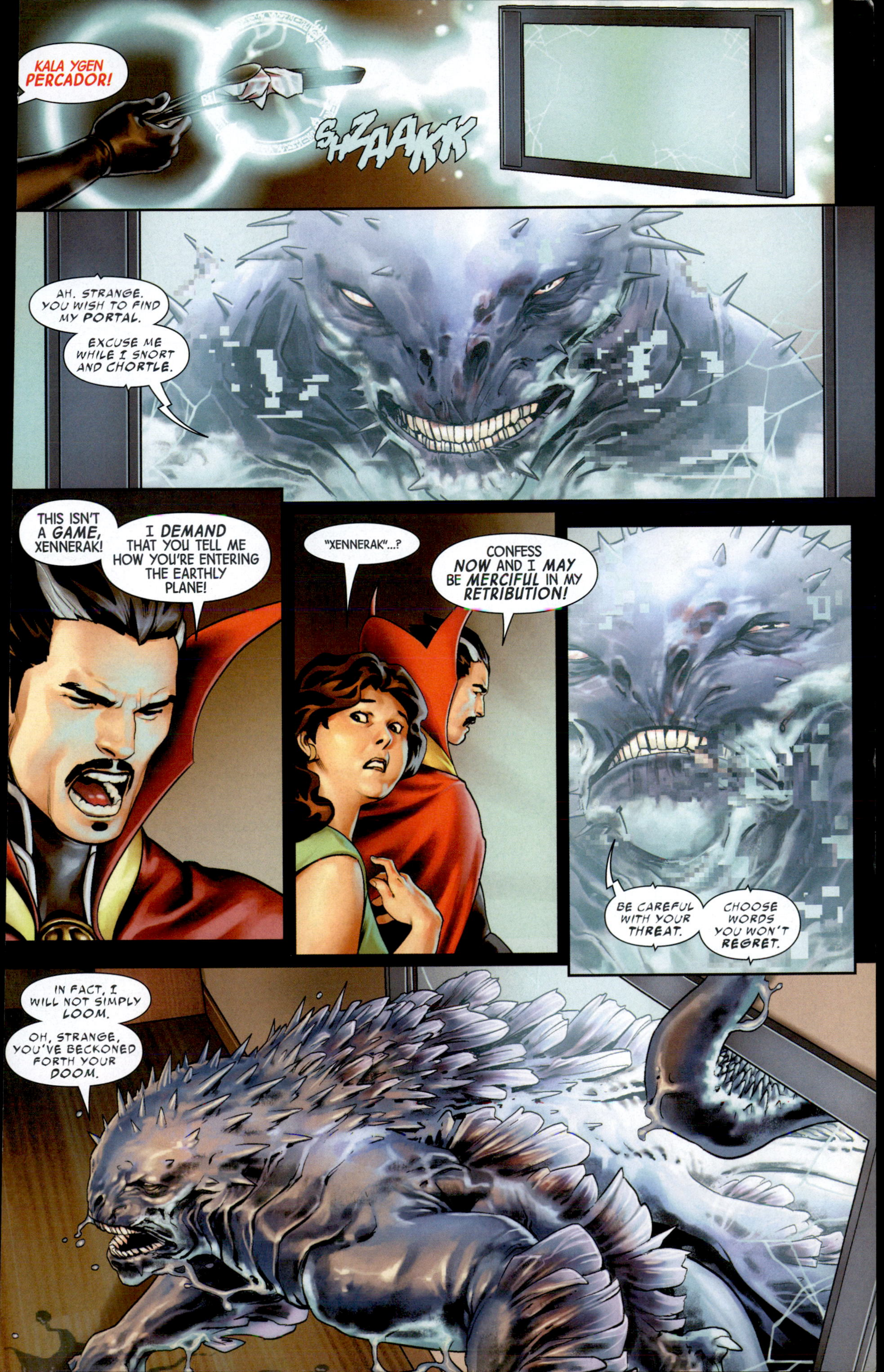
KALA YGEN PERCADOR!
SHZAAKK
AH. STRANGE. YOU WISH TO FIND MY PORTAL.
EXCUSE ME WHILE I SNORT AND CHORTLE.
THIS ISN'T A GAME, XENNERAK!
I DEMAND THAT YOU TELL ME HOW YOU'RE ENTERING THE EARTHLY PLANE!
"XENNERAK"...?
CONFESS NOW AND I MAY BE MERCIFUL IN MY RETRIBUTION!
BE CAREFUL WITH YOUR THREAT.
CHOOSE WORDS YOU WON'T REGRET.
IN FACT, I WILL NOT SIMPLY LOOM.
OH, STRANGE, YOU'VE BECKONED FORTH YOUR DOOM.

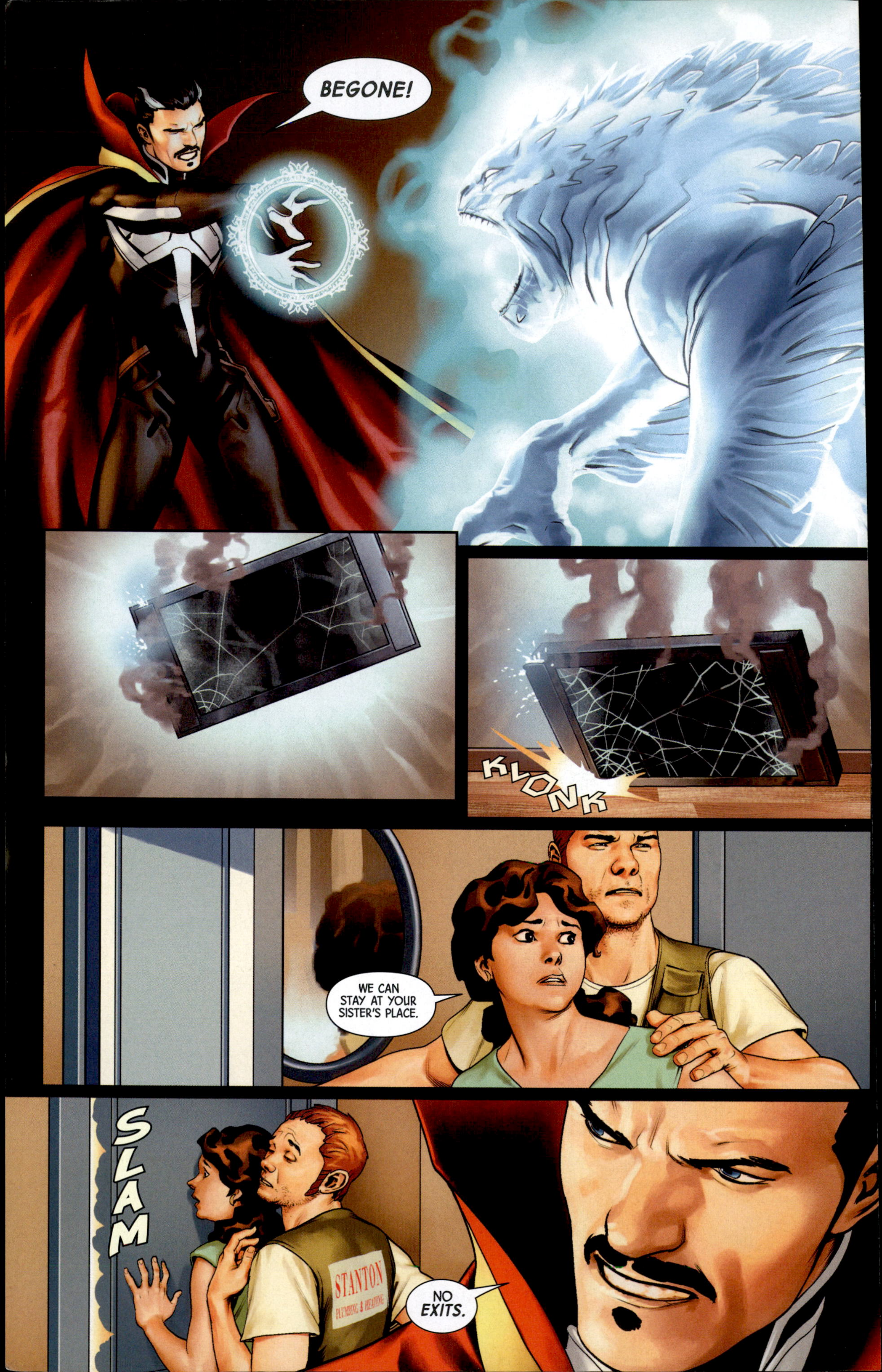
BEGONE!
KVONK
WE CAN STAY AT YOUR SISTER'S PLACE.
SLAM
STANTON PLUMBING & HEATING
NO EXITS.

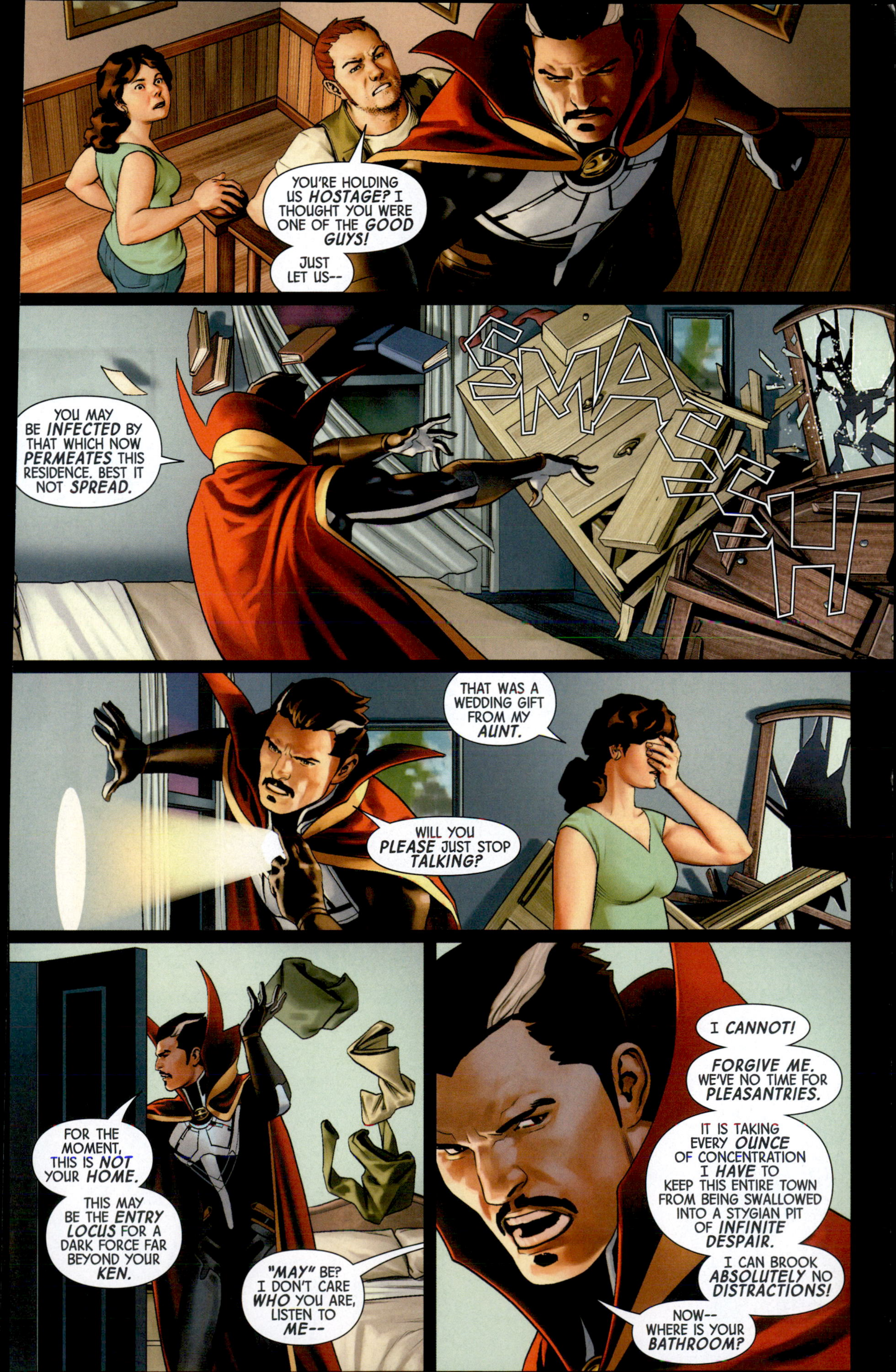

YOU'RE HOLDING US *HOSTAGE?* I THOUGHT YOU WERE ONE OF THE *GOOD GUYS!*
JUST LET US--
YOU MAY BE *INFECTED* BY THAT WHICH NOW *PERMEATES* THIS RESIDENCE. BEST IT NOT *SPREAD.*
SMASH
THAT WAS A WEDDING GIFT FROM MY *AUNT.*
WILL YOU *PLEASE* JUST STOP *TALKING?*
FOR THE MOMENT, THIS IS *NOT* YOUR *HOME.*
THIS MAY BE THE *ENTRY LOCUS* FOR A DARK FORCE FAR BEYOND YOUR *KEN.*
"MAY" BE? I DON'T CARE *WHO* YOU ARE, LISTEN TO *ME--*
I *CANNOT!*
FORGIVE ME. WE'VE NO TIME FOR *PLEASANTRIES.*
IT IS TAKING EVERY *OUNCE* OF CONCENTRATION *I HAVE* TO KEEP THIS ENTIRE TOWN FROM BEING SWALLOWED INTO A STYGIAN PIT OF *INFINITE DESPAIR.*
I CAN BROOK *ABSOLUTELY* NO *DISTRACTIONS!*
NOW-- WHERE IS YOUR *BATHROOM?*

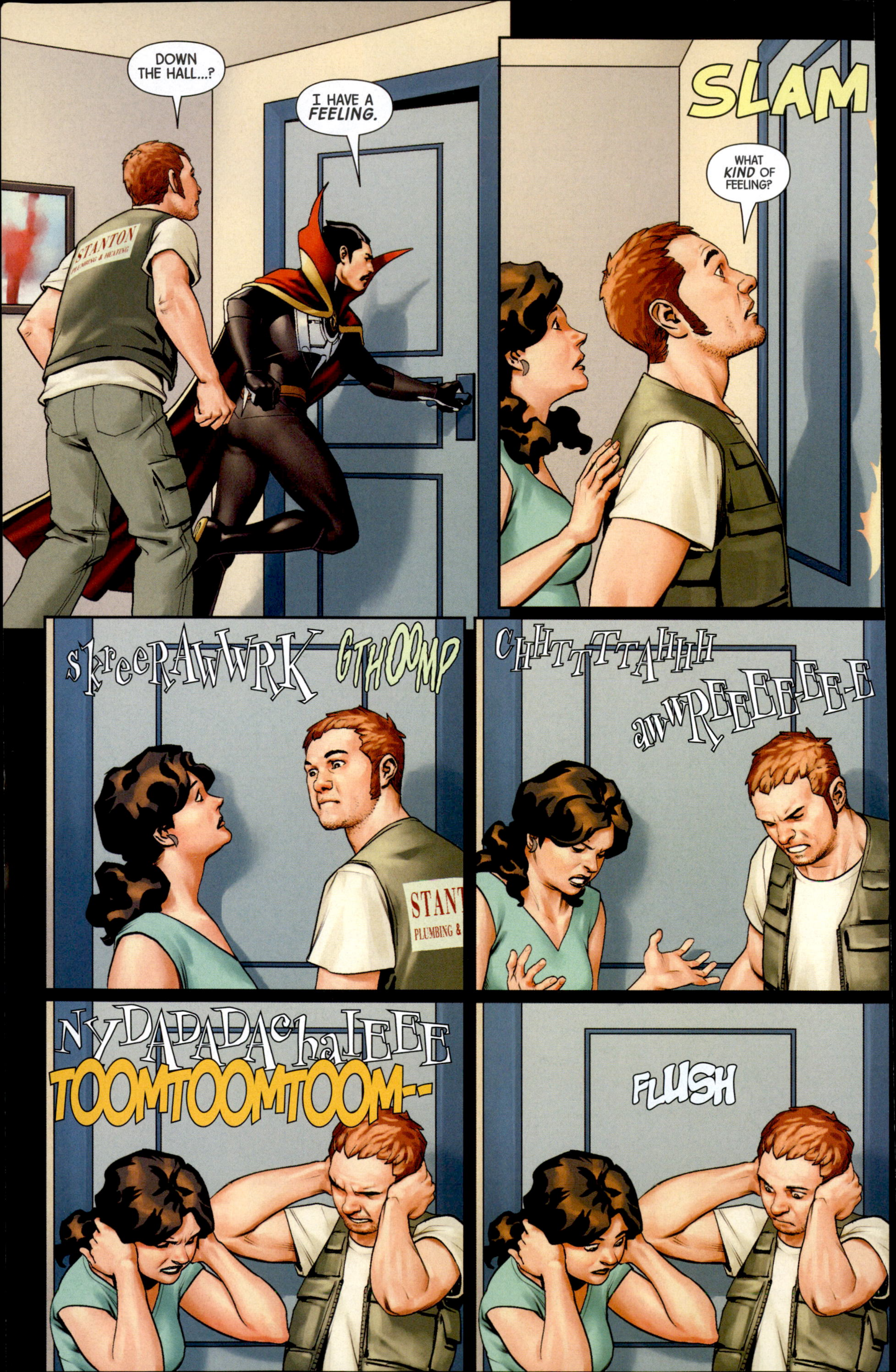
DOWN THE HALL...?
I HAVE A FEELING.
STANTON PLUMBING & HEATING
SLAM
WHAT KIND OF FEELING?
SKREERAWWRK
GTHOOMP
STANT PLUMBING &
CHHTTTTTAHHH
AWWREEEEE-EE-E
NYDADADACHAIEEE
TOOMTOOMTOOM--
FLUSH

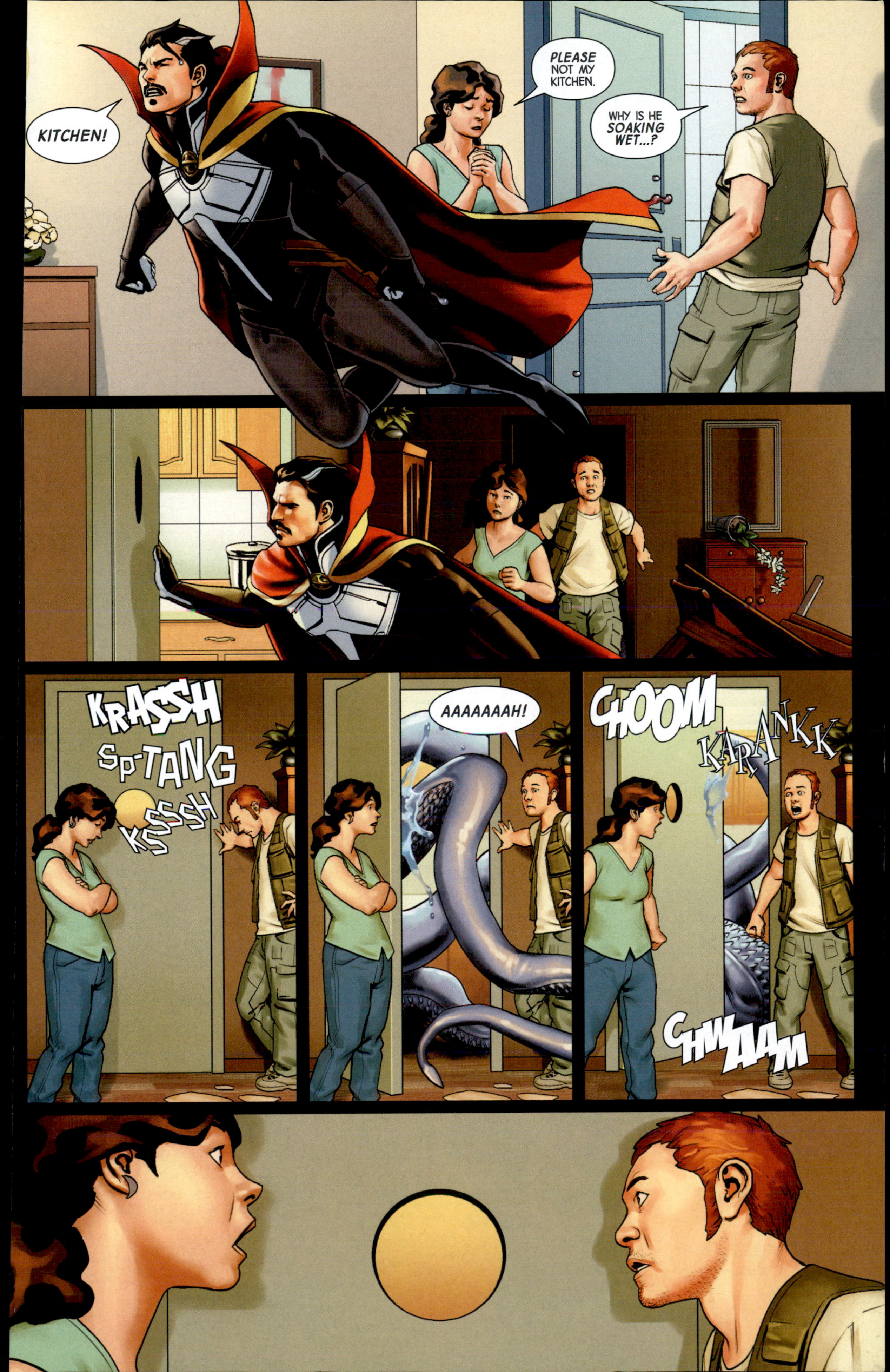
KITCHEN!
PLEASE NOT MY KITCHEN.
WHY IS HE SOAKING WET...?
KRASSH
SP-TANG
KSSSSH
AAAAAAAH!
CHOOM
KARANKK
CHWAAM

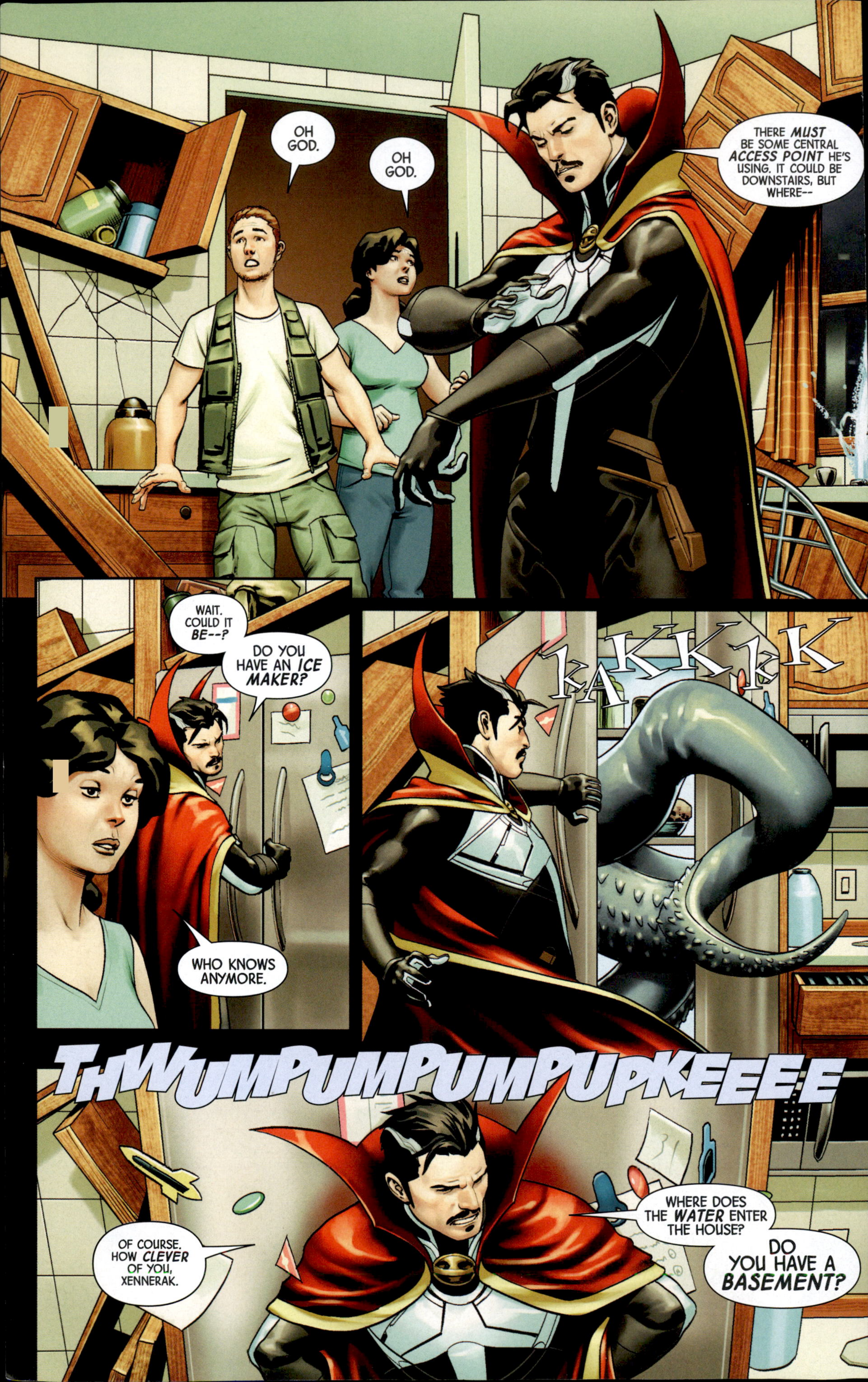
OH GOD.
OH GOD.
THERE MUST BE SOME CENTRAL ACCESS POINT HE'S USING. IT COULD BE DOWNSTAIRS, BUT WHERE--
WAIT. COULD IT BE--?
DO YOU HAVE AN ICE MAKER?
WHO KNOWS ANYMORE.
KAKKKKK
THWUMPUMPUMPUPKEEEEE
OF COURSE. HOW CLEVER OF YOU, XENNERAK.
WHERE DOES THE WATER ENTER THE HOUSE?
DO YOU HAVE A BASEMENT?

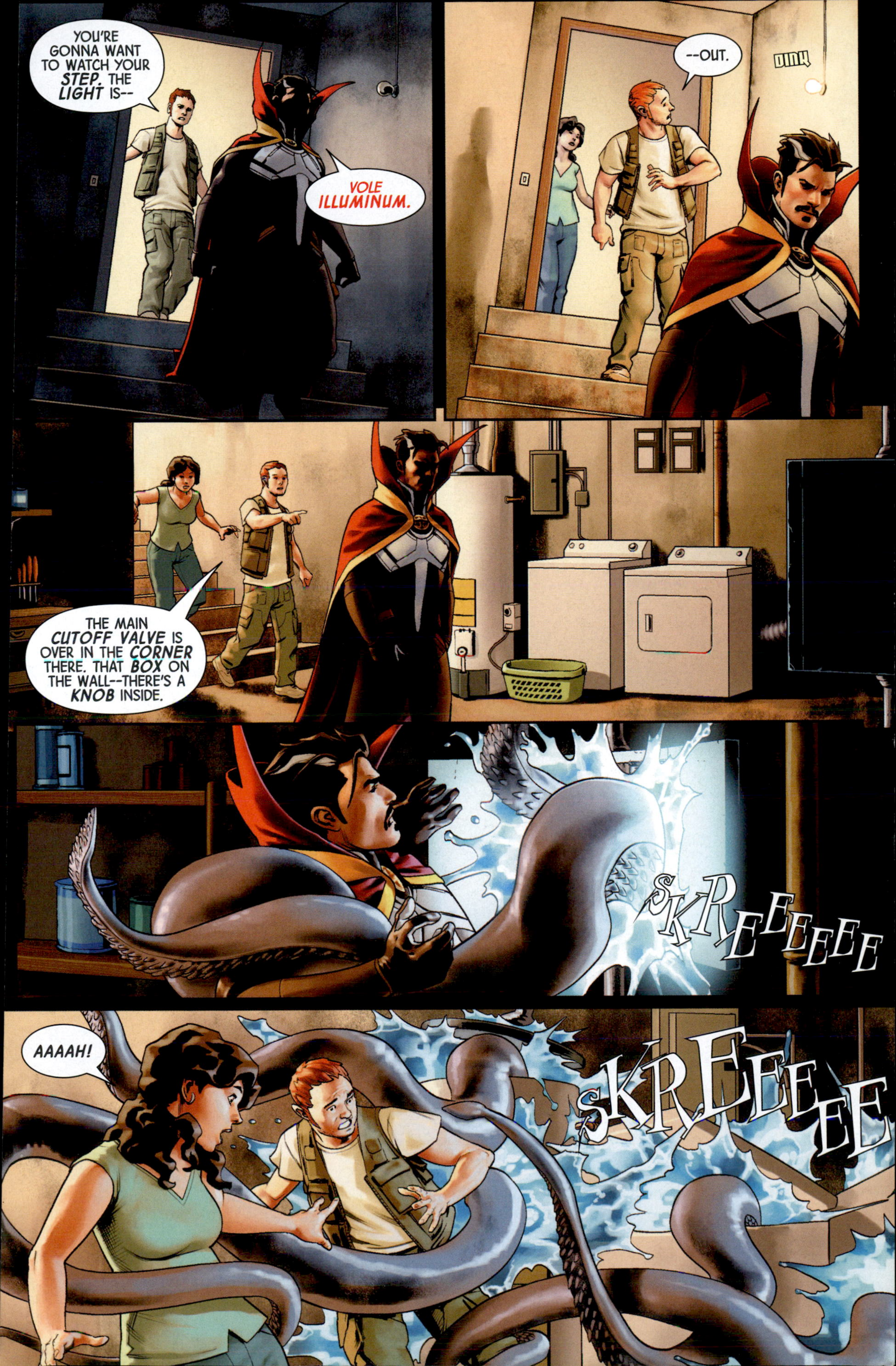
YOU'RE GONNA WANT TO WATCH YOUR STEP. THE LIGHT IS--
VOLE ILLUMINUM.
--OUT.
DINK
THE MAIN CUTOFF VALVE IS OVER IN THE CORNER THERE. THAT BOX ON THE WALL--THERE'S A KNOB INSIDE.
SKREEEEEEE
AAAAH!
SKREEEEEE

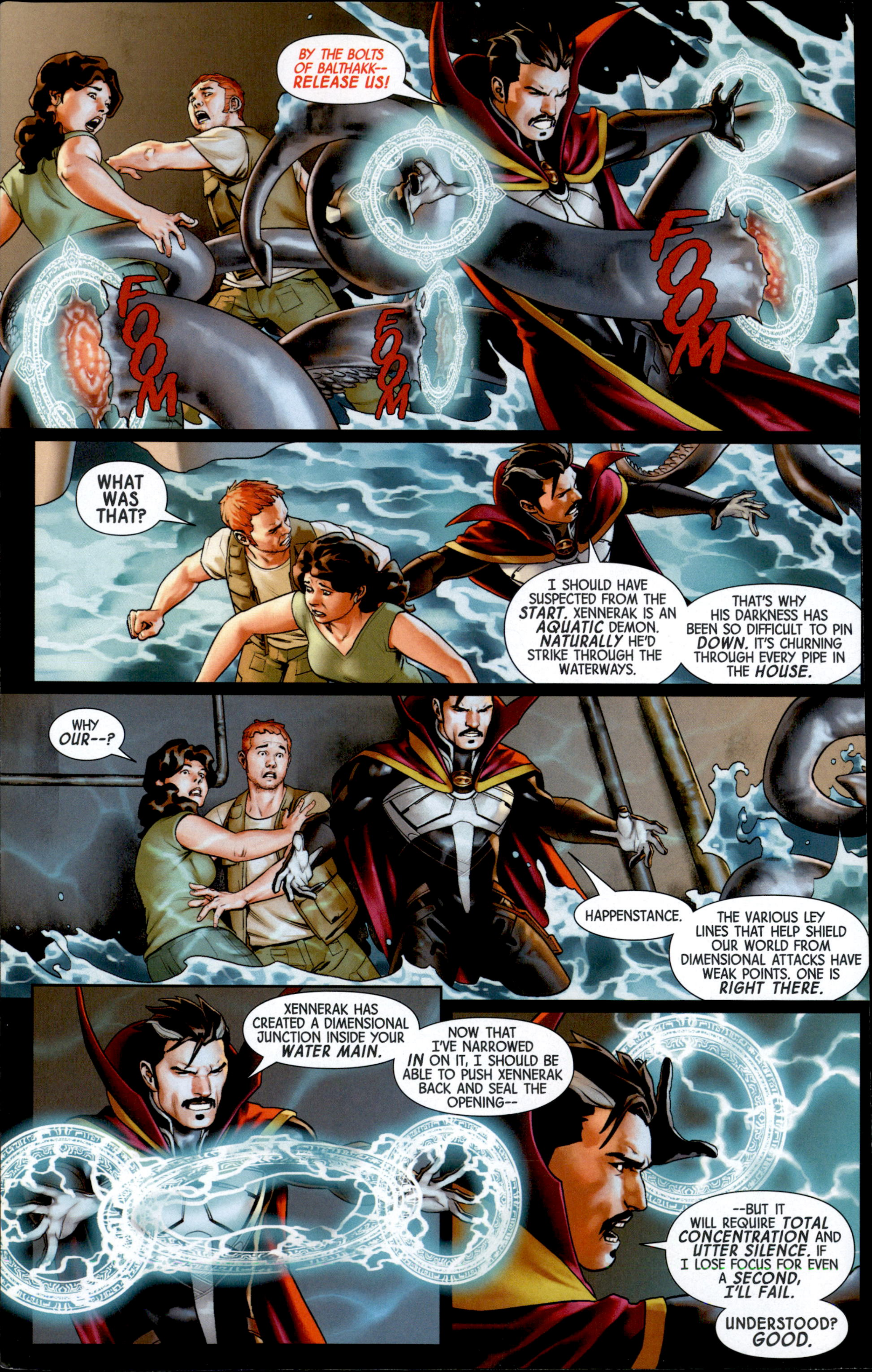
BY THE BOLTS OF BALTHAKK-- RELEASE US!
FOOM
FOOM
FOOM
WHAT WAS THAT?
I SHOULD HAVE SUSPECTED FROM THE START. XENNERAK IS AN AQUATIC DEMON. NATURALLY HE'D STRIKE THROUGH THE WATERWAYS.
THAT'S WHY HIS DARKNESS HAS BEEN SO DIFFICULT TO PIN DOWN. IT'S CHURNING THROUGH EVERY PIPE IN THE HOUSE.
WHY OUR--?
HAPPENSTANCE.
THE VARIOUS LEY LINES THAT HELP SHIELD OUR WORLD FROM DIMENSIONAL ATTACKS HAVE WEAK POINTS. ONE IS RIGHT THERE.
XENNERAK HAS CREATED A DIMENSIONAL JUNCTION INSIDE YOUR WATER MAIN.
NOW THAT I'VE NARROWED IN ON IT, I SHOULD BE ABLE TO PUSH XENNERAK BACK AND SEAL THE OPENING--
--BUT IT WILL REQUIRE TOTAL CONCENTRATION AND UTTER SILENCE. IF I LOSE FOCUS FOR EVEN A SECOND, I'LL FAIL.
UNDERSTOOD? GOOD.

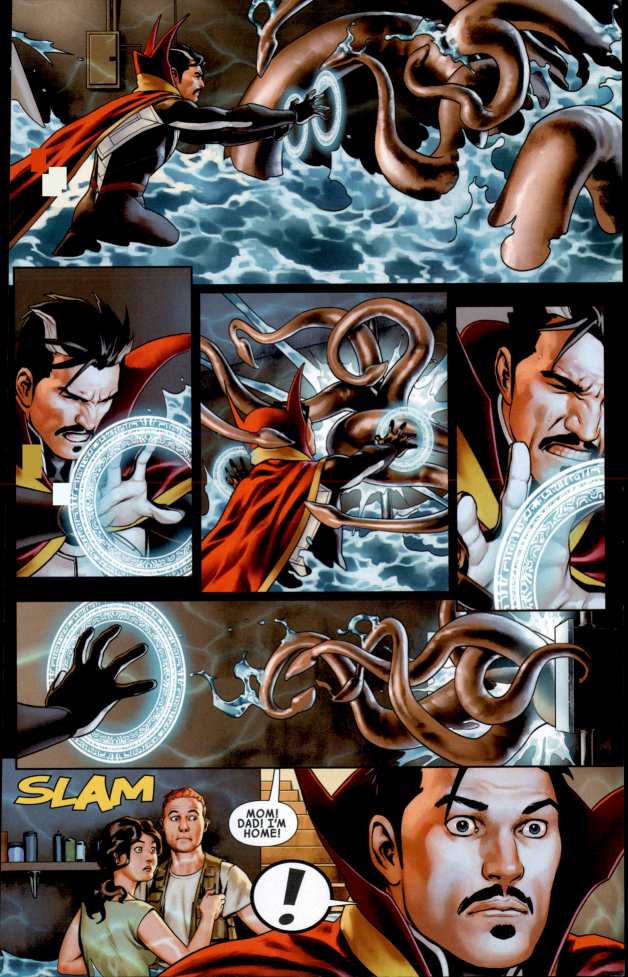

SLAM

MOM! DAD! I'M HOME!

!

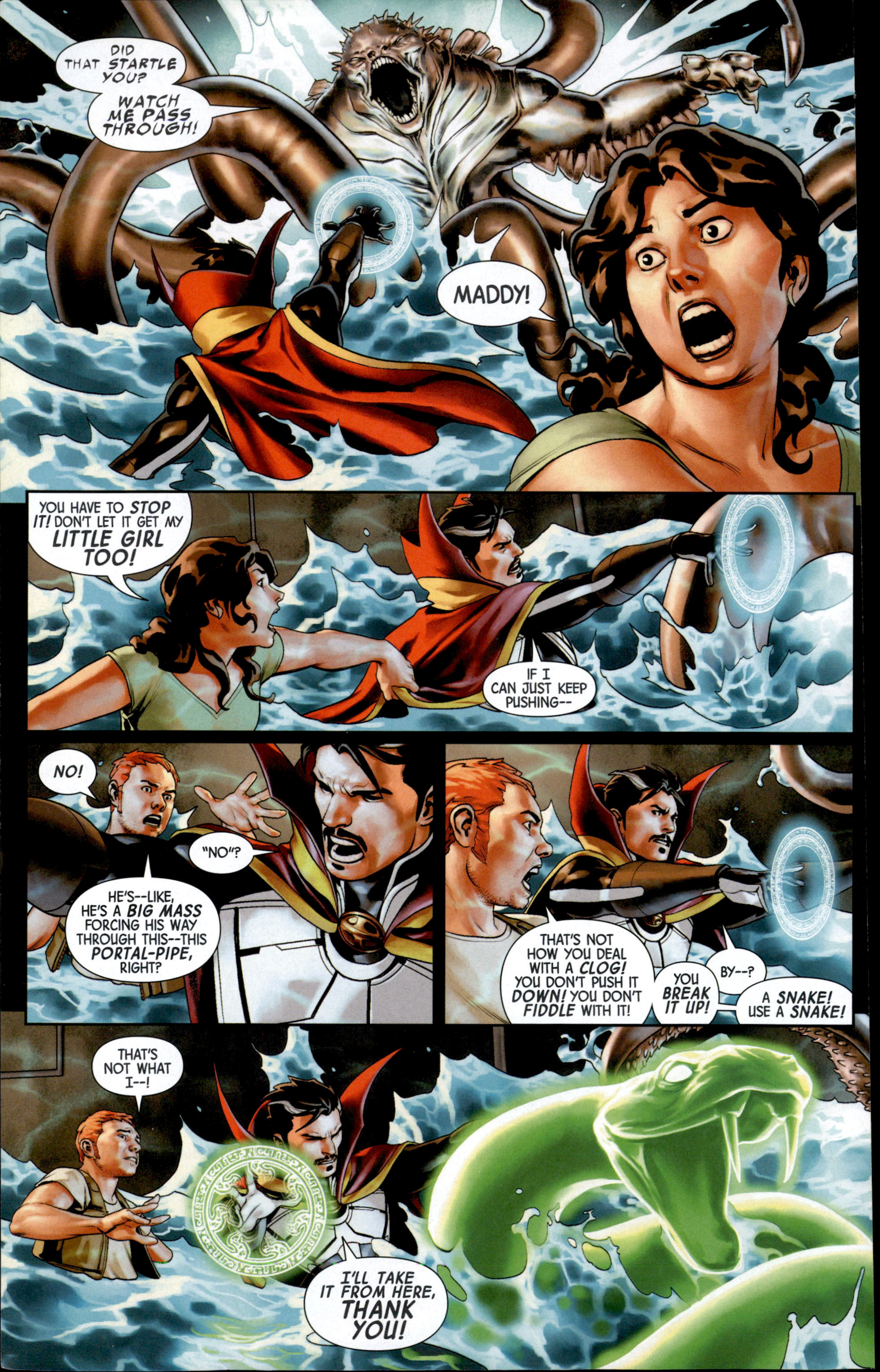
DID THAT STARTLE YOU?
WATCH ME PASS THROUGH!
MADDY!
YOU HAVE TO STOP IT! DON'T LET IT GET MY LITTLE GIRL TOO!
IF I CAN JUST KEEP PUSHING--
NO!
"NO"?
HE'S--LIKE, HE'S A BIG MASS FORCING HIS WAY THROUGH THIS--THIS PORTAL-PIPE, RIGHT?
THAT'S NOT HOW YOU DEAL WITH A CLOG! YOU DON'T PUSH IT DOWN! YOU DON'T FIDDLE WITH IT!
YOU BREAK IT UP!
BY--?
A SNAKE! USE A SNAKE!
THAT'S NOT WHAT I--!
I'LL TAKE IT FROM HERE, THANK YOU!

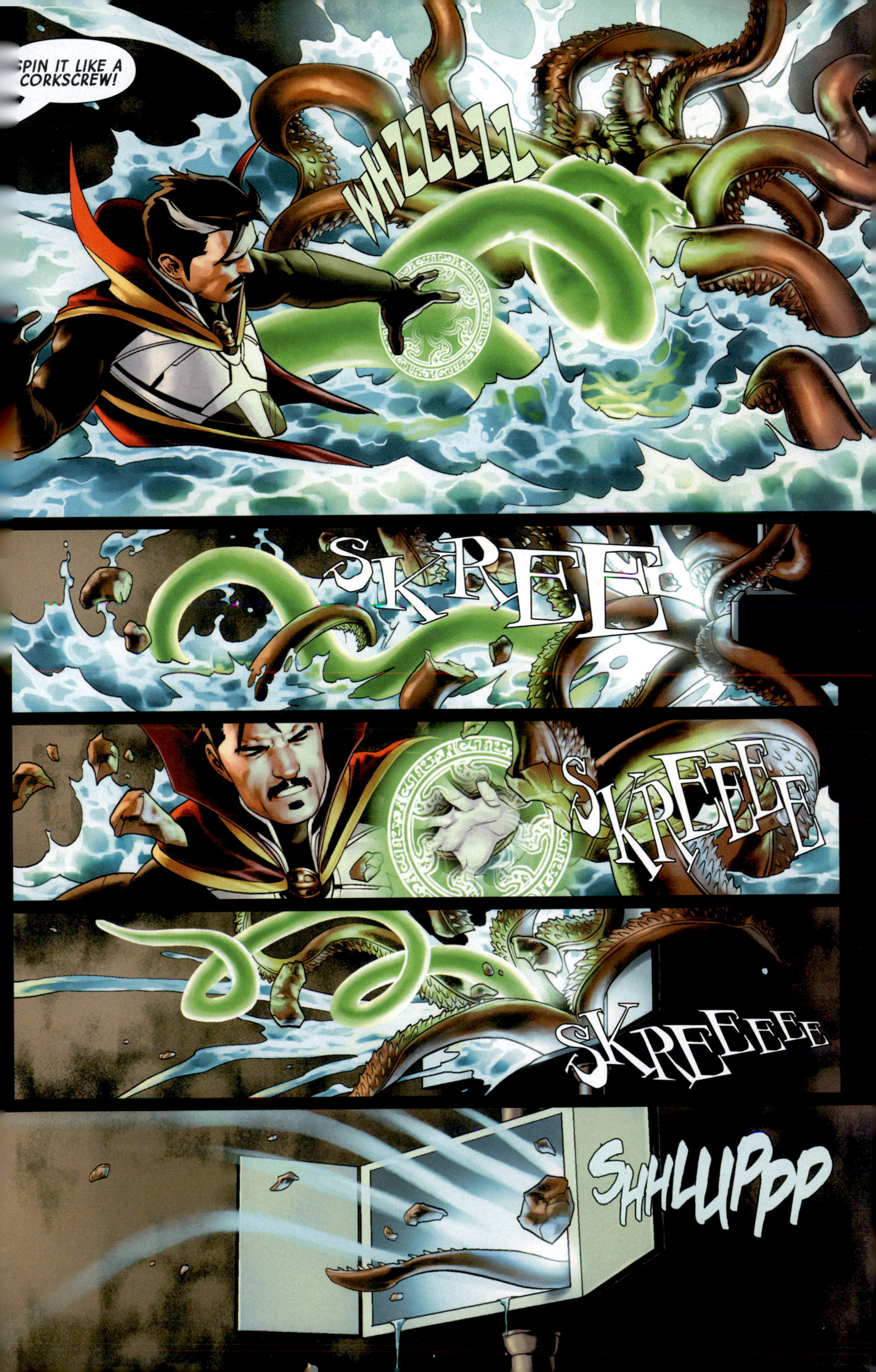
SPIN IT LIKE A CORKSCREW!
WHZZZZZZ
SKREEE
SKREEEE
SKREEEEE
SHHLUPPP

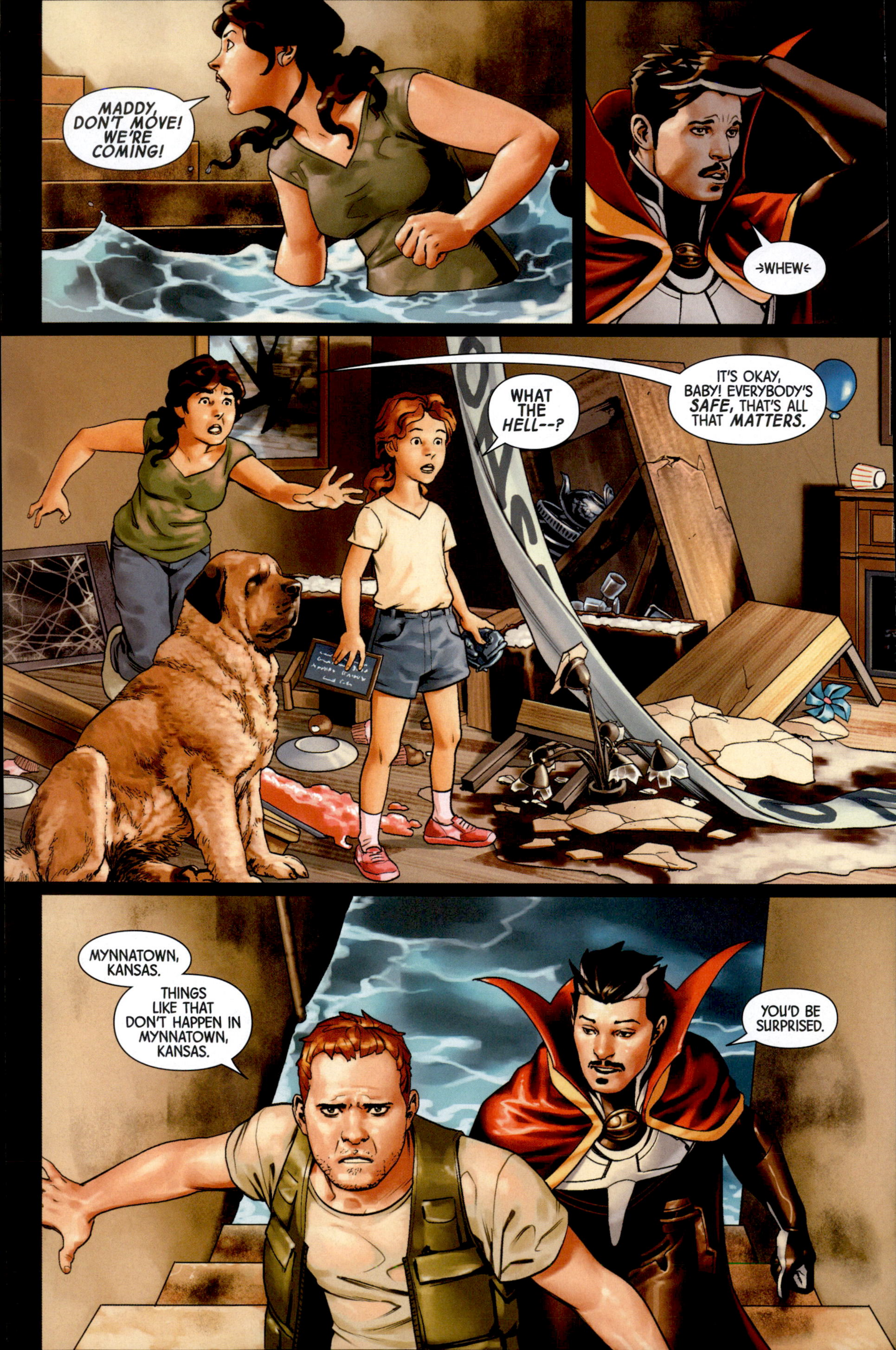
MADDY, DON'T MOVE! WE'RE COMING!
›WHEW‹
IT'S OKAY, BABY! EVERYBODY'S SAFE, THAT'S ALL THAT MATTERS.
WHAT THE HELL--?
MYNNATOWN, KANSAS.
THINGS LIKE THAT DON'T HAPPEN IN MYNNATOWN, KANSAS.
YOU'D BE SURPRISED.

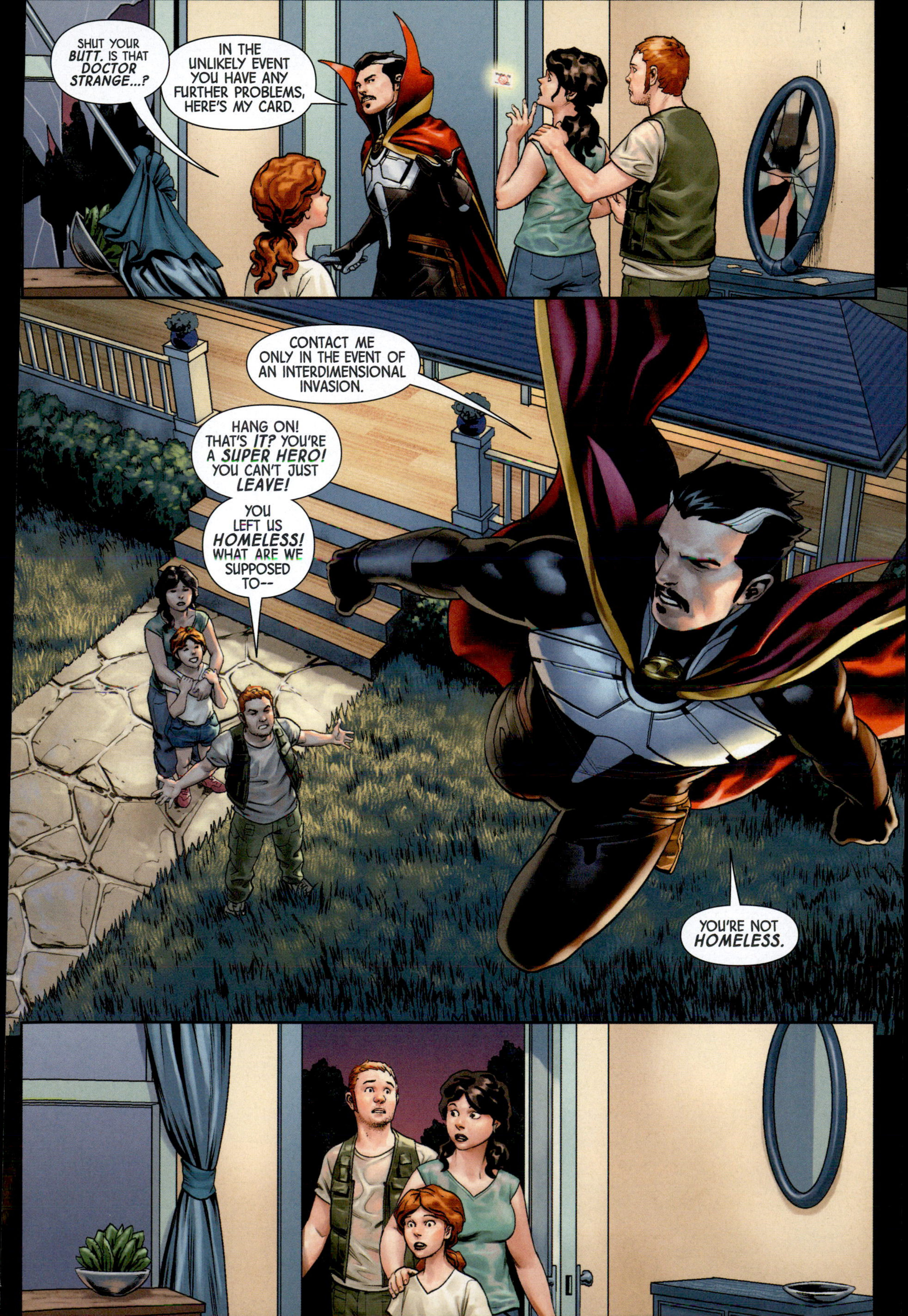
SHUT YOUR BUTT. IS THAT DOCTOR STRANGE...?
IN THE UNLIKELY EVENT YOU HAVE ANY FURTHER PROBLEMS, HERE'S MY CARD.
CONTACT ME ONLY IN THE EVENT OF AN INTERDIMENSIONAL INVASION.
HANG ON! THAT'S IT? YOU'RE A SUPER HERO! YOU CAN'T JUST LEAVE!
YOU LEFT US HOMELESS! WHAT ARE WE SUPPOSED TO--
YOU'RE NOT HOMELESS.

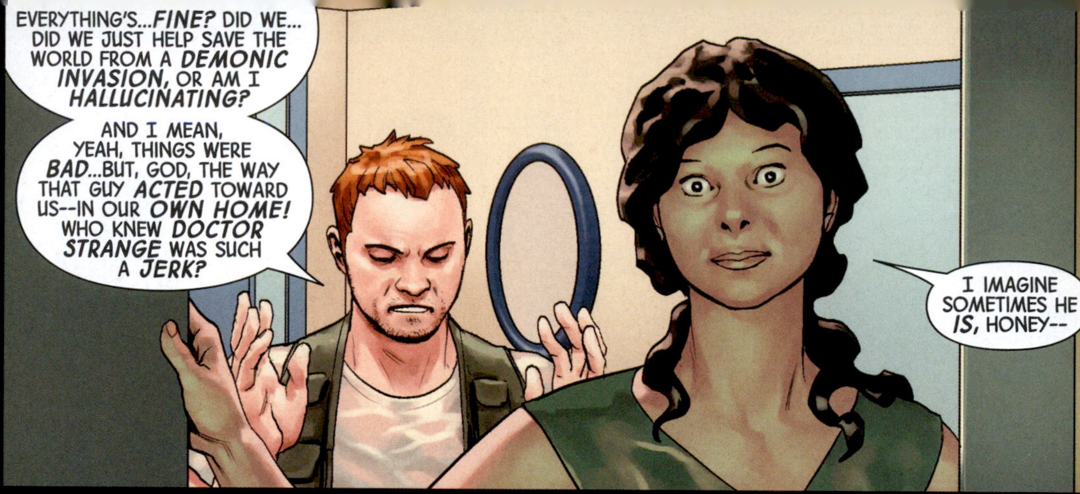
EVERYTHING'S...FINE? DID WE... DID WE JUST HELP SAVE THE WORLD FROM A DEMONIC INVASION, OR AM I HALLUCINATING?
AND I MEAN, YEAH, THINGS WERE BAD...BUT, GOD, THE WAY THAT GUY ACTED TOWARD US--IN OUR OWN HOME! WHO KNEW DOCTOR STRANGE WAS SUCH A JERK?
I IMAGINE SOMETIMES HE IS, HONEY--

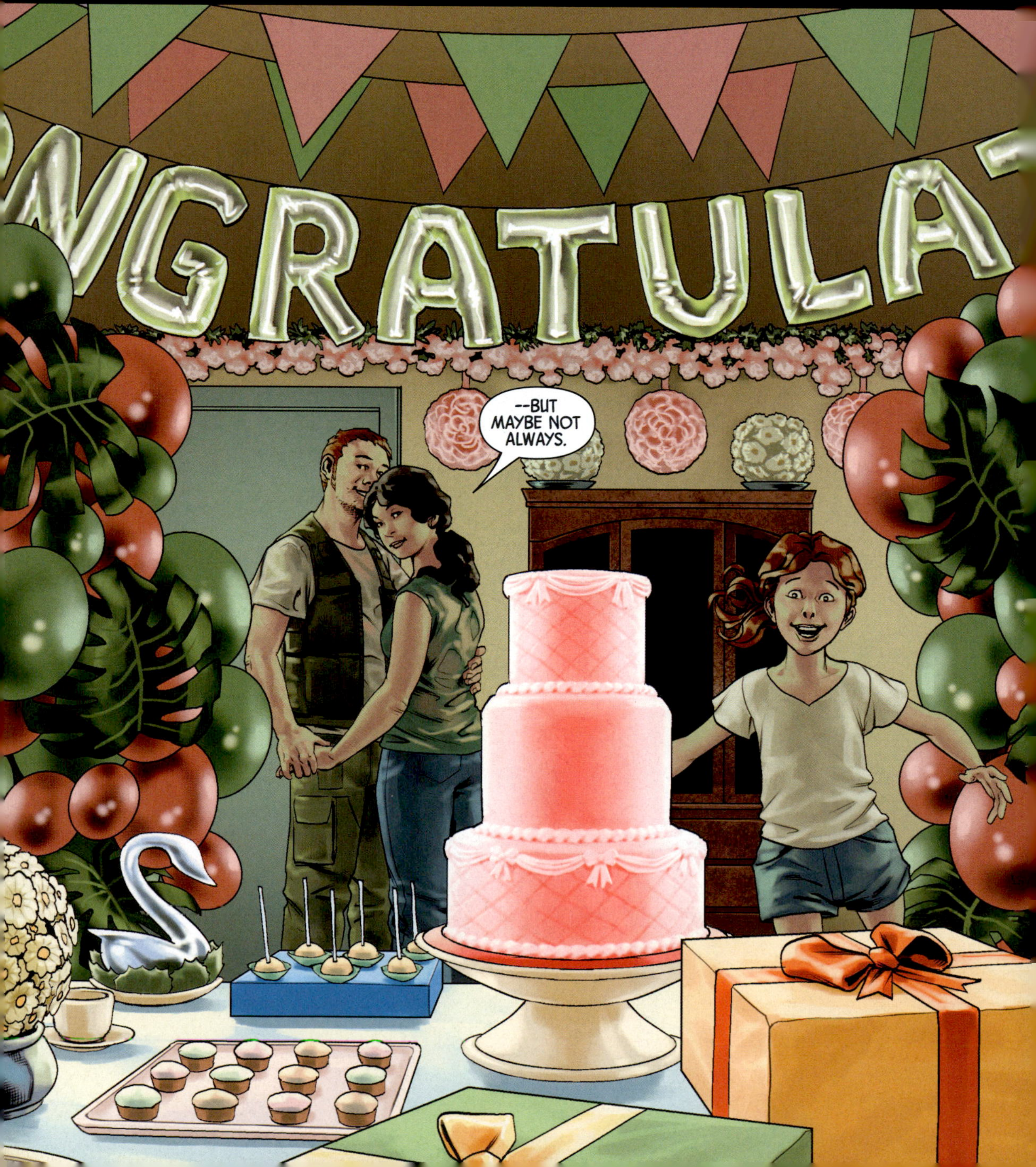
NGRATULAT
--BUT MAYBE NOT ALWAYS.

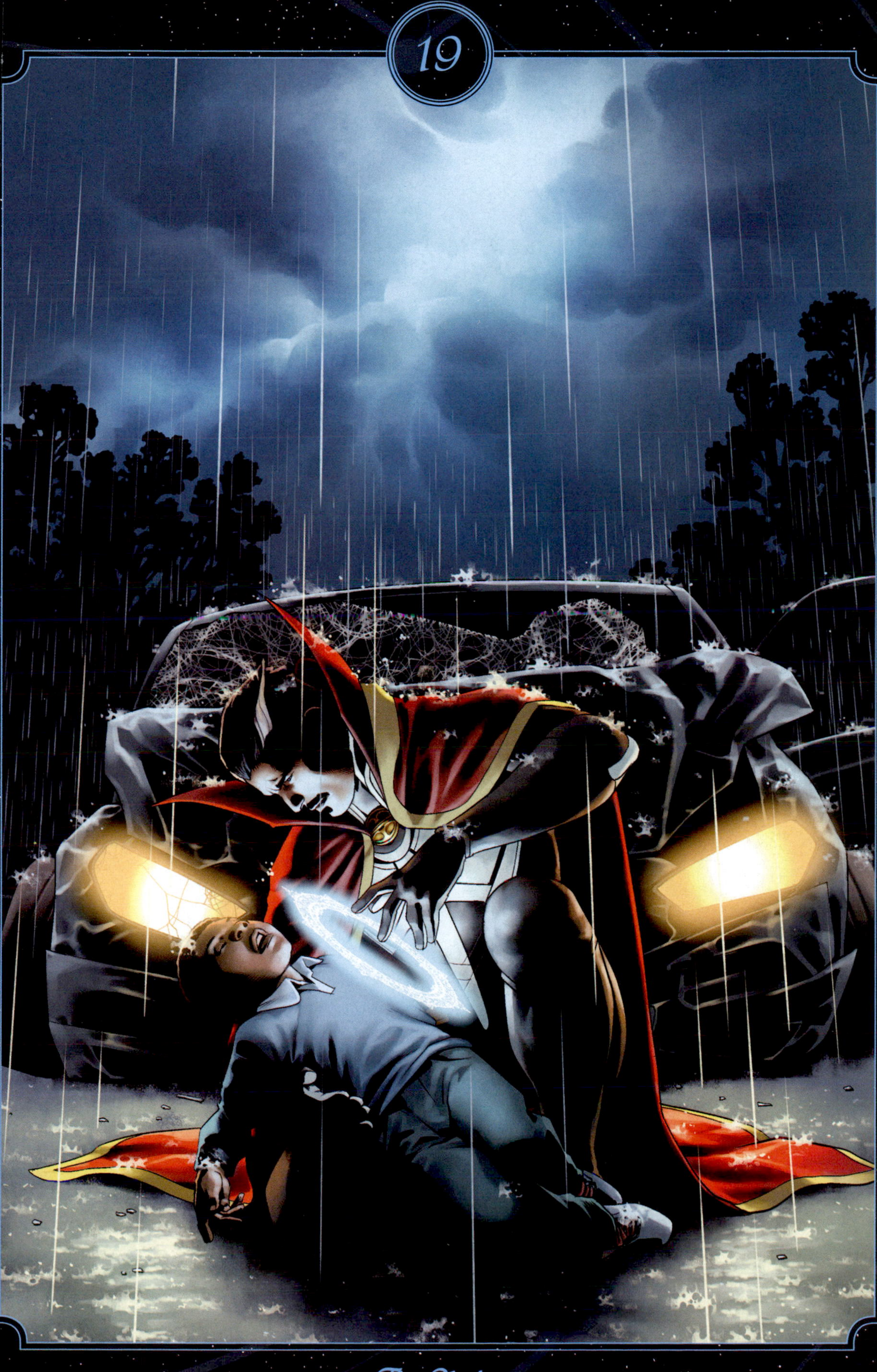
19

The Choice

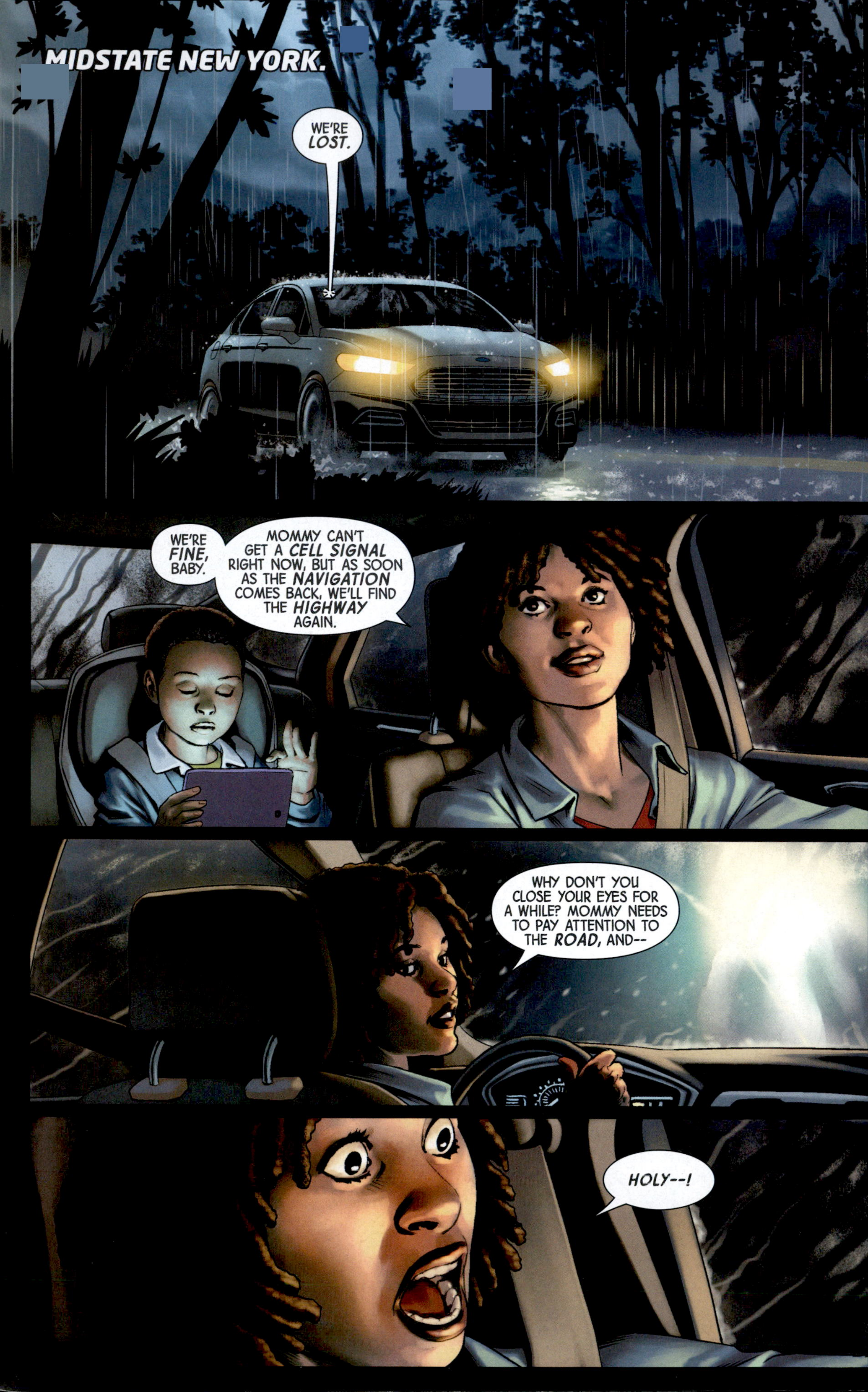
MIDSTATE NEW YORK.
WE'RE LOST.
WE'RE FINE, BABY.
MOMMY CAN'T GET A CELL SIGNAL RIGHT NOW, BUT AS SOON AS THE NAVIGATION COMES BACK, WE'LL FIND THE HIGHWAY AGAIN.
WHY DON'T YOU CLOSE YOUR EYES FOR A WHILE? MOMMY NEEDS TO PAY ATTENTION TO THE ROAD, AND--
HOLY--!

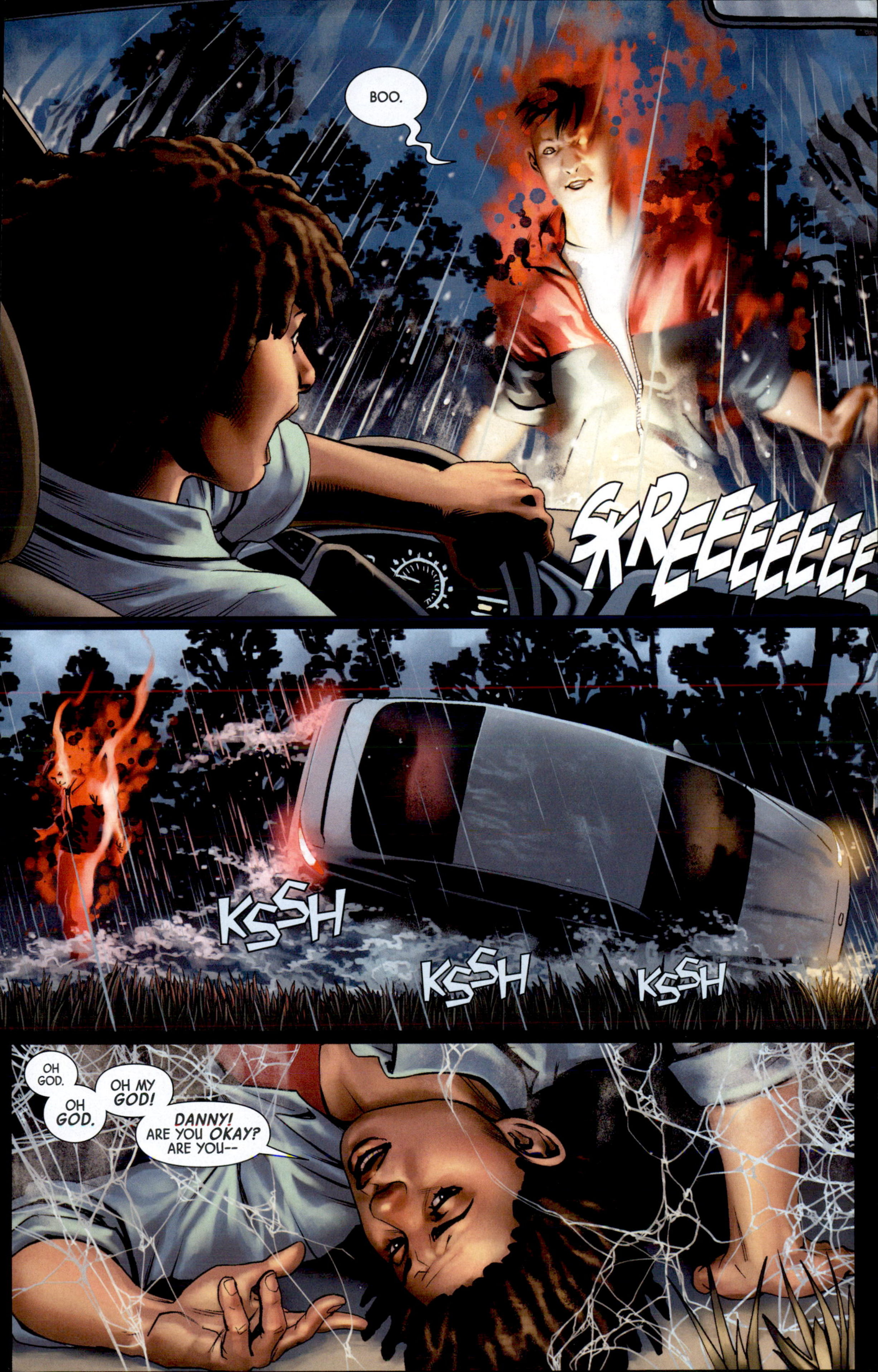
BOO.
SKREEEEEEEEE
KSSH
KSSH
KSSH
OH GOD.
OH GOD.
OH MY GOD!
DANNY! ARE YOU OKAY? ARE YOU--

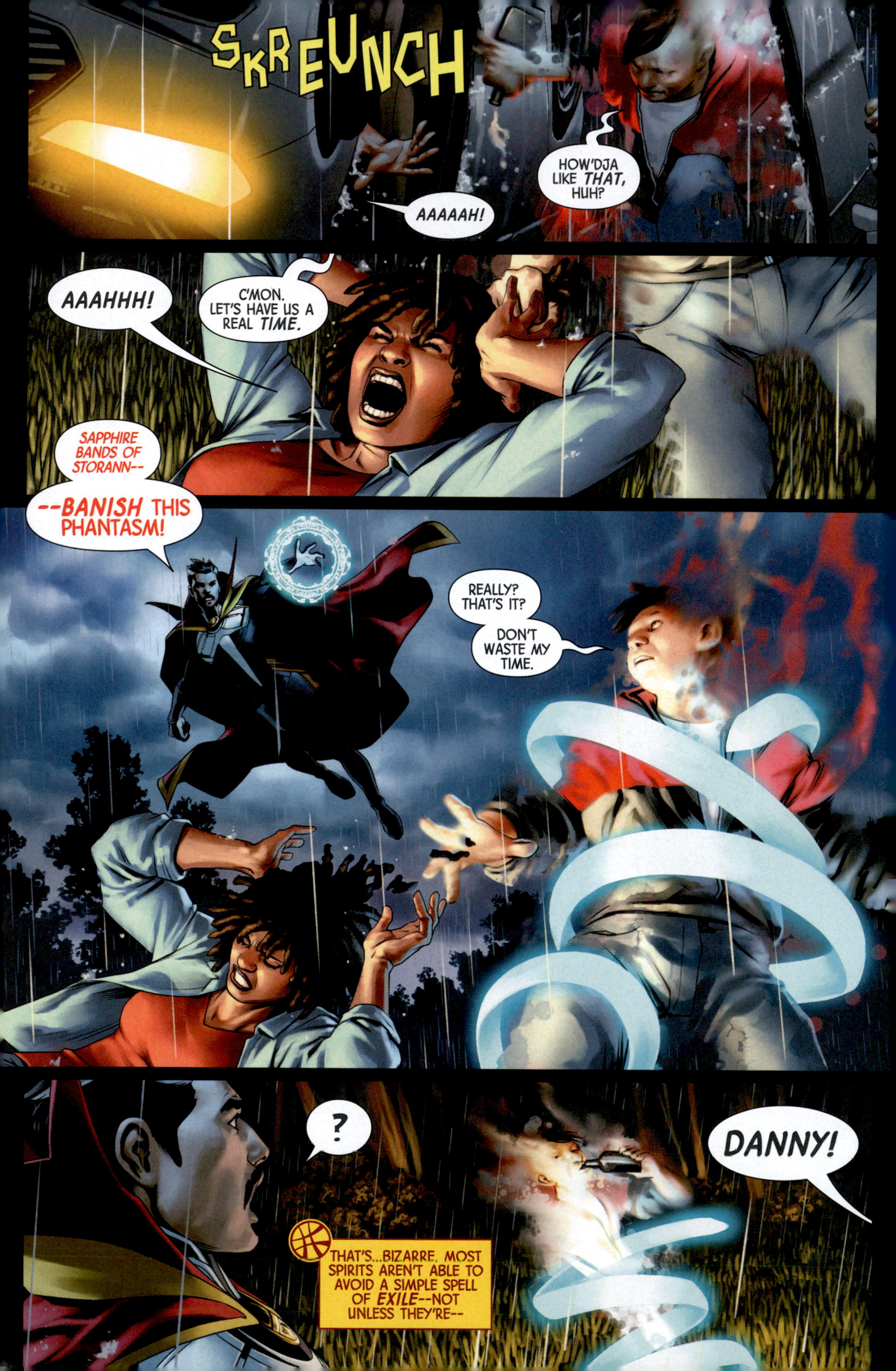
SKREUNCH
AAAAAH!
HOW'DJA LIKE THAT, HUH?
AAAHHH!
C'MON. LET'S HAVE US A REAL TIME.
SAPPHIRE BANDS OF STORANN--
--BANISH THIS PHANTASM!
REALLY? THAT'S IT?
DON'T WASTE MY TIME.
?
DANNY!
THAT'S...BIZARRE. MOST SPIRITS AREN'T ABLE TO AVOID A SIMPLE SPELL OF EXILE--NOT UNLESS THEY'RE--

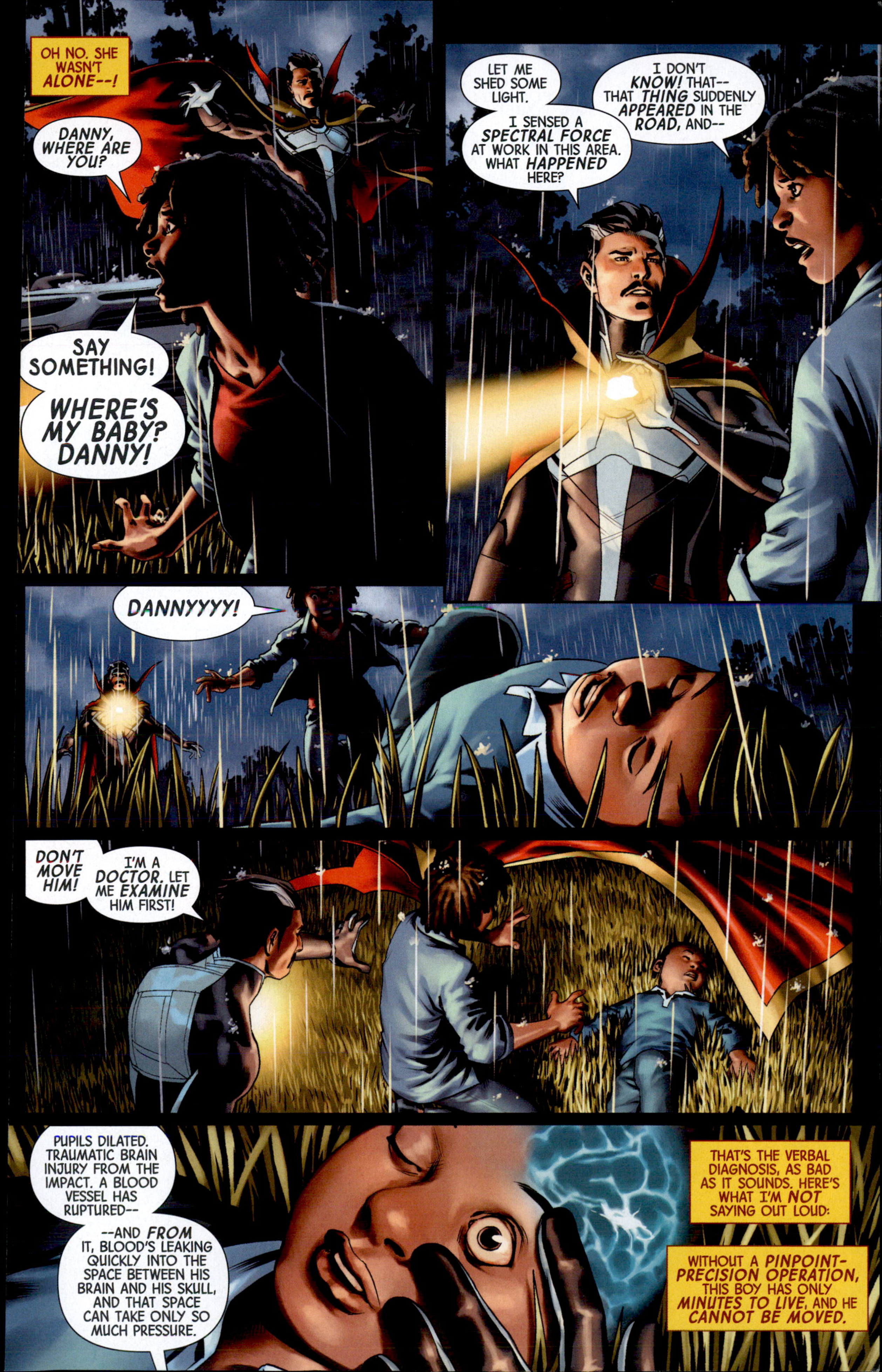
OH NO. SHE WASN'T ALONE--!
DANNY, WHERE ARE YOU?
SAY SOMETHING!
WHERE'S MY BABY? DANNY!
LET ME SHED SOME LIGHT.
I SENSED A SPECTRAL FORCE AT WORK IN THIS AREA. WHAT HAPPENED HERE?
I DON'T KNOW! THAT-- THAT THING SUDDENLY APPEARED IN THE ROAD, AND--
DANNYYYY!
DON'T MOVE HIM!
I'M A DOCTOR. LET ME EXAMINE HIM FIRST!
PUPILS DILATED. TRAUMATIC BRAIN INJURY FROM THE IMPACT. A BLOOD VESSEL HAS RUPTURED--
--AND FROM IT, BLOOD'S LEAKING QUICKLY INTO THE SPACE BETWEEN HIS BRAIN AND HIS SKULL, AND THAT SPACE CAN TAKE ONLY SO MUCH PRESSURE.
THAT'S THE VERBAL DIAGNOSIS, AS BAD AS IT SOUNDS. HERE'S WHAT I'M NOT SAYING OUT LOUD:
WITHOUT A PINPOINT-PRECISION OPERATION, THIS BOY HAS ONLY MINUTES TO LIVE, AND HE CANNOT BE MOVED.

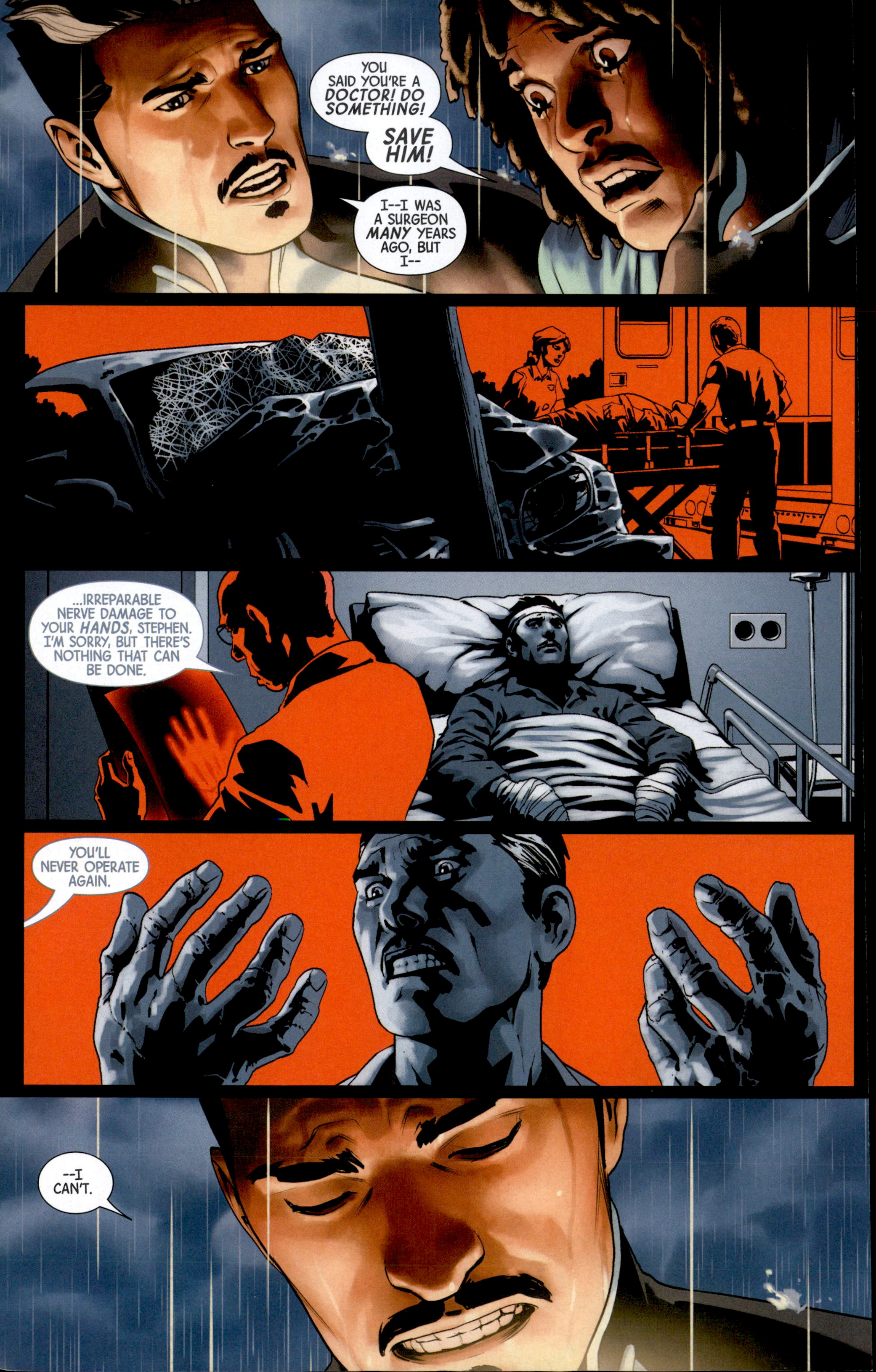
YOU SAID YOU'RE A DOCTOR! DO SOMETHING!
SAVE HIM!
I--I WAS A SURGEON MANY YEARS AGO, BUT I--
...IRREPARABLE NERVE DAMAGE TO YOUR HANDS, STEPHEN. I'M SORRY, BUT THERE'S NOTHING THAT CAN BE DONE.
YOU'LL NEVER OPERATE AGAIN.
--I CAN'T.

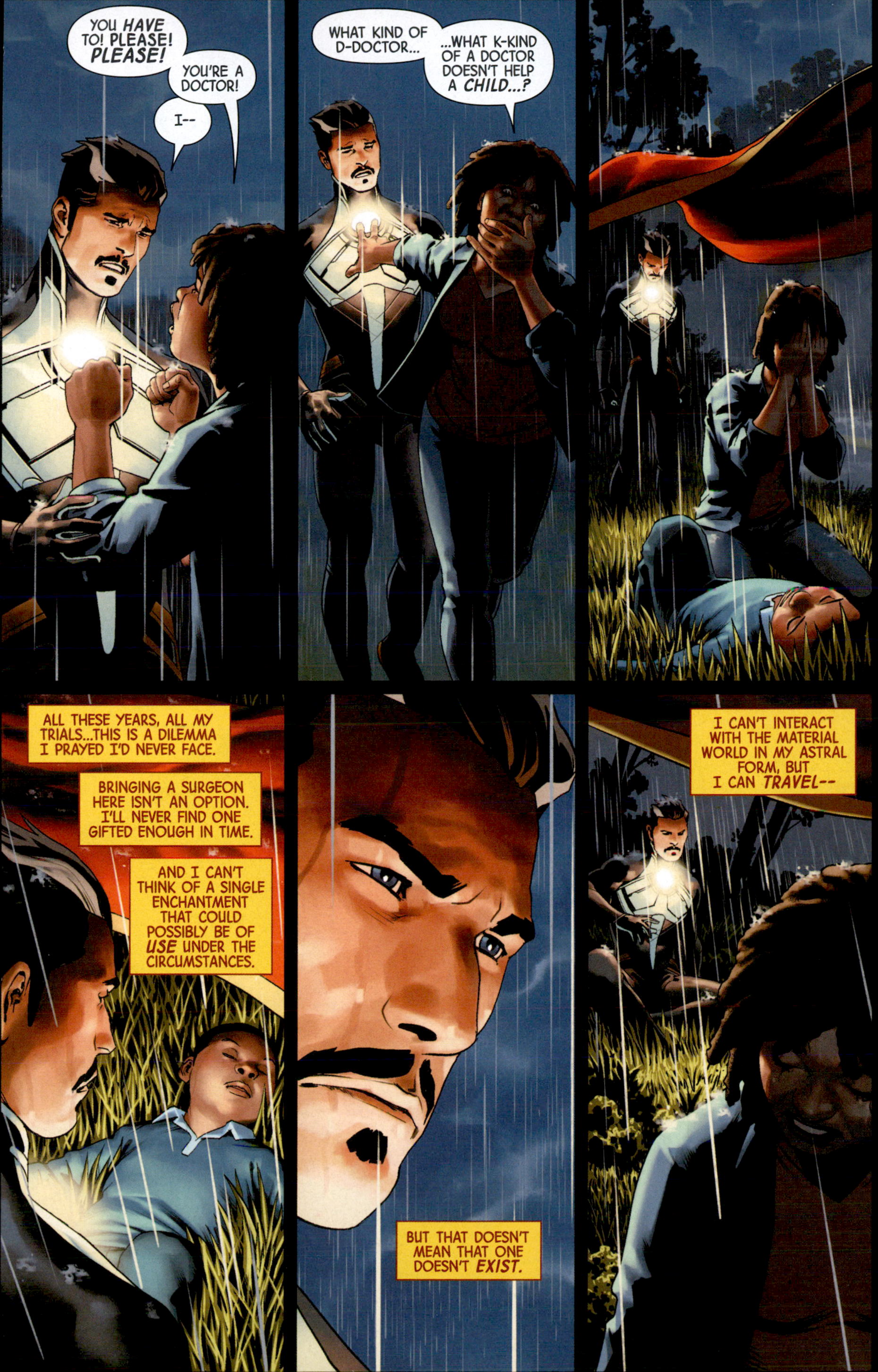
YOU HAVE TO! PLEASE! PLEASE!
YOU'RE A DOCTOR!
I--
WHAT KIND OF D-DOCTOR...
...WHAT K-KIND OF A DOCTOR DOESN'T HELP A CHILD...?
ALL THESE YEARS, ALL MY TRIALS...THIS IS A DILEMMA I PRAYED I'D NEVER FACE.
BRINGING A SURGEON HERE ISN'T AN OPTION. I'LL NEVER FIND ONE GIFTED ENOUGH IN TIME.
AND I CAN'T THINK OF A SINGLE ENCHANTMENT THAT COULD POSSIBLY BE OF USE UNDER THE CIRCUMSTANCES.
BUT THAT DOESN'T MEAN THAT ONE DOESN'T EXIST.
I CAN'T INTERACT WITH THE MATERIAL WORLD IN MY ASTRAL FORM, BUT I CAN TRAVEL--

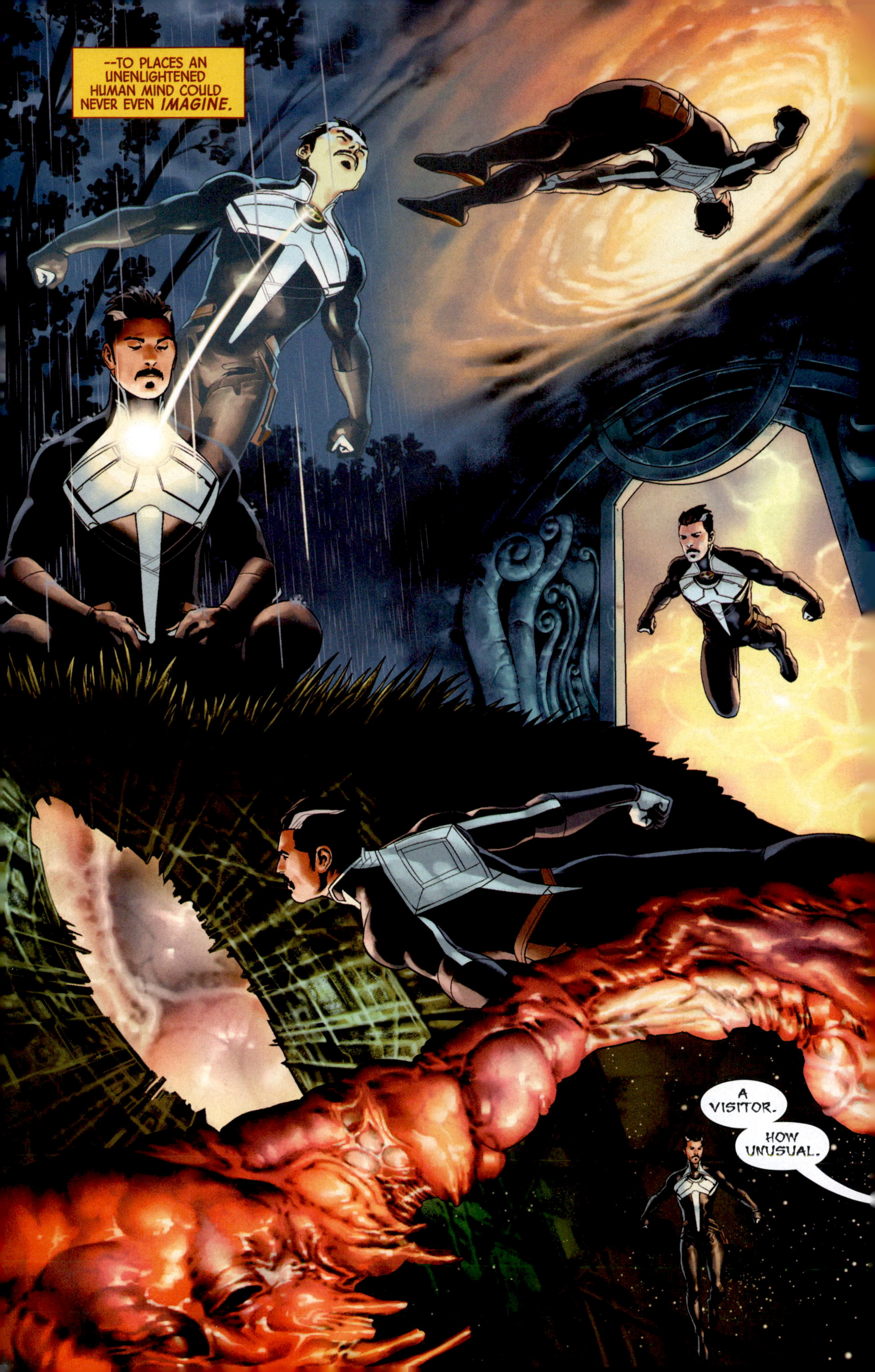
--TO PLACES AN UNENLIGHTENED HUMAN MIND COULD NEVER EVEN IMAGINE.
A VISITOR.
HOW UNUSUAL.

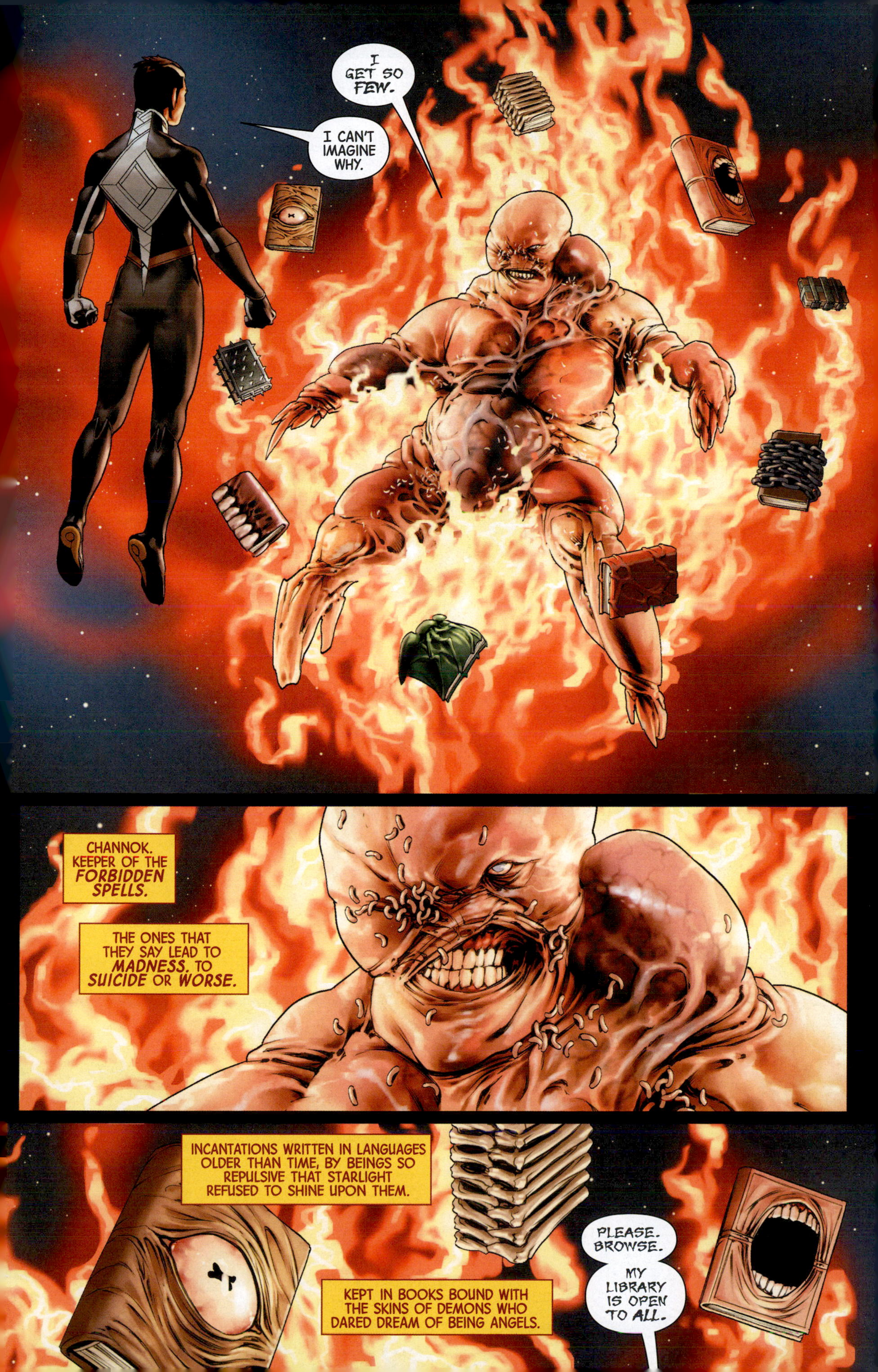
I GET SO FEW.
I CAN'T IMAGINE WHY.
CHANNOK. KEEPER OF THE FORBIDDEN SPELLS.
THE ONES THAT THEY SAY LEAD TO MADNESS, TO SUICIDE OR WORSE.
INCANTATIONS WRITTEN IN LANGUAGES OLDER THAN TIME, BY BEINGS SO REPULSIVE THAT STARLIGHT REFUSED TO SHINE UPON THEM.
KEPT IN BOOKS BOUND WITH THE SKINS OF DEMONS WHO DARED DREAM OF BEING ANGELS.
PLEASE. BROWSE.
MY LIBRARY IS OPEN TO ALL.

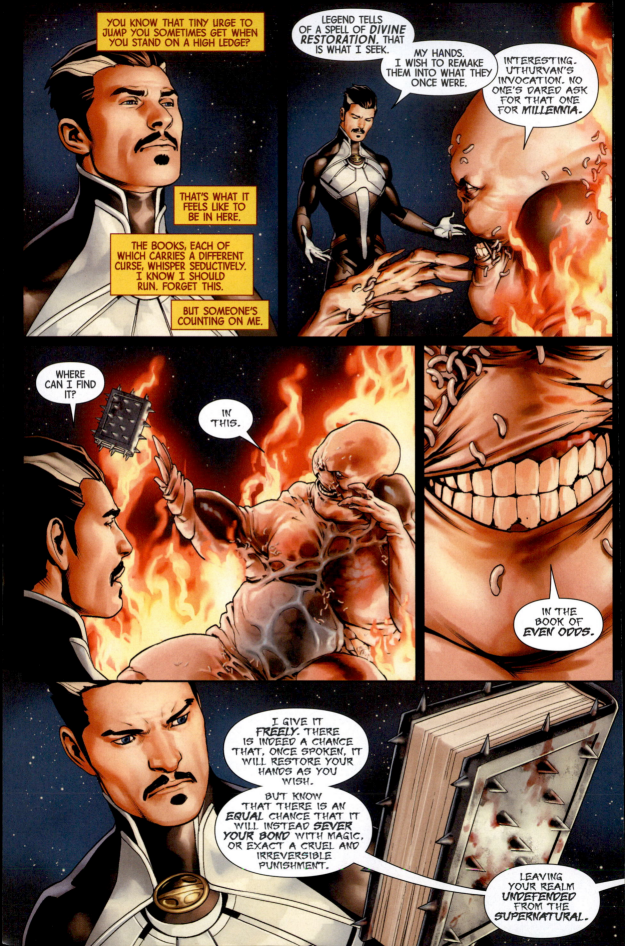

YOU KNOW THAT TINY URGE TO JUMP YOU SOMETIMES GET WHEN YOU STAND ON A HIGH LEDGE?

LEGEND TELLS OF A SPELL OF *DIVINE RESTORATION.* THAT IS WHAT I SEEK.

MY HANDS. I WISH TO REMAKE THEM INTO WHAT THEY ONCE WERE.

INTERESTING. UTHURVAN'S INVOCATION. NO ONE'S DARED ASK FOR THAT ONE FOR *MILLENNIA.*

THAT'S WHAT IT FEELS LIKE TO BE IN HERE.

THE BOOKS, EACH OF WHICH CARRIES A DIFFERENT CURSE, WHISPER SEDUCTIVELY. I KNOW I SHOULD RUN. FORGET THIS.

BUT SOMEONE'S COUNTING ON ME.

WHERE CAN I FIND IT?

IN THIS.

IN THE BOOK OF *EVEN ODDS.*

I GIVE IT *FREELY.* THERE IS INDEED A CHANCE THAT, ONCE SPOKEN, IT WILL RESTORE YOUR HANDS AS YOU WISH.

BUT KNOW THAT THERE IS AN *EQUAL* CHANCE THAT IT WILL INSTEAD *SEVER YOUR BOND* WITH MAGIC, OR EXACT A CRUEL AND IRREVERSIBLE PUNISHMENT.

LEAVING YOUR REALM *UNDEFENDED* FROM THE *SUPERNATURAL.*

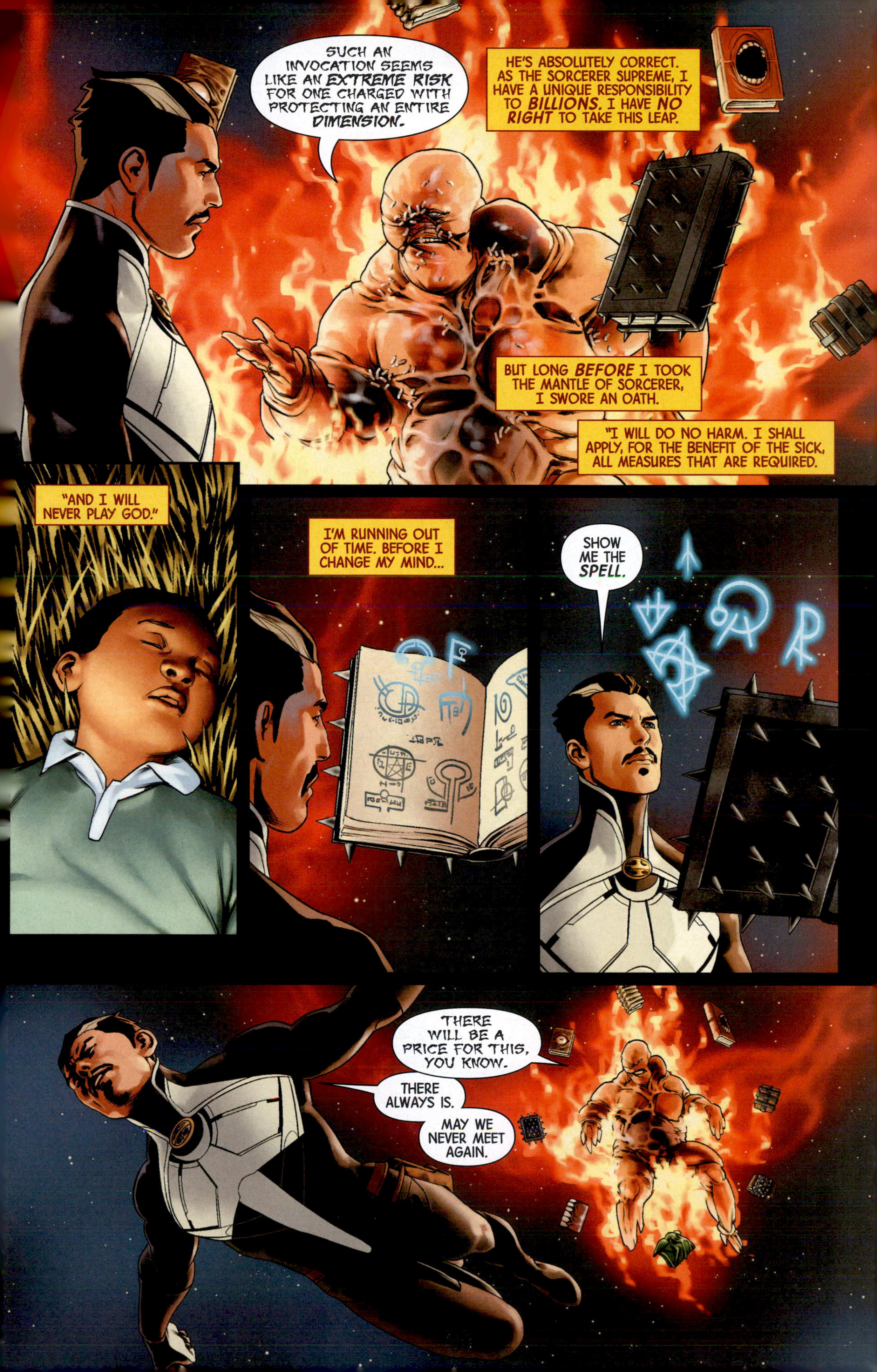
SUCH AN INVOCATION SEEMS LIKE AN EXTREME RISK FOR ONE CHARGED WITH PROTECTING AN ENTIRE DIMENSION.
HE'S ABSOLUTELY CORRECT. AS THE SORCERER SUPREME, I HAVE A UNIQUE RESPONSIBILITY TO BILLIONS. I HAVE NO RIGHT TO TAKE THIS LEAP.
BUT LONG BEFORE I TOOK THE MANTLE OF SORCERER, I SWORE AN OATH.
"I WILL DO NO HARM. I SHALL APPLY, FOR THE BENEFIT OF THE SICK, ALL MEASURES THAT ARE REQUIRED.
"AND I WILL NEVER PLAY GOD."
I'M RUNNING OUT OF TIME. BEFORE I CHANGE MY MIND...
SHOW ME THE SPELL.
THERE WILL BE A PRICE FOR THIS, YOU KNOW.
THERE ALWAYS IS.
MAY WE NEVER MEET AGAIN.

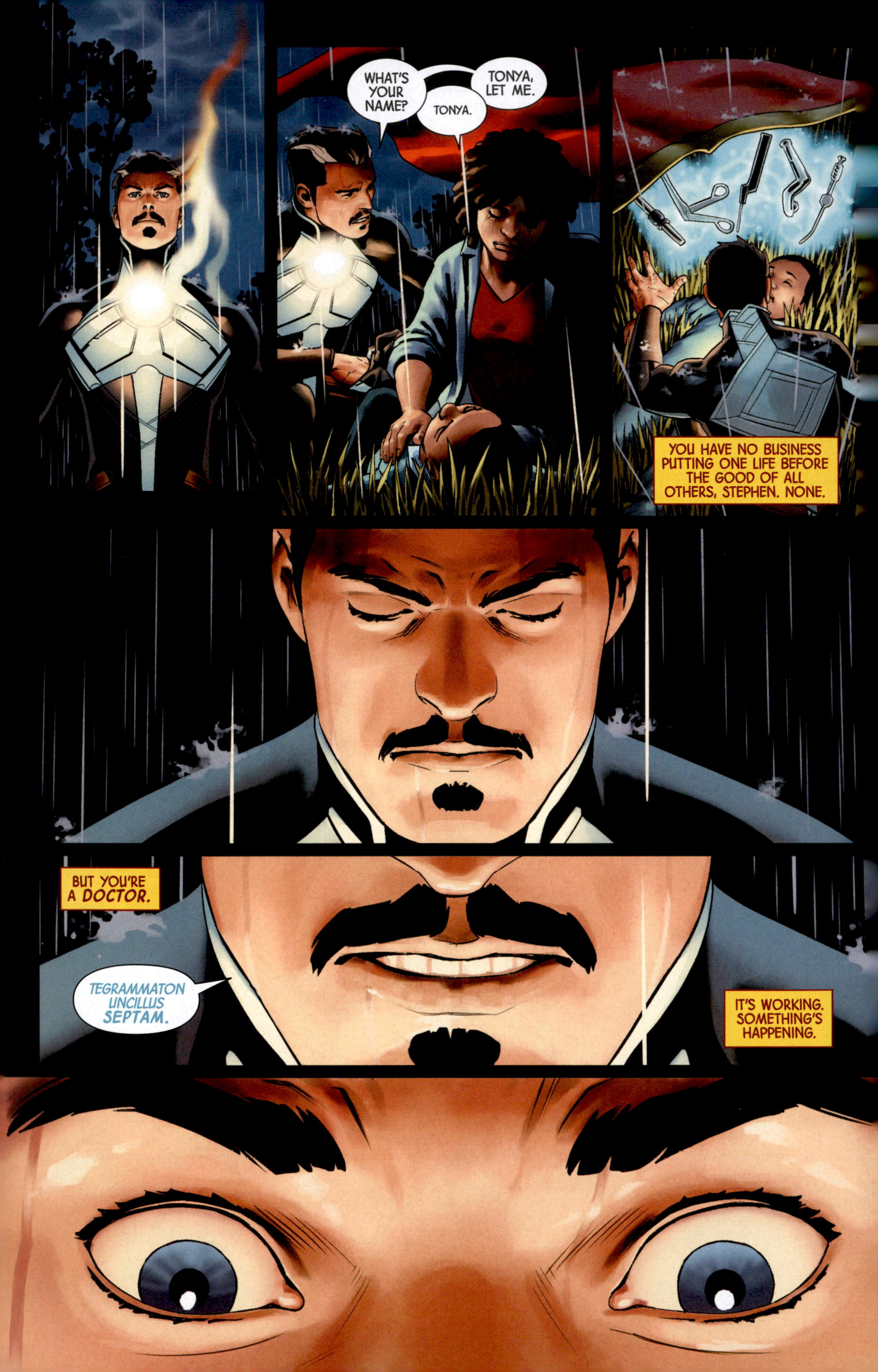
WHAT'S YOUR NAME?
TONYA.
TONYA, LET ME.
YOU HAVE NO BUSINESS PUTTING ONE LIFE BEFORE THE GOOD OF ALL OTHERS, STEPHEN. NONE.
BUT YOU'RE A DOCTOR.
TEGRAMMATON UNCILLUS SEPTAM.
IT'S WORKING. SOMETHING'S HAPPENING.

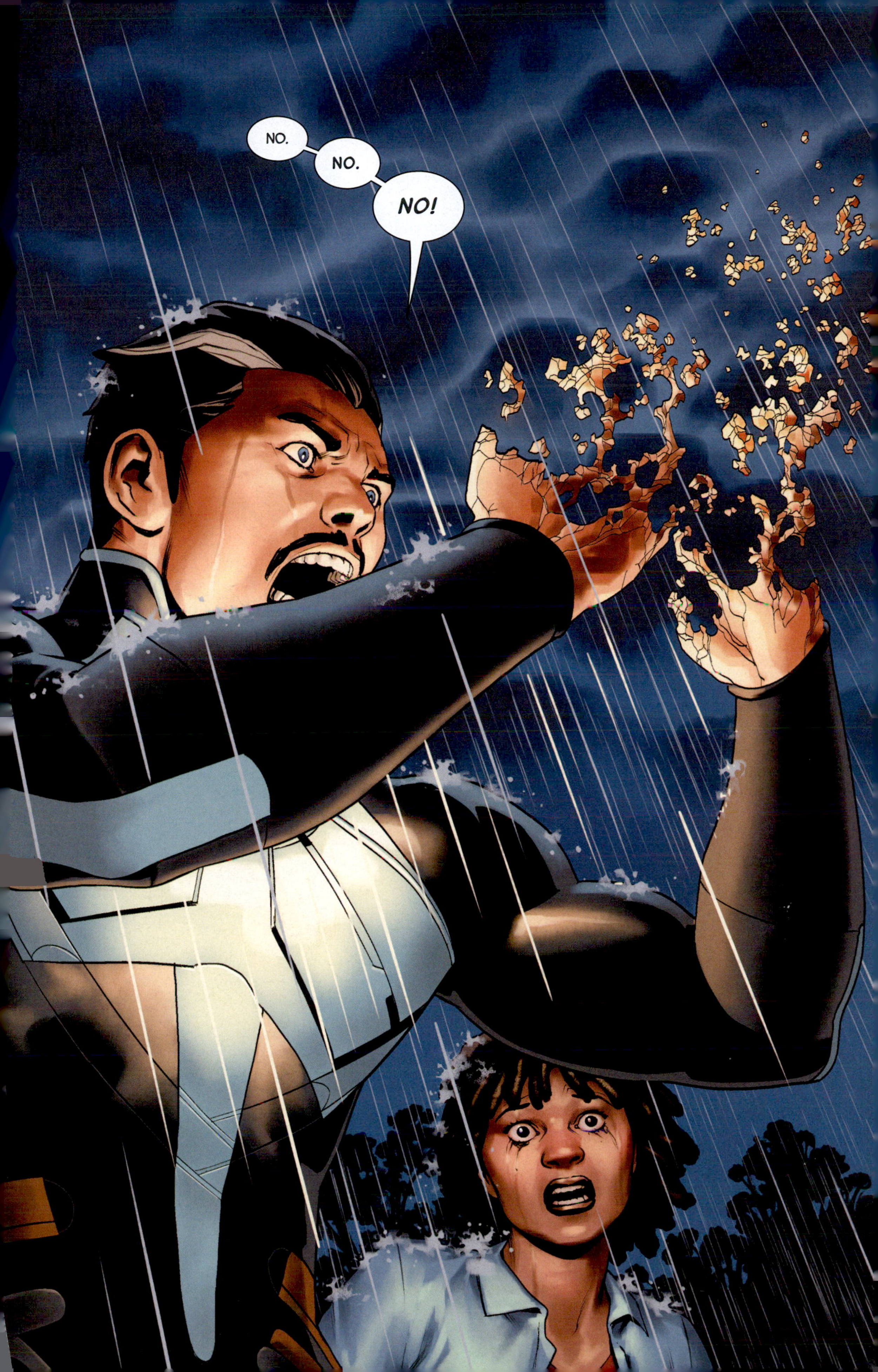
NO.
NO.
NO!

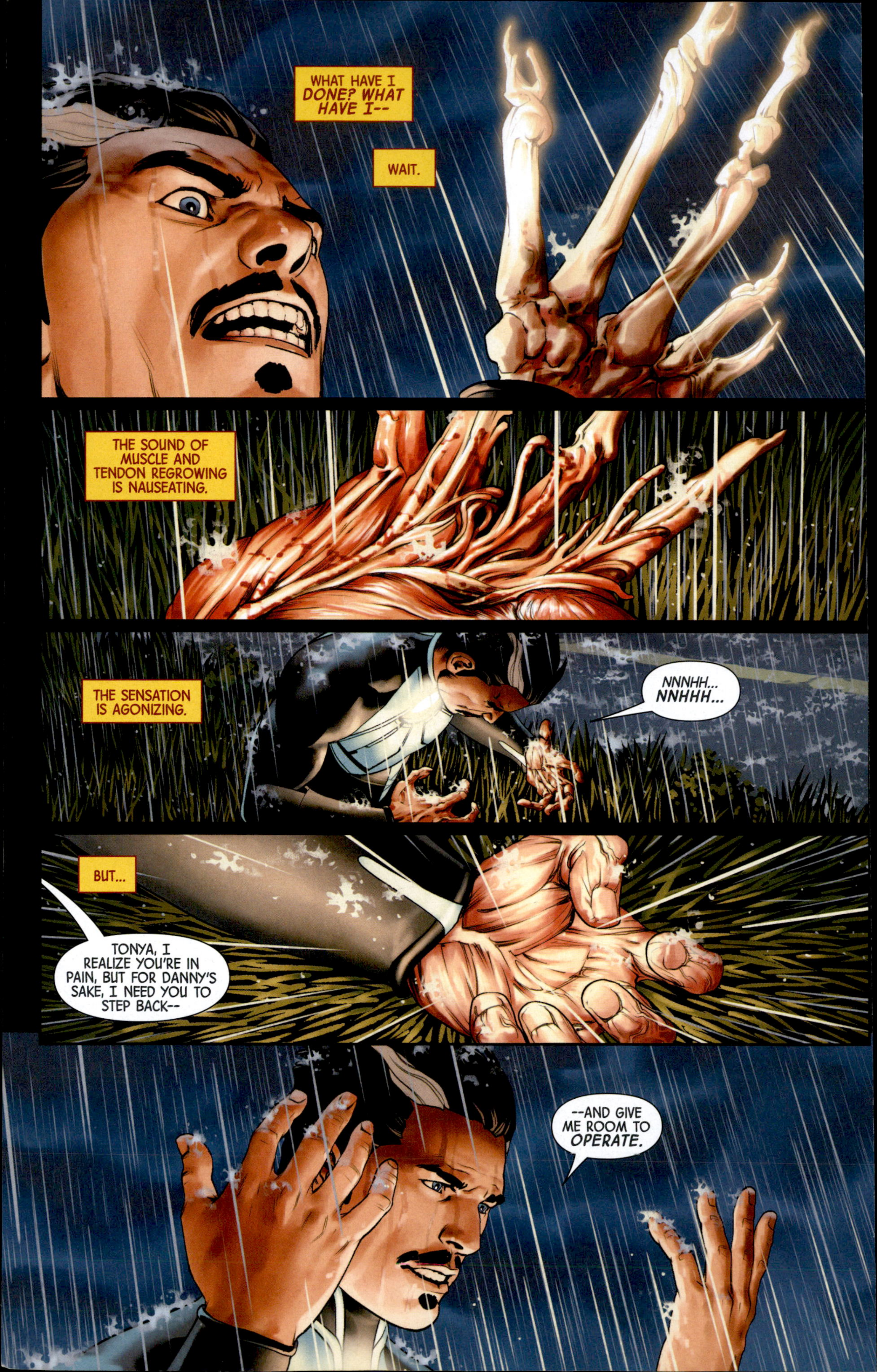
WHAT HAVE I DONE? WHAT HAVE I--
WAIT.
THE SOUND OF MUSCLE AND TENDON REGROWING IS NAUSEATING.
THE SENSATION IS AGONIZING.
NNNHH... NNHHH...
BUT...
TONYA, I REALIZE YOU'RE IN PAIN, BUT FOR DANNY'S SAKE, I NEED YOU TO STEP BACK--
--AND GIVE ME ROOM TO OPERATE.

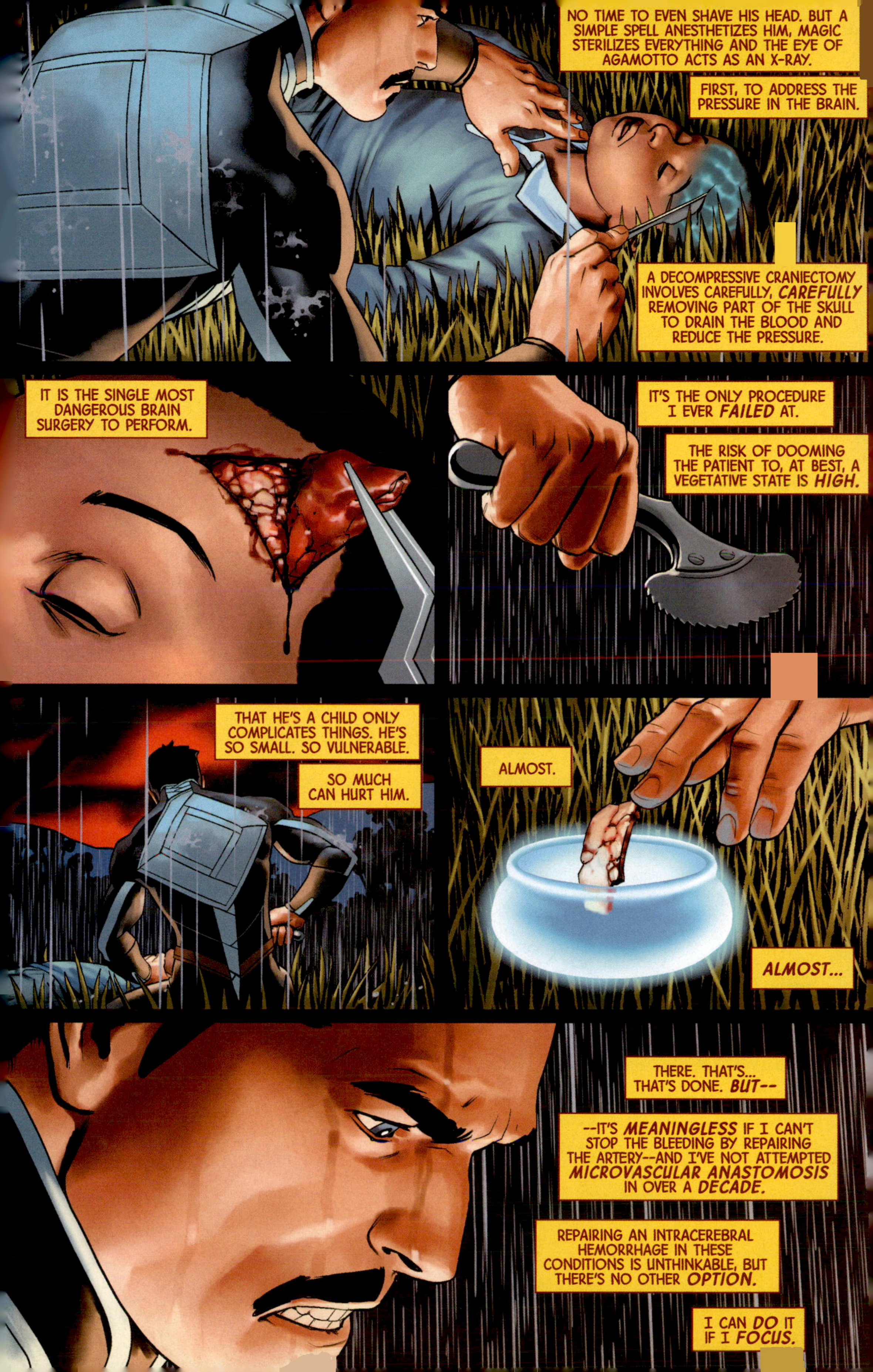
NO TIME TO EVEN SHAVE HIS HEAD. BUT A SIMPLE SPELL ANESTHETIZES HIM, MAGIC STERILIZES EVERYTHING AND THE EYE OF AGAMOTTO ACTS AS AN X-RAY.
FIRST, TO ADDRESS THE PRESSURE IN THE BRAIN.
A DECOMPRESSIVE CRANIECTOMY INVOLVES CAREFULLY, *CAREFULLY* REMOVING PART OF THE SKULL TO DRAIN THE BLOOD AND REDUCE THE PRESSURE.
IT IS THE SINGLE MOST DANGEROUS BRAIN SURGERY TO PERFORM.
IT'S THE ONLY PROCEDURE I EVER *FAILED* AT.
THE RISK OF DOOMING THE PATIENT TO, AT BEST, A VEGETATIVE STATE IS *HIGH*.
THAT HE'S A CHILD ONLY COMPLICATES THINGS. HE'S SO SMALL. SO VULNERABLE.
SO MUCH CAN HURT HIM.
ALMOST.
ALMOST...
THERE. THAT'S... THAT'S DONE. *BUT--*
--IT'S *MEANINGLESS* IF I CAN'T STOP THE BLEEDING BY REPAIRING THE ARTERY--AND I'VE NOT ATTEMPTED *MICROVASCULAR ANASTOMOSIS* IN OVER A *DECADE*.
REPAIRING AN INTRACEREBRAL HEMORRHAGE IN THESE CONDITIONS IS UNTHINKABLE, BUT THERE'S NO OTHER *OPTION*.
I CAN *DO* IT IF I *FOCUS*.

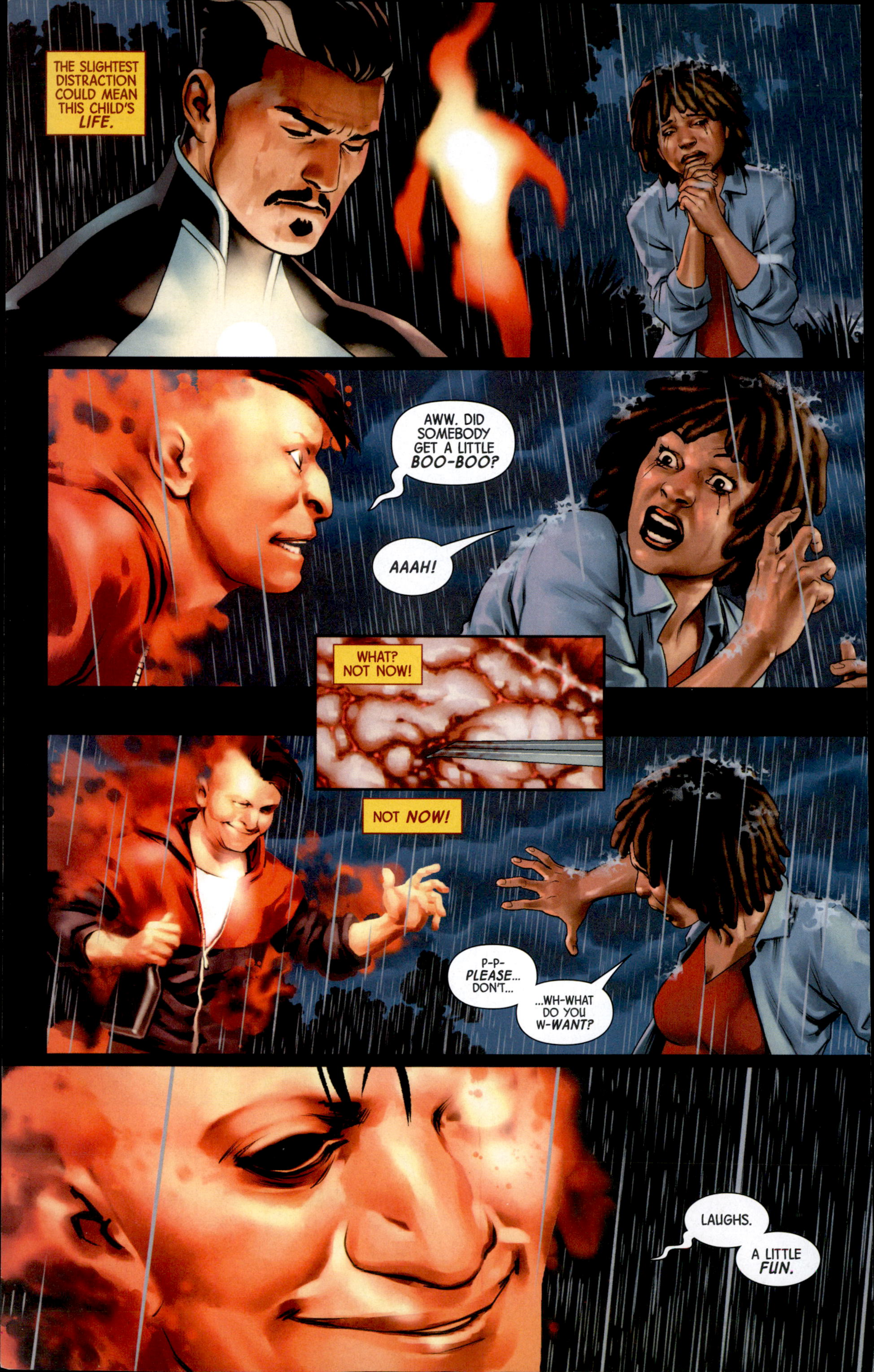
THE SLIGHTEST DISTRACTION COULD MEAN THIS CHILD'S *LIFE.*
AWW. DID SOMEBODY GET A LITTLE *BOO-BOO?*
AAAH!
WHAT? NOT NOW!
NOT *NOW!*
P-P- *PLEASE*... DON'T...
...WH-WHAT DO YOU W-*WANT?*
LAUGHS.
A LITTLE *FUN.*

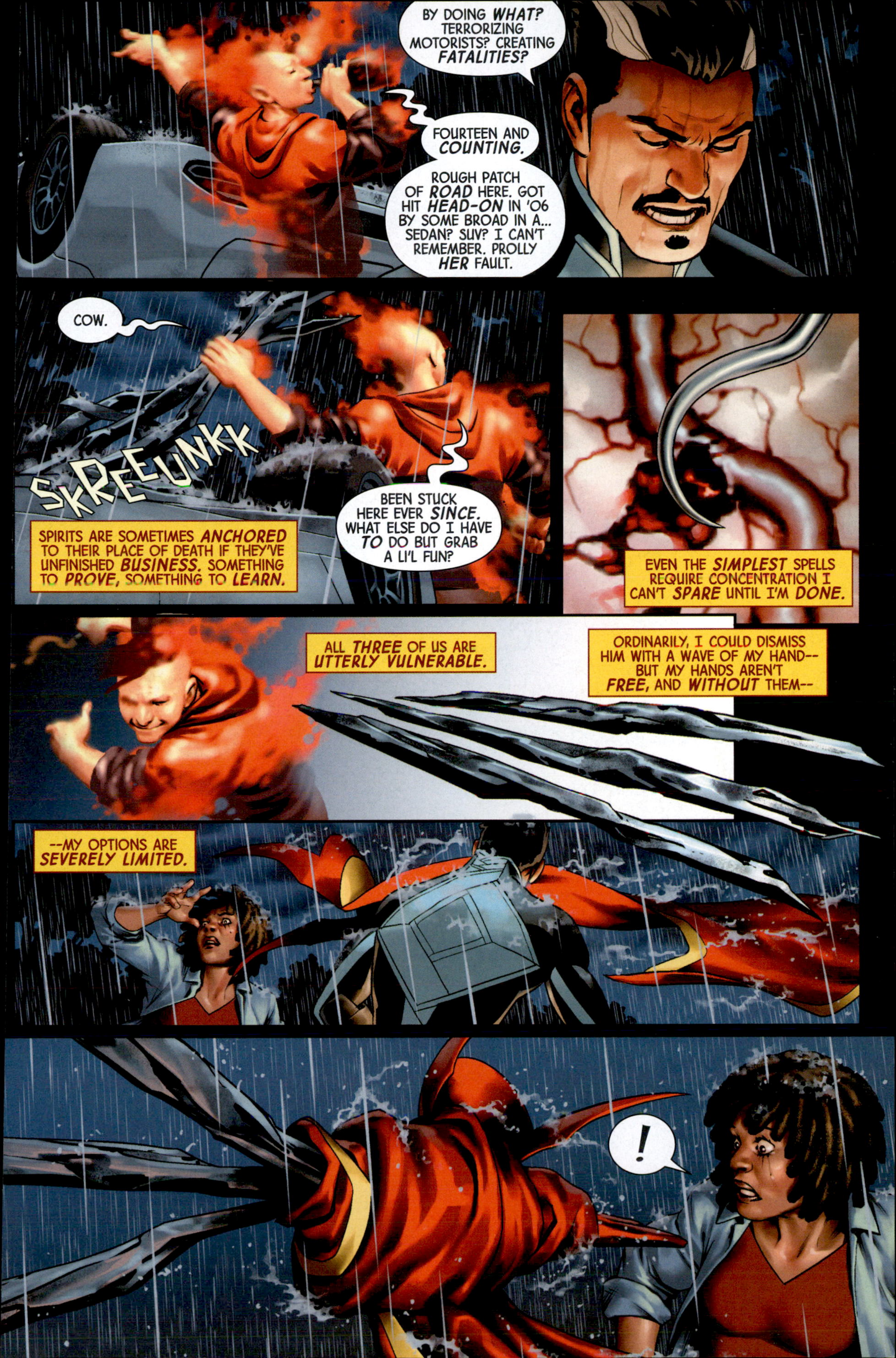
BY DOING WHAT? TERRORIZING MOTORISTS? CREATING FATALITIES?
FOURTEEN AND COUNTING.
ROUGH PATCH OF ROAD HERE. GOT HIT HEAD-ON IN '06 BY SOME BROAD IN A... SEDAN? SUV? I CAN'T REMEMBER. PROLLY HER FAULT.
COW.
SKREEUNKK
SPIRITS ARE SOMETIMES ANCHORED TO THEIR PLACE OF DEATH IF THEY'VE UNFINISHED BUSINESS. SOMETHING TO PROVE, SOMETHING TO LEARN.
BEEN STUCK HERE EVER SINCE. WHAT ELSE DO I HAVE TO DO BUT GRAB A LI'L FUN?
EVEN THE SIMPLEST SPELLS REQUIRE CONCENTRATION I CAN'T SPARE UNTIL I'M DONE.
ALL THREE OF US ARE UTTERLY VULNERABLE.
ORDINARILY, I COULD DISMISS HIM WITH A WAVE OF MY HAND--BUT MY HANDS AREN'T FREE, AND WITHOUT THEM--
--MY OPTIONS ARE SEVERELY LIMITED.
!

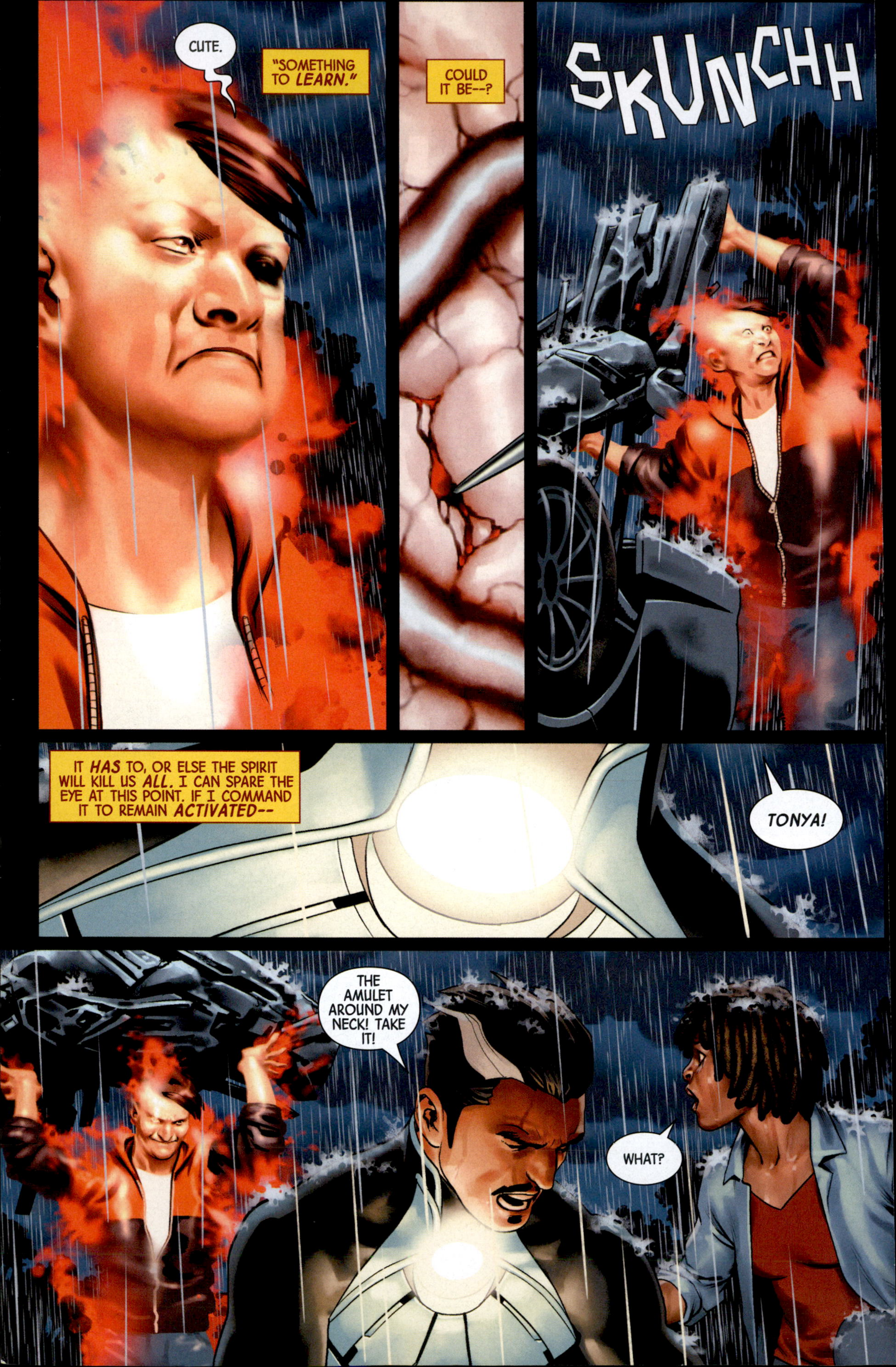
CUTE.
"SOMETHING TO LEARN."
COULD IT BE--?
SKUNCHH
IT HAS TO, OR ELSE THE SPIRIT WILL KILL US ALL. I CAN SPARE THE EYE AT THIS POINT. IF I COMMAND IT TO REMAIN ACTIVATED--
TONYA!
THE AMULET AROUND MY NECK! TAKE IT!
WHAT?

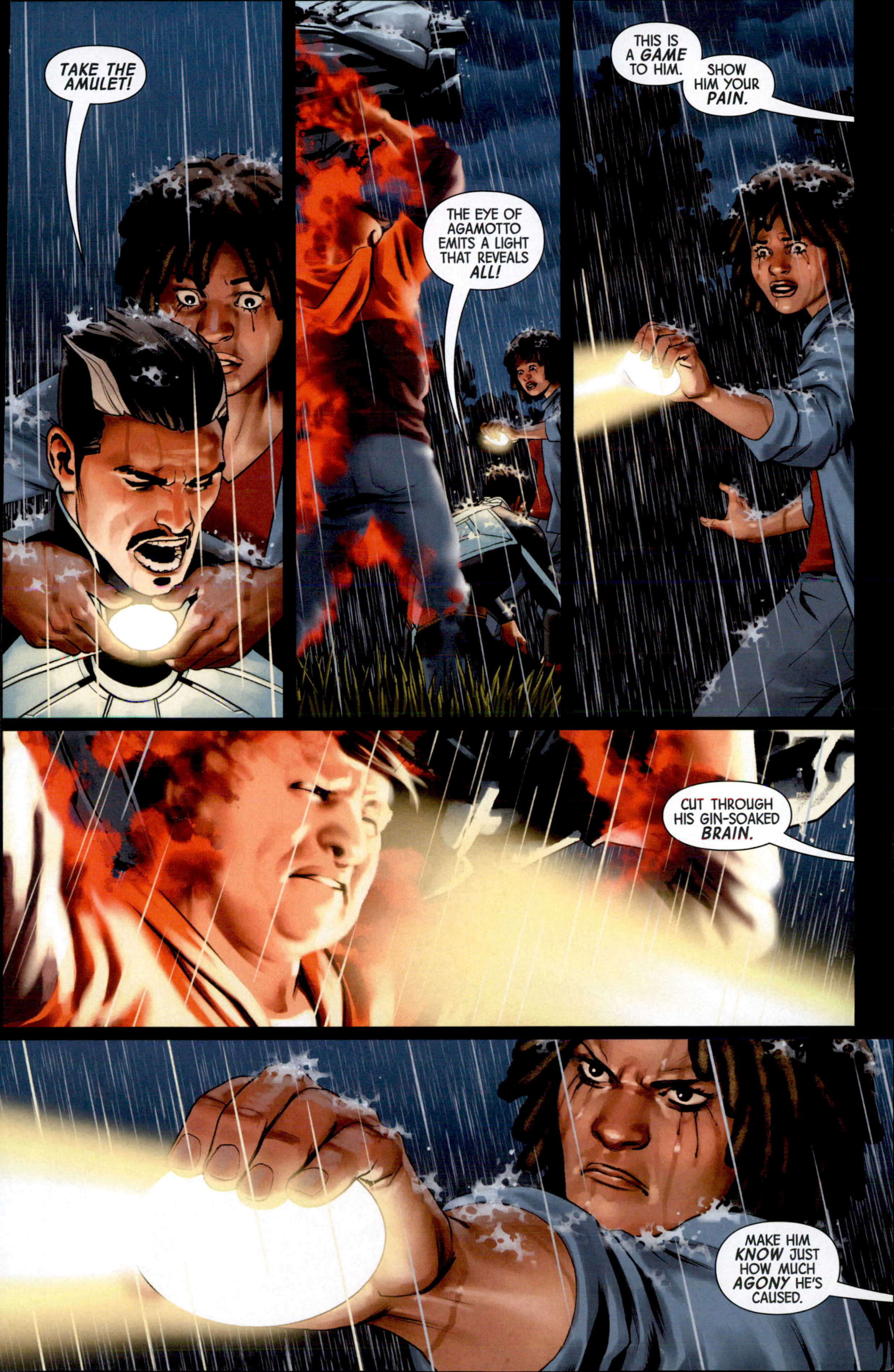
TAKE THE AMULET!
THE EYE OF AGAMOTTO EMITS A LIGHT THAT REVEALS ALL!
THIS IS A GAME TO HIM.
SHOW HIM YOUR PAIN.
CUT THROUGH HIS GIN-SOAKED BRAIN.
MAKE HIM KNOW JUST HOW MUCH AGONY HE'S CAUSED.

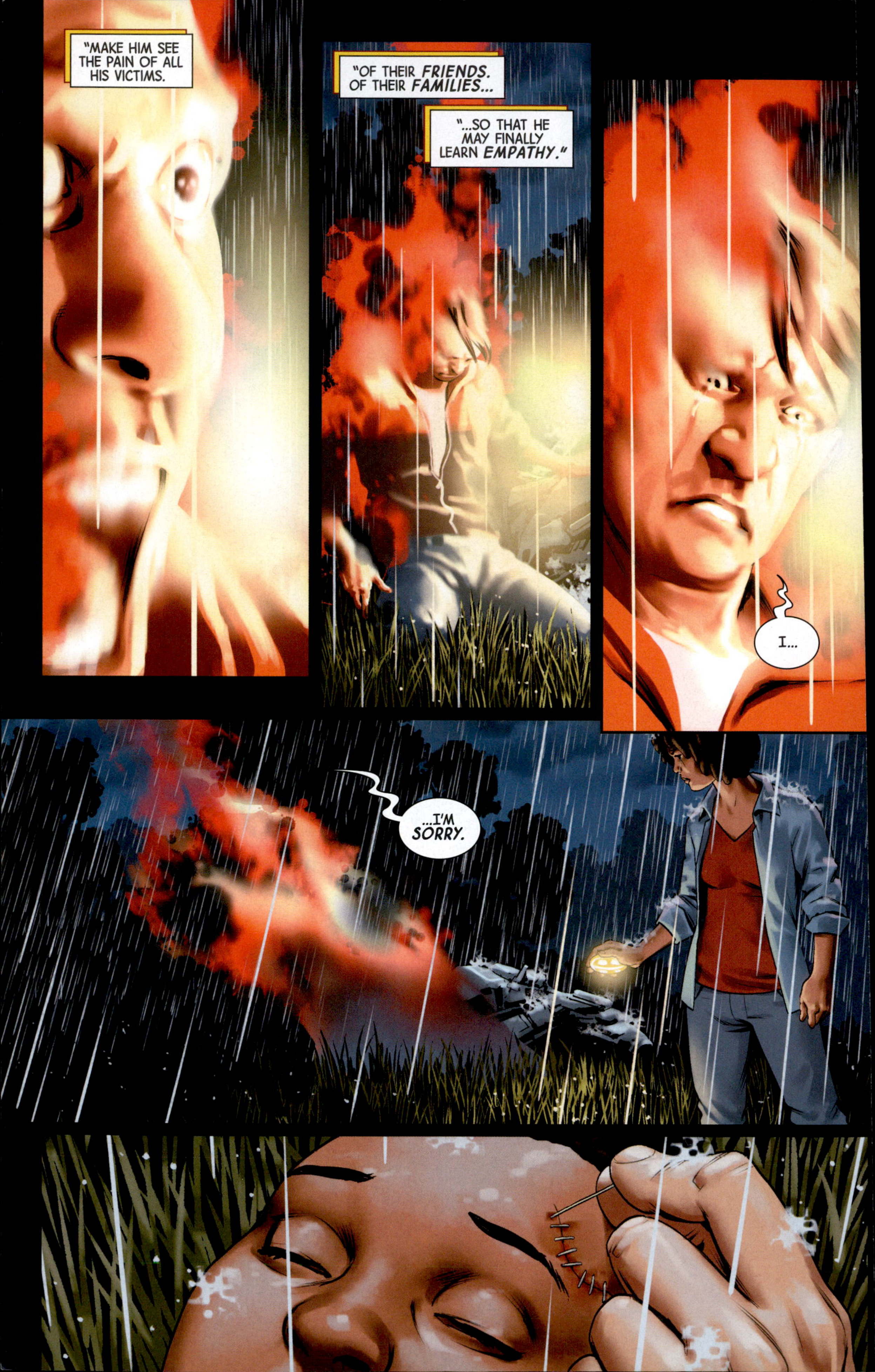
"MAKE HIM SEE THE PAIN OF ALL HIS VICTIMS.
"OF THEIR FRIENDS. OF THEIR FAMILIES...
"...SO THAT HE MAY FINALLY LEARN EMPATHY."
I...
...I'M SORRY.

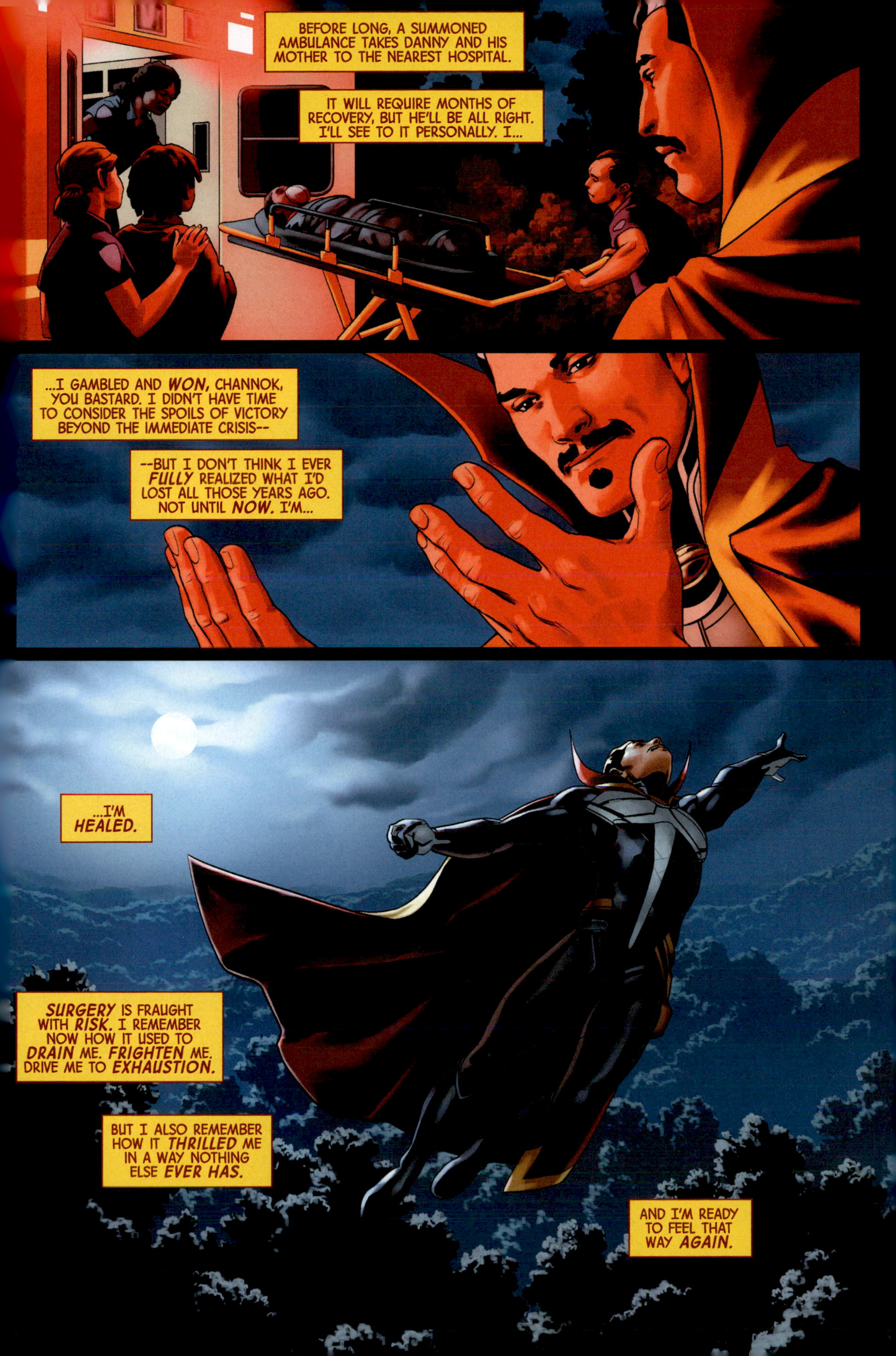
BEFORE LONG, A SUMMONED AMBULANCE TAKES DANNY AND HIS MOTHER TO THE NEAREST HOSPITAL.
IT WILL REQUIRE MONTHS OF RECOVERY, BUT HE'LL BE ALL RIGHT. I'LL SEE TO IT PERSONALLY. I...
...I GAMBLED AND WON, CHANNOK, YOU BASTARD. I DIDN'T HAVE TIME TO CONSIDER THE SPOILS OF VICTORY BEYOND THE IMMEDIATE CRISIS--
--BUT I DON'T THINK I EVER FULLY REALIZED WHAT I'D LOST ALL THOSE YEARS AGO. NOT UNTIL NOW. I'M...
...I'M HEALED.
SURGERY IS FRAUGHT WITH RISK. I REMEMBER NOW HOW IT USED TO DRAIN ME. FRIGHTEN ME. DRIVE ME TO EXHAUSTION.
BUT I ALSO REMEMBER HOW IT THRILLED ME IN A WAY NOTHING ELSE EVER HAS.
AND I'M READY TO FEEL THAT WAY AGAIN.

20

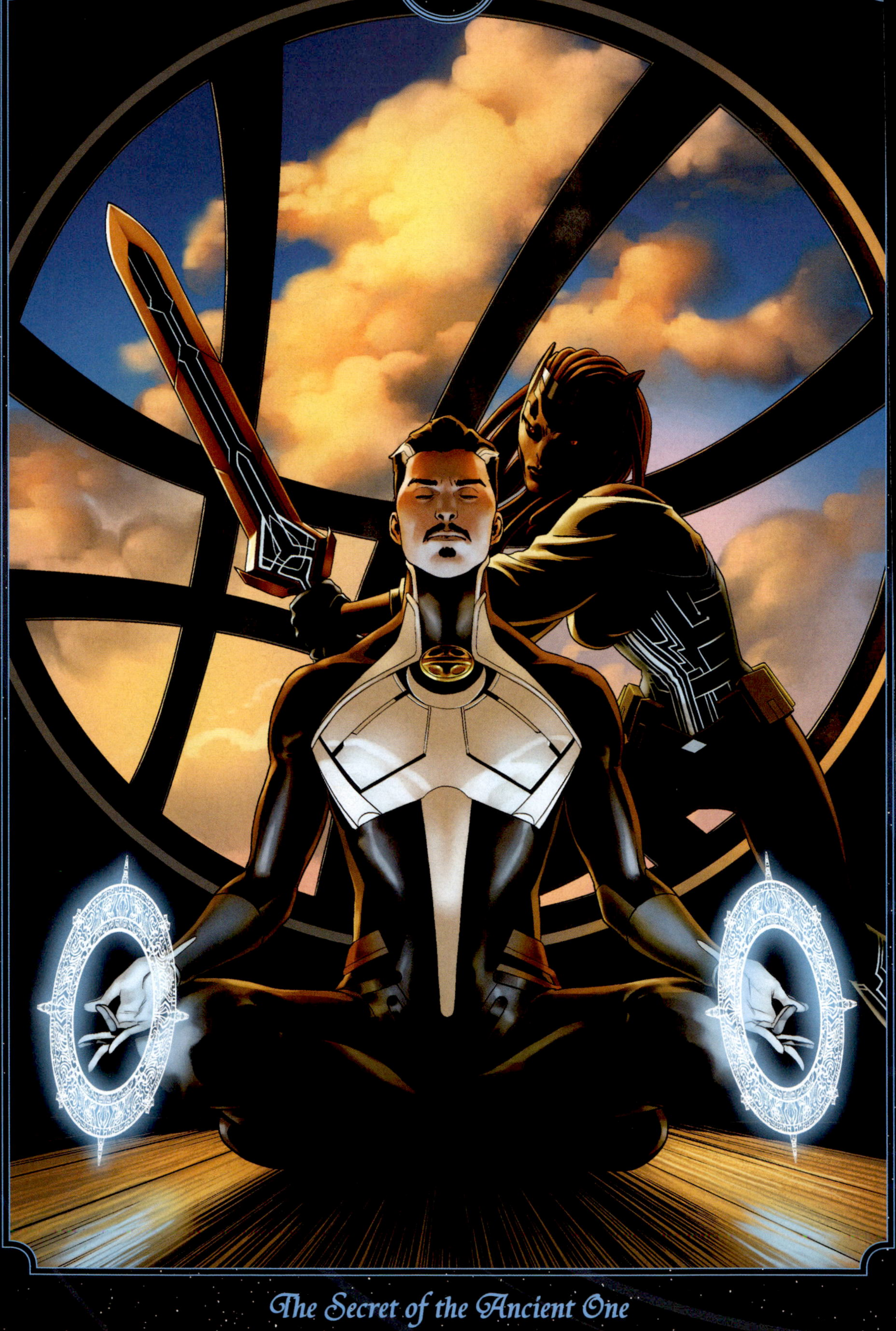

The Secret of the Ancient One

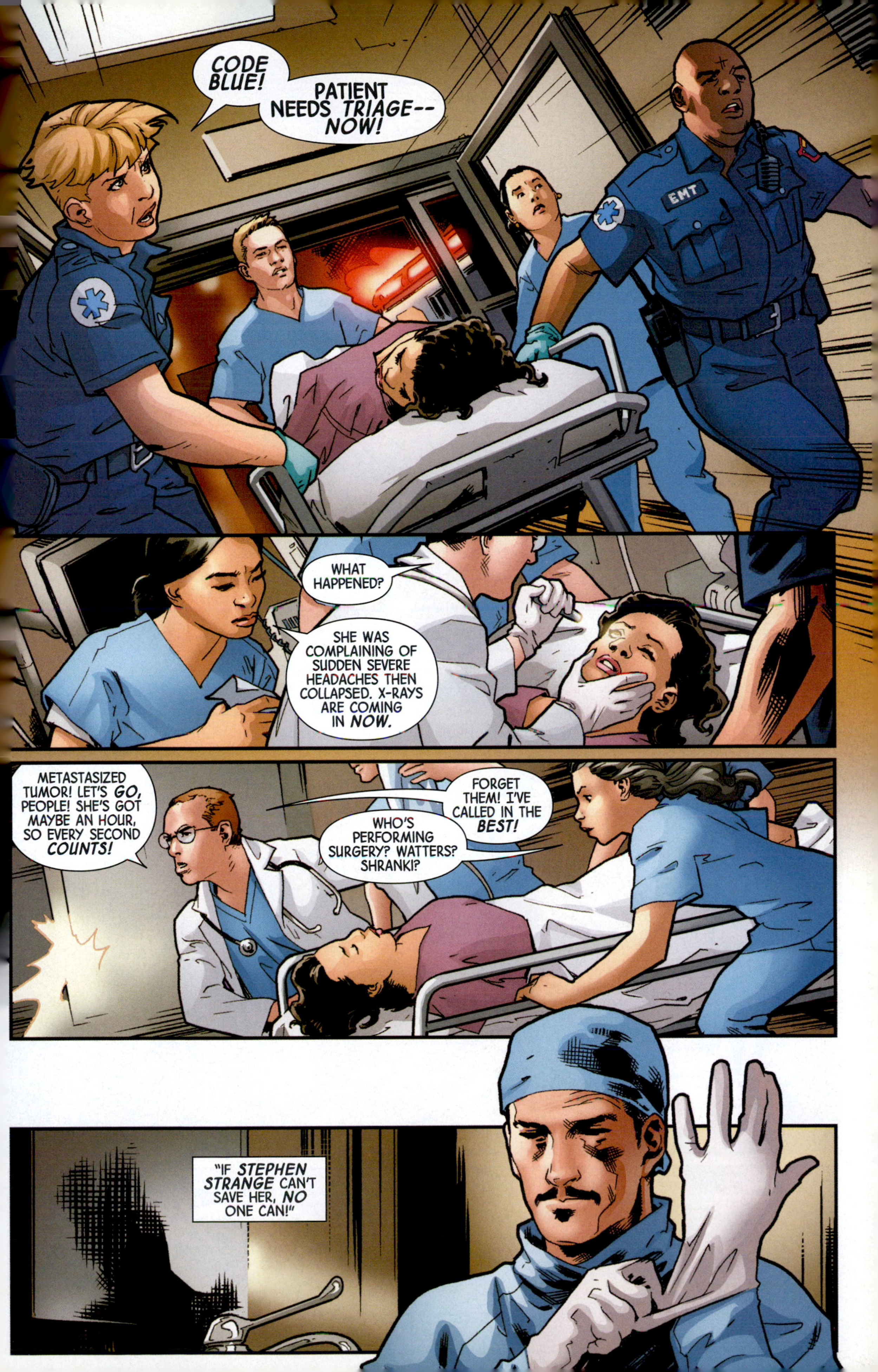

CODE BLUE!
PATIENT NEEDS TRIAGE-- NOW!
EMT
WHAT HAPPENED?
SHE WAS COMPLAINING OF SUDDEN SEVERE HEADACHES THEN COLLAPSED. X-RAYS ARE COMING IN NOW.
METASTASIZED TUMOR! LET'S GO, PEOPLE! SHE'S GOT MAYBE AN HOUR, SO EVERY SECOND COUNTS!
WHO'S PERFORMING SURGERY? WATTERS? SHRANKI?
FORGET THEM! I'VE CALLED IN THE BEST!
"IF STEPHEN STRANGE CAN'T SAVE HER, NO ONE CAN!"

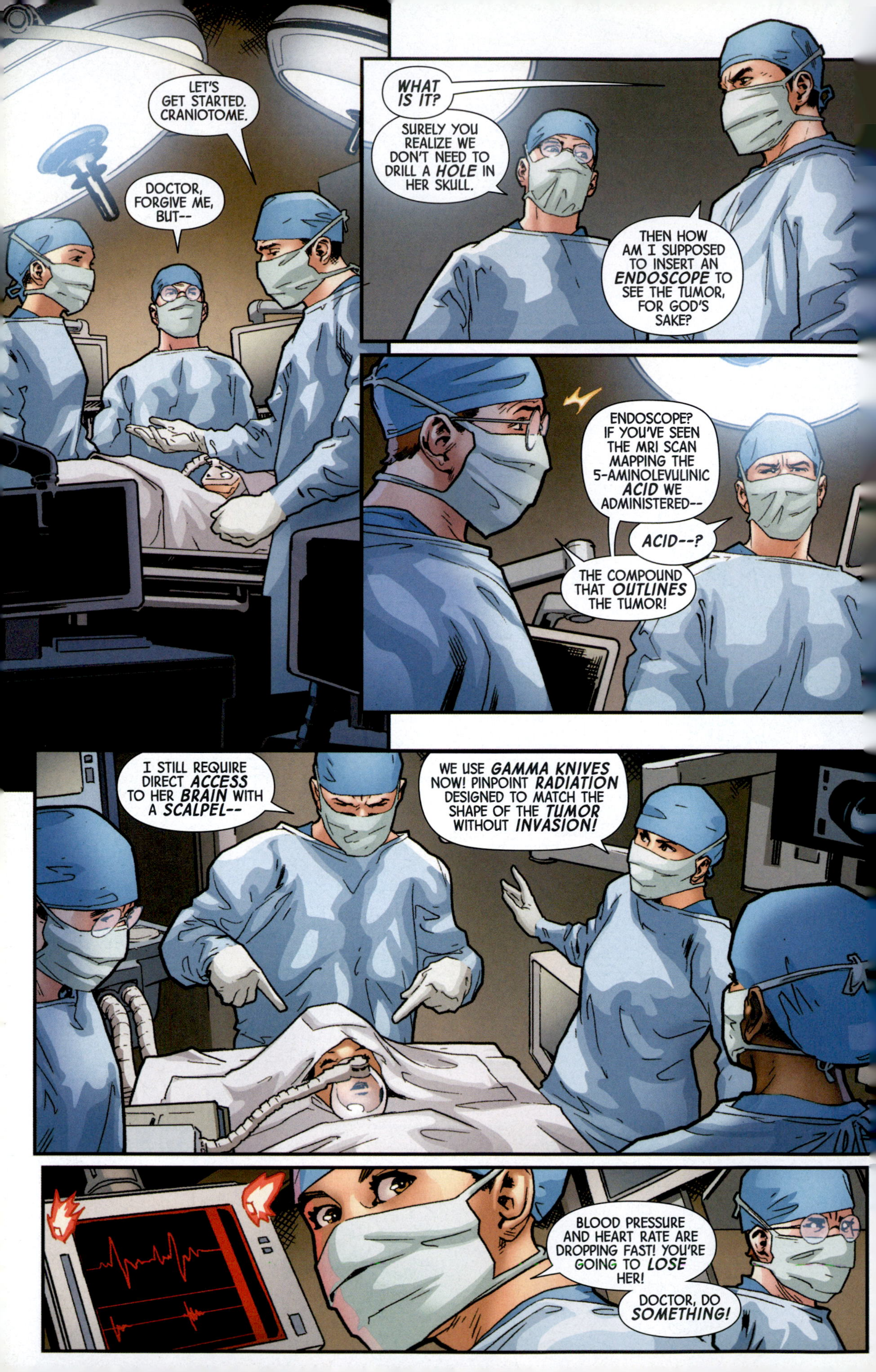
LET'S GET STARTED. CRANIOTOME.
DOCTOR, FORGIVE ME, BUT--
WHAT IS IT?
SURELY YOU REALIZE WE DON'T NEED TO DRILL A HOLE IN HER SKULL.
THEN HOW AM I SUPPOSED TO INSERT AN ENDOSCOPE TO SEE THE TUMOR, FOR GOD'S SAKE?
ENDOSCOPE? IF YOU'VE SEEN THE MRI SCAN MAPPING THE 5-AMINOLEVULINIC ACID WE ADMINISTERED--
ACID--?
THE COMPOUND THAT OUTLINES THE TUMOR!
I STILL REQUIRE DIRECT ACCESS TO HER BRAIN WITH A SCALPEL--
WE USE GAMMA KNIVES NOW! PINPOINT RADIATION DESIGNED TO MATCH THE SHAPE OF THE TUMOR WITHOUT INVASION!
BLOOD PRESSURE AND HEART RATE ARE DROPPING FAST! YOU'RE GOING TO LOSE HER!
DOCTOR, DO SOMETHING!

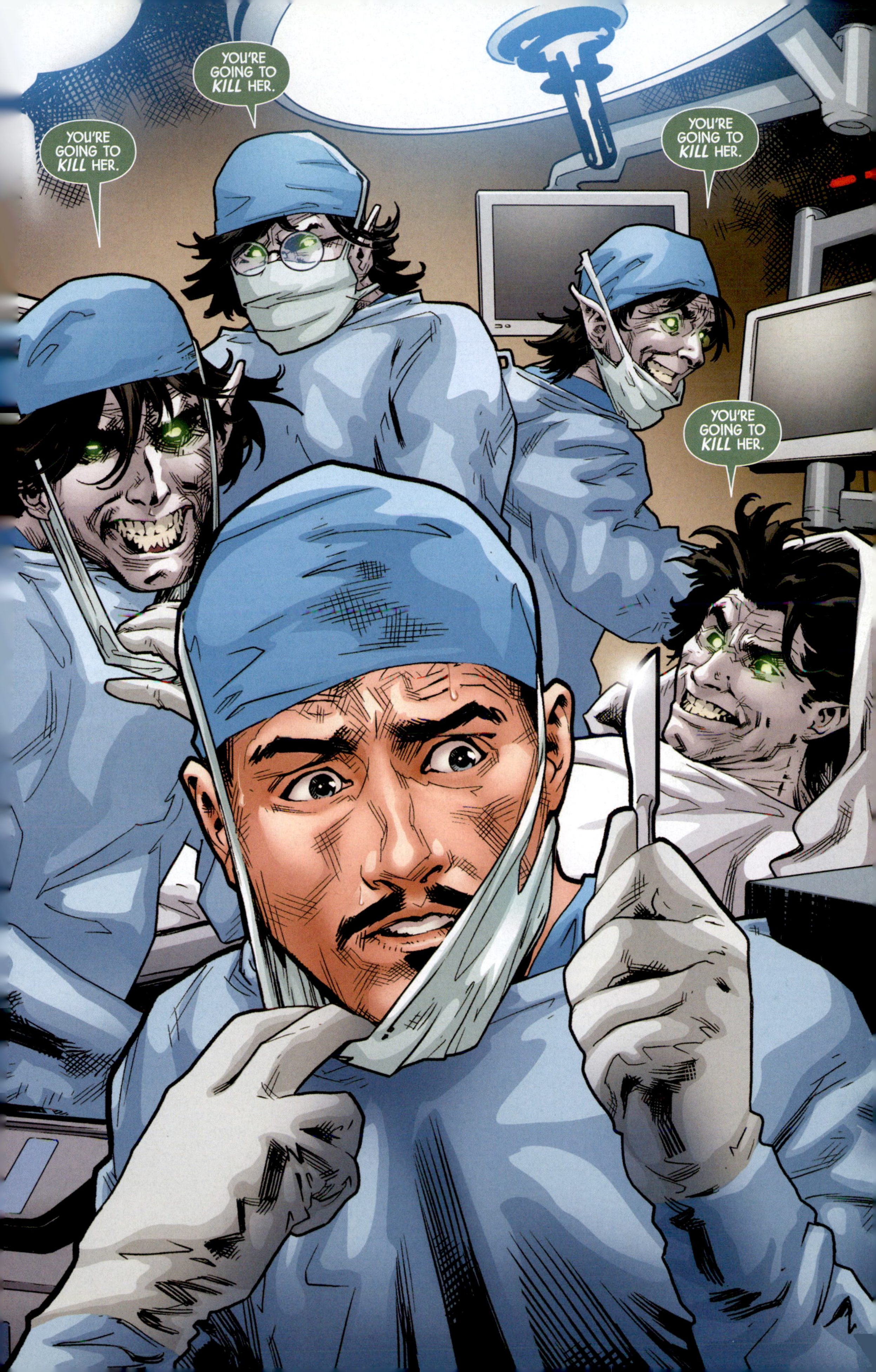
YOU'RE GOING TO KILL HER.
YOU'RE GOING TO KILL HER.
YOU'RE GOING TO KILL HER.
YOU'RE GOING TO KILL HER.

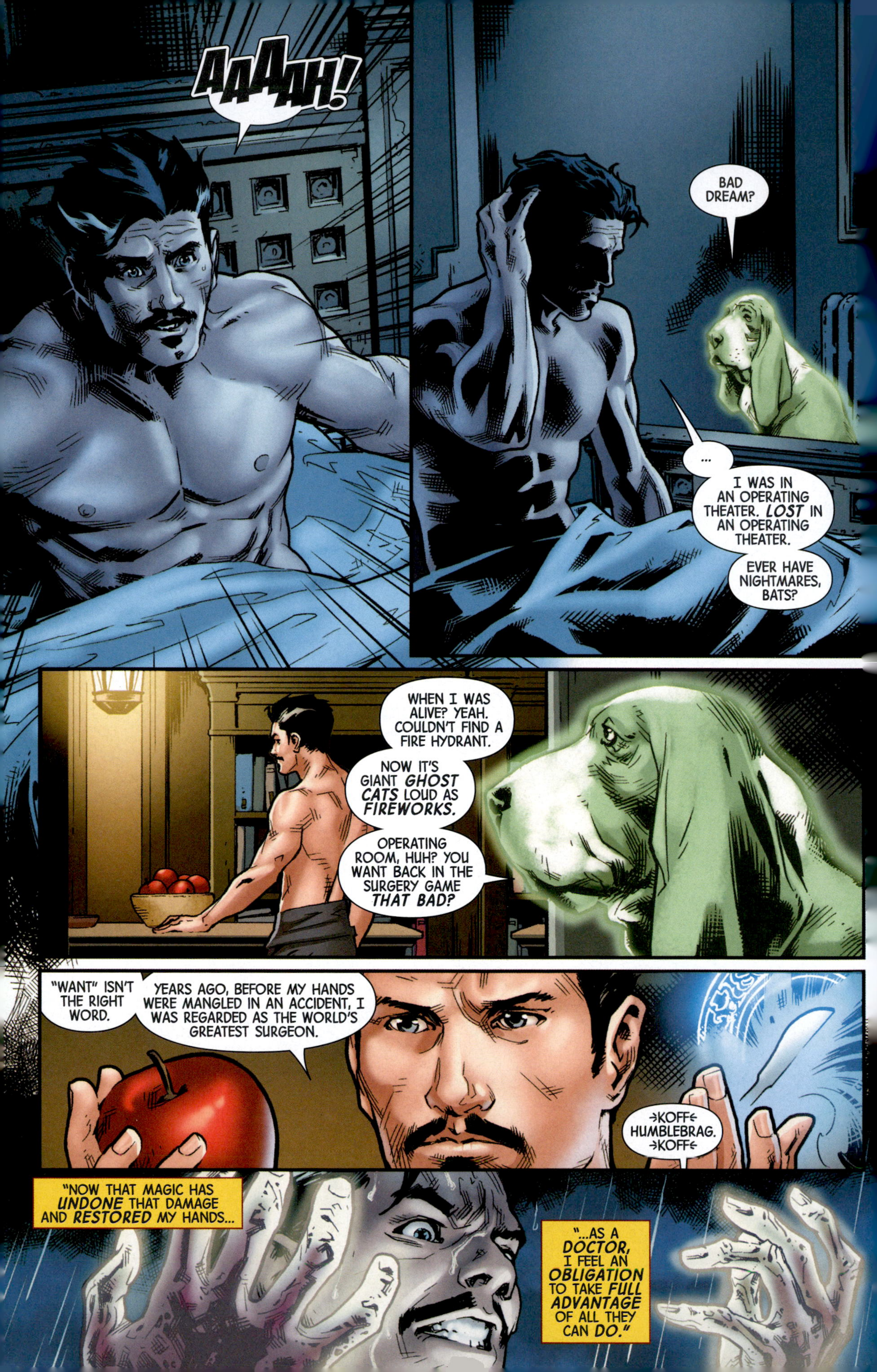
AAAAH!
BAD DREAM?
...
I WAS IN AN OPERATING THEATER. LOST IN AN OPERATING THEATER.
EVER HAVE NIGHTMARES, BATS?
WHEN I WAS ALIVE? YEAH. COULDN'T FIND A FIRE HYDRANT.
NOW IT'S GIANT GHOST CATS LOUD AS FIREWORKS.
OPERATING ROOM, HUH? YOU WANT BACK IN THE SURGERY GAME THAT BAD?
"WANT" ISN'T THE RIGHT WORD.
YEARS AGO, BEFORE MY HANDS WERE MANGLED IN AN ACCIDENT, I WAS REGARDED AS THE WORLD'S GREATEST SURGEON.
KOFF HUMBLEBRAG. *KOFF*
"NOW THAT MAGIC HAS UNDONE THAT DAMAGE AND RESTORED MY HANDS...
"...AS A DOCTOR, I FEEL AN OBLIGATION TO TAKE FULL ADVANTAGE OF ALL THEY CAN DO."

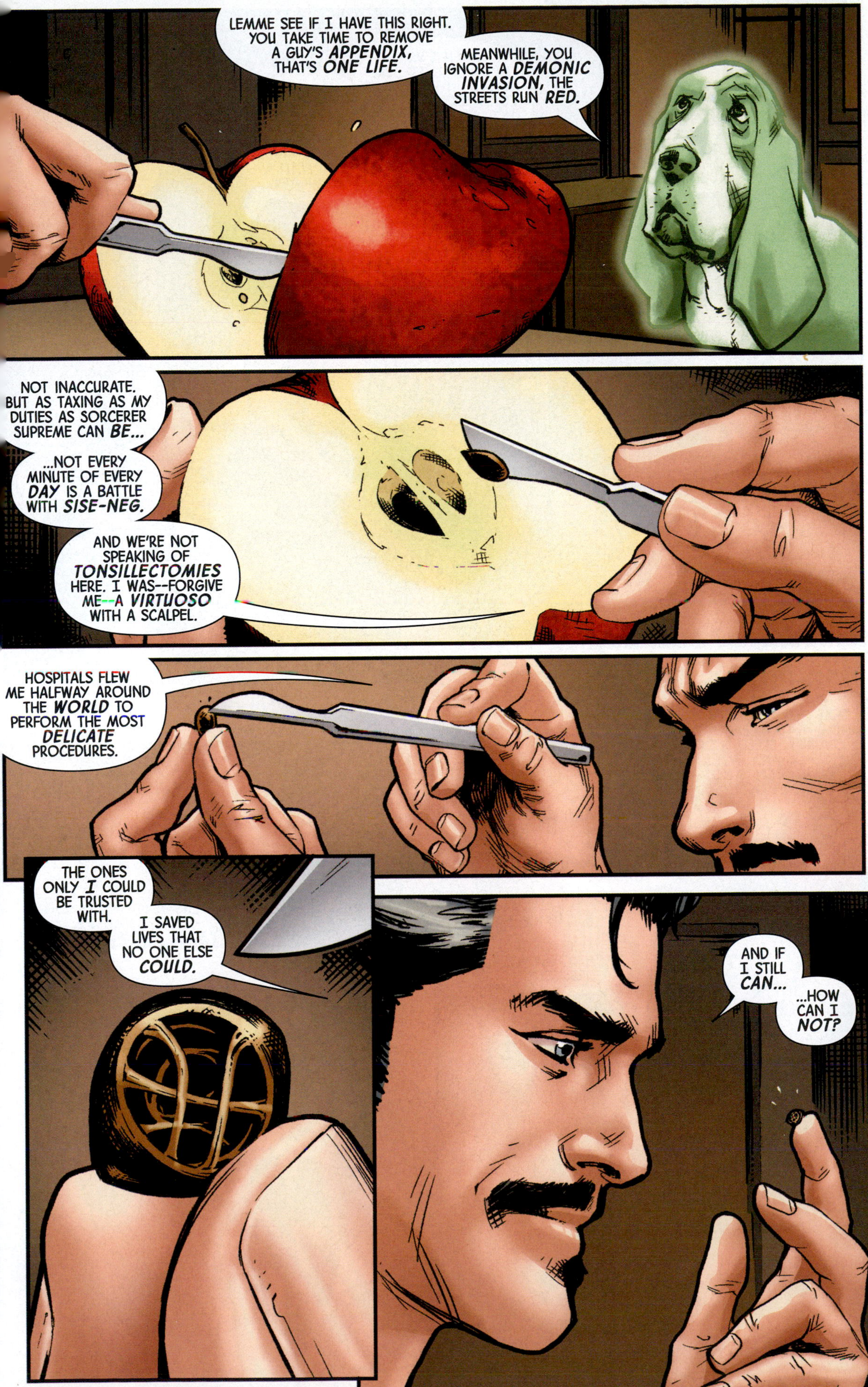

LEMME SEE IF I HAVE THIS RIGHT. YOU TAKE TIME TO REMOVE A GUY'S APPENDIX, THAT'S ONE LIFE.
MEANWHILE, YOU IGNORE A DEMONIC INVASION, THE STREETS RUN RED.
NOT INACCURATE. BUT AS TAXING AS MY DUTIES AS SORCERER SUPREME CAN BE...
...NOT EVERY MINUTE OF EVERY DAY IS A BATTLE WITH SISE-NEG.
AND WE'RE NOT SPEAKING OF TONSILLECTOMIES HERE. I WAS--FORGIVE ME--A VIRTUOSO WITH A SCALPEL.
HOSPITALS FLEW ME HALFWAY AROUND THE WORLD TO PERFORM THE MOST DELICATE PROCEDURES.
THE ONES ONLY I COULD BE TRUSTED WITH.
I SAVED LIVES THAT NO ONE ELSE COULD.
AND IF I STILL CAN...
...HOW CAN I NOT?

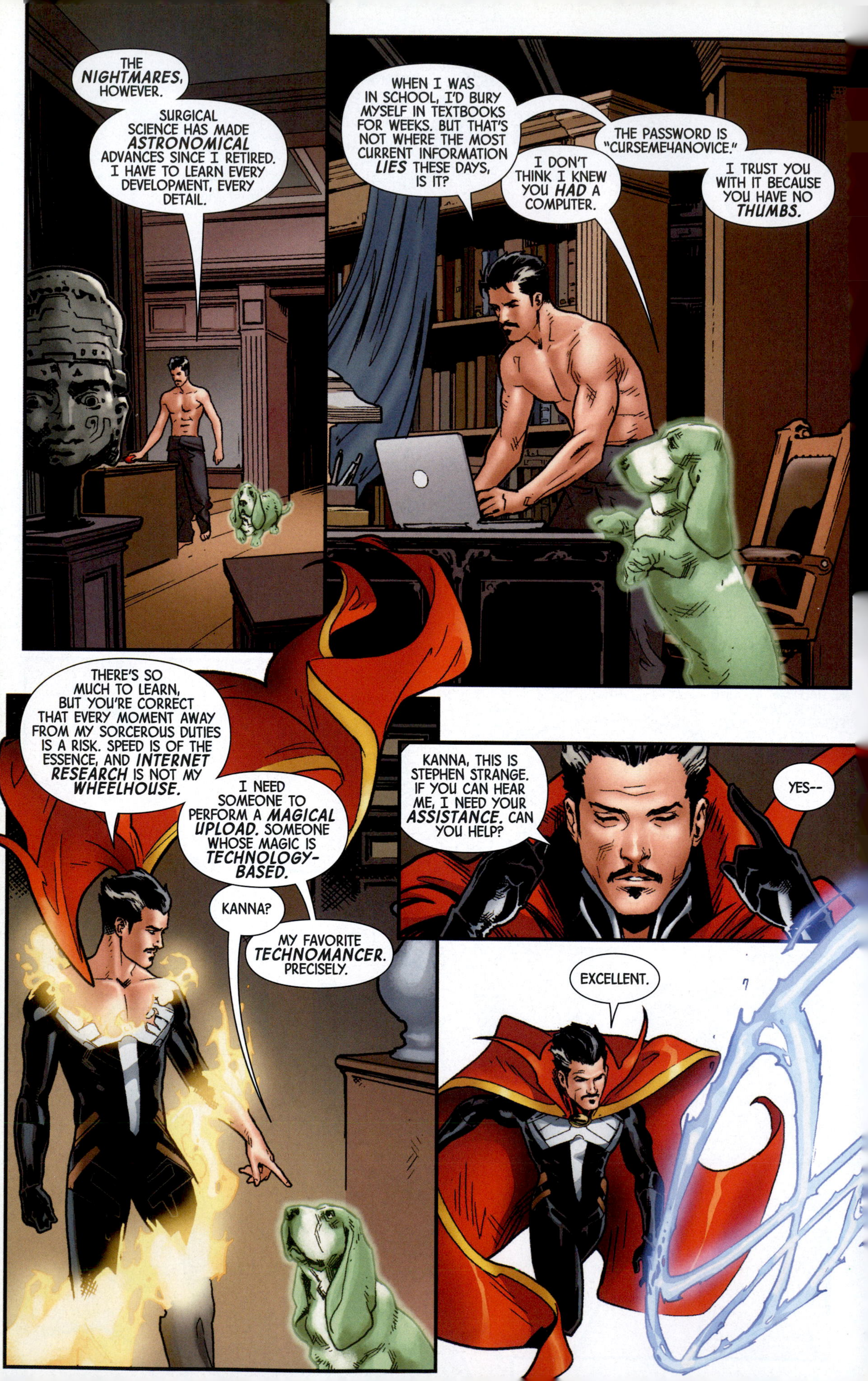
THE NIGHTMARES, HOWEVER.
SURGICAL SCIENCE HAS MADE ASTRONOMICAL ADVANCES SINCE I RETIRED. I HAVE TO LEARN EVERY DEVELOPMENT, EVERY DETAIL.
WHEN I WAS IN SCHOOL, I'D BURY MYSELF IN TEXTBOOKS FOR WEEKS. BUT THAT'S NOT WHERE THE MOST CURRENT INFORMATION LIES THESE DAYS, IS IT?
I DON'T THINK I KNEW YOU HAD A COMPUTER.
THE PASSWORD IS "CURSEME4ANOVICE."
I TRUST YOU WITH IT BECAUSE YOU HAVE NO THUMBS.
THERE'S SO MUCH TO LEARN, BUT YOU'RE CORRECT THAT EVERY MOMENT AWAY FROM MY SORCEROUS DUTIES IS A RISK. SPEED IS OF THE ESSENCE, AND INTERNET RESEARCH IS NOT MY WHEELHOUSE.
I NEED SOMEONE TO PERFORM A MAGICAL UPLOAD. SOMEONE WHOSE MAGIC IS TECHNOLOGY-BASED.
KANNA?
MY FAVORITE TECHNOMANCER. PRECISELY.
KANNA, THIS IS STEPHEN STRANGE. IF YOU CAN HEAR ME, I NEED YOUR ASSISTANCE. CAN YOU HELP?
YES--
EXCELLENT.

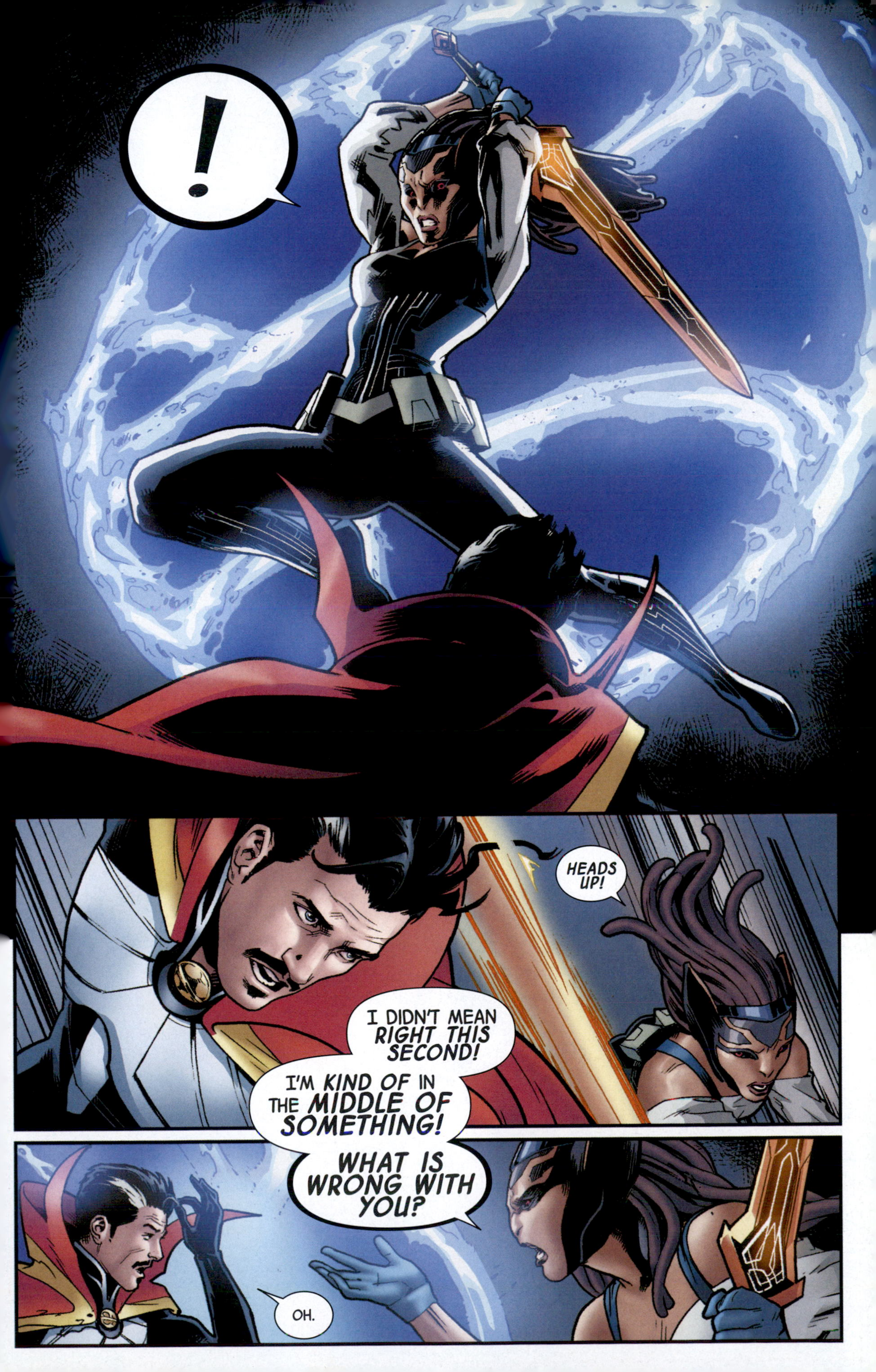
!
HEADS UP!
I DIDN'T MEAN RIGHT THIS SECOND!
I'M KIND OF IN THE MIDDLE OF SOMETHING!
WHAT IS WRONG WITH YOU?
OH.

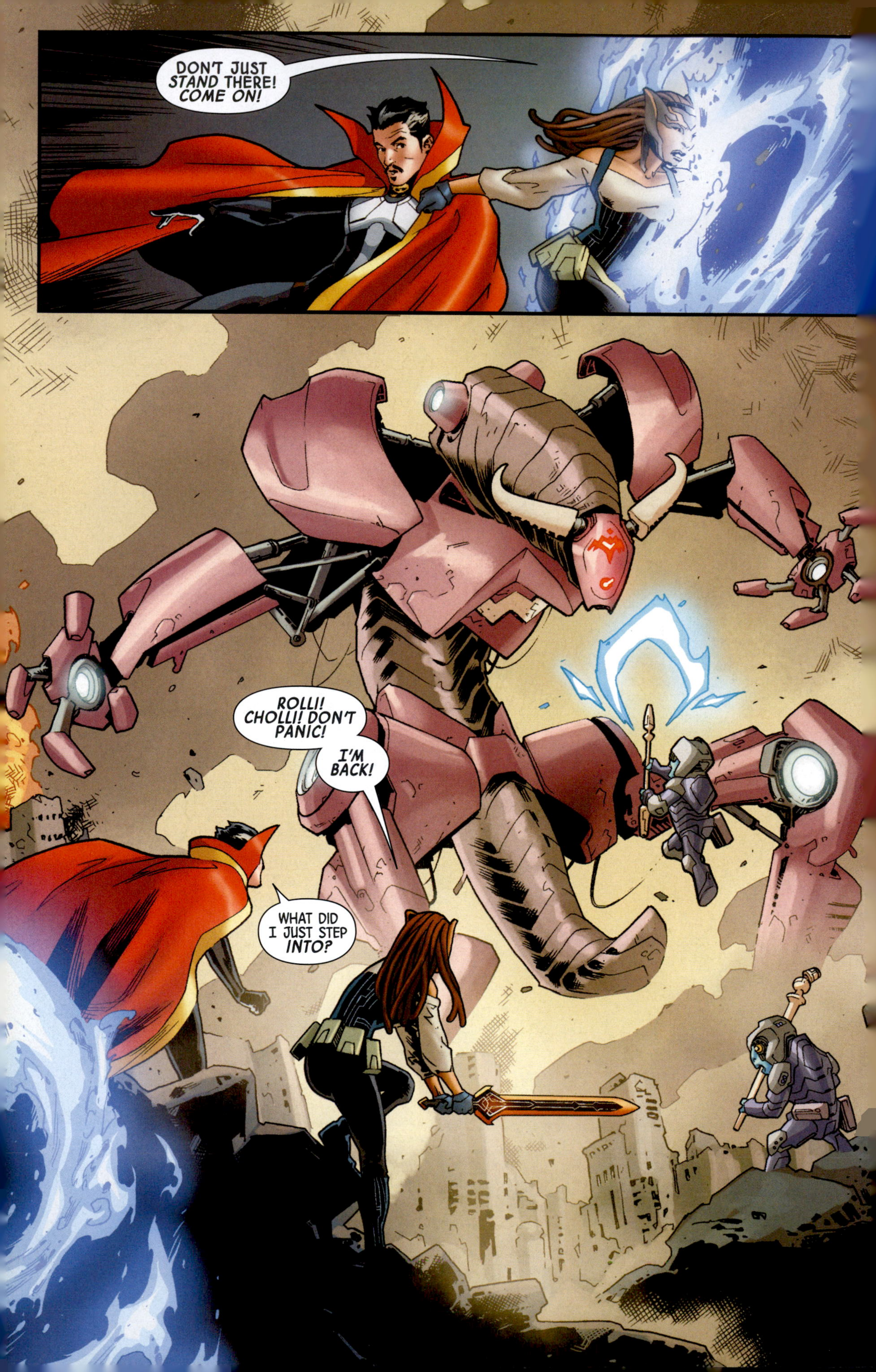
DON'T JUST STAND THERE! COME ON!
ROLLI! CHOLLI! DON'T PANIC!
I'M BACK!
WHAT DID I JUST STEP INTO?

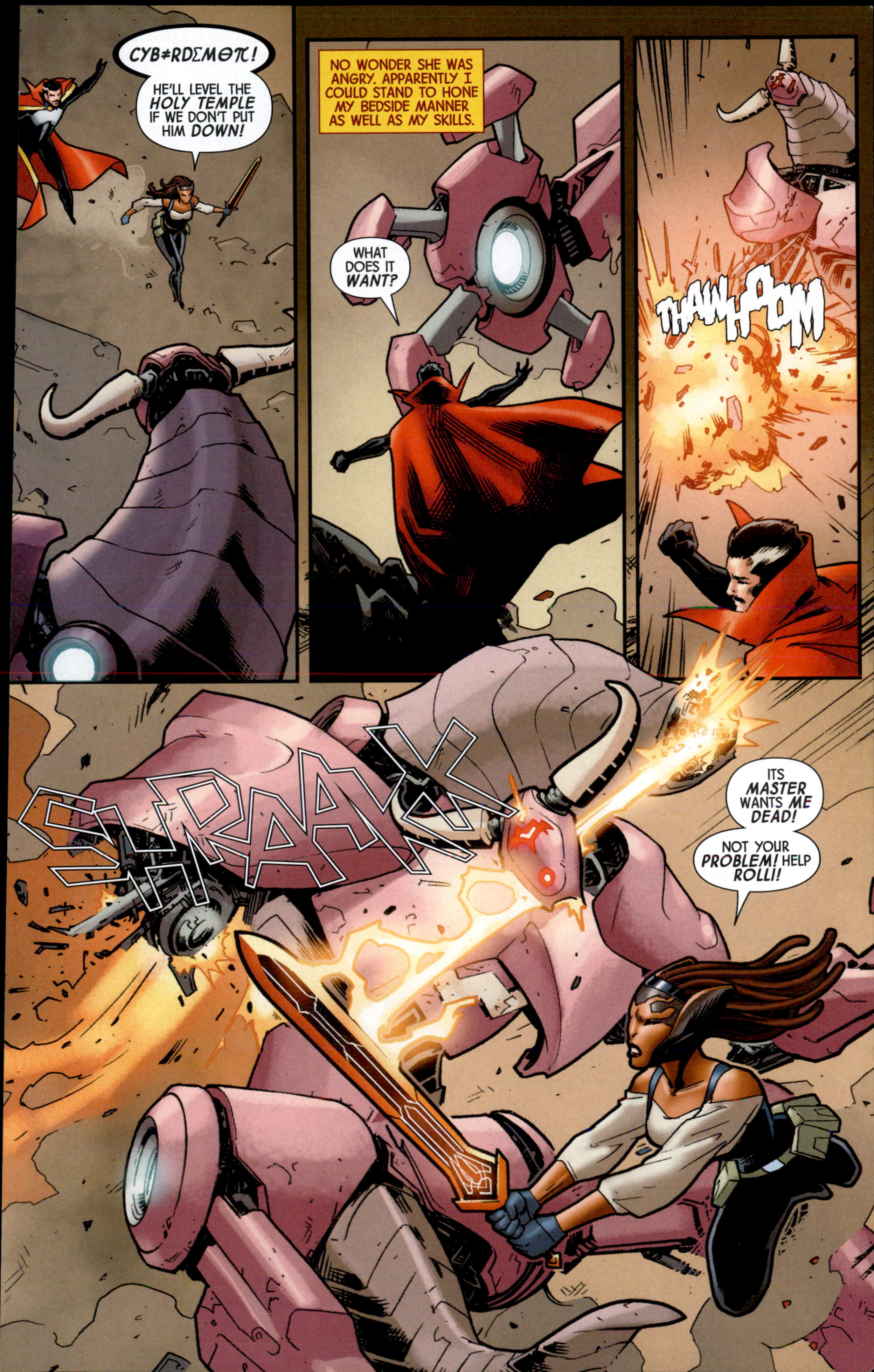
CYB≠RDΣMΘπ!
HE'LL LEVEL THE HOLY TEMPLE IF WE DON'T PUT HIM DOWN!
NO WONDER SHE WAS ANGRY. APPARENTLY I COULD STAND TO HONE MY BEDSIDE MANNER AS WELL AS MY SKILLS.
WHAT DOES IT WANT?
THAWHOOM
SHRAAKK
ITS MASTER WANTS ME DEAD!
NOT YOUR PROBLEM! HELP ROLLI!

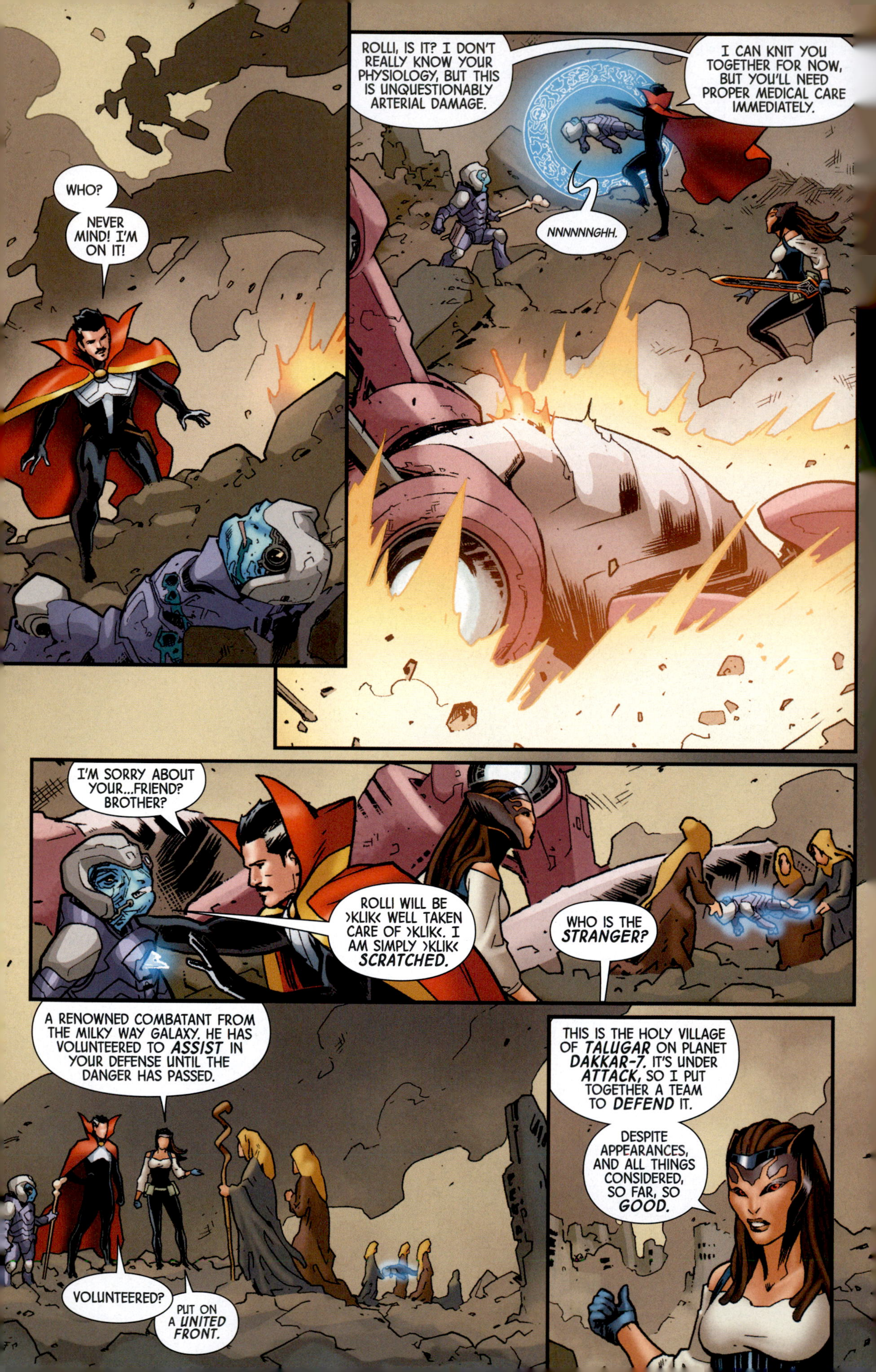
WHO?
NEVER MIND! I'M ON IT!
ROLLI, IS IT? I DON'T REALLY KNOW YOUR PHYSIOLOGY, BUT THIS IS UNQUESTIONABLY ARTERIAL DAMAGE.
I CAN KNIT YOU TOGETHER FOR NOW, BUT YOU'LL NEED PROPER MEDICAL CARE IMMEDIATELY.
NNNNNNGHH.
I'M SORRY ABOUT YOUR...FRIEND? BROTHER?
ROLLI WILL BE ›KLIK‹ WELL TAKEN CARE OF ›KLIK‹. I AM SIMPLY ›KLIK‹ SCRATCHED.
WHO IS THE STRANGER?
A RENOWNED COMBATANT FROM THE MILKY WAY GALAXY. HE HAS VOLUNTEERED TO ASSIST IN YOUR DEFENSE UNTIL THE DANGER HAS PASSED.
VOLUNTEERED?
PUT ON A UNITED FRONT.
THIS IS THE HOLY VILLAGE OF TALUGAR ON PLANET DAKKAR-7. IT'S UNDER ATTACK, SO I PUT TOGETHER A TEAM TO DEFEND IT.
DESPITE APPEARANCES, AND ALL THINGS CONSIDERED, SO FAR, SO GOOD.

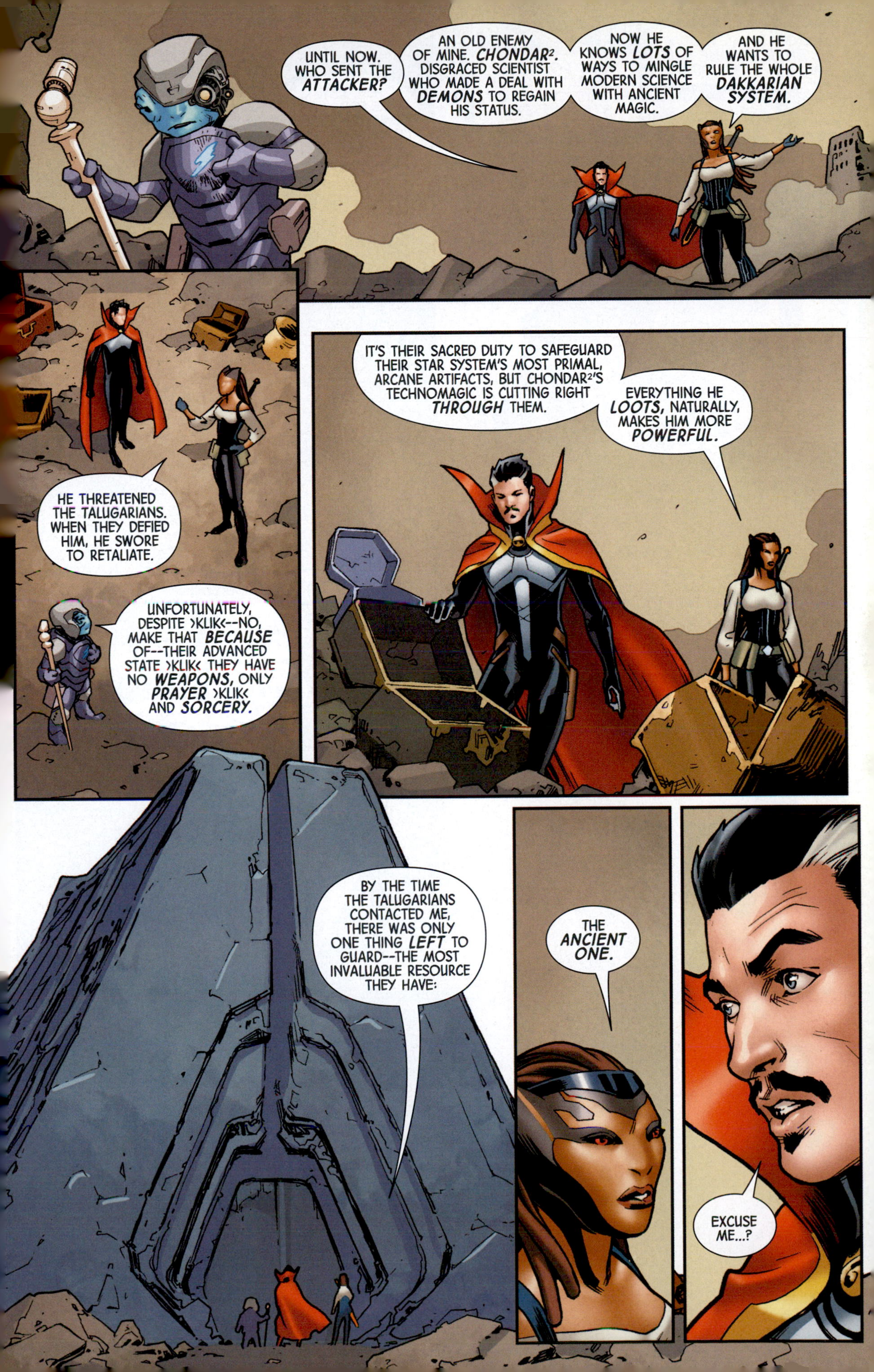
UNTIL NOW. WHO SENT THE ATTACKER?
AN OLD ENEMY OF MINE. CHONDAR². DISGRACED SCIENTIST WHO MADE A DEAL WITH DEMONS TO REGAIN HIS STATUS.
NOW HE KNOWS LOTS OF WAYS TO MINGLE MODERN SCIENCE WITH ANCIENT MAGIC.
AND HE WANTS TO RULE THE WHOLE DAKKARIAN SYSTEM.
HE THREATENED THE TALUGARIANS. WHEN THEY DEFIED HIM, HE SWORE TO RETALIATE.
UNFORTUNATELY, DESPITE ›KLIK‹--NO, MAKE THAT BECAUSE OF--THEIR ADVANCED STATE ›KLIK‹ THEY HAVE NO WEAPONS, ONLY PRAYER ›KLIK‹ AND SORCERY.
IT'S THEIR SACRED DUTY TO SAFEGUARD THEIR STAR SYSTEM'S MOST PRIMAL, ARCANE ARTIFACTS, BUT CHONDAR²'S TECHNOMAGIC IS CUTTING RIGHT THROUGH THEM.
EVERYTHING HE LOOTS, NATURALLY, MAKES HIM MORE POWERFUL.
BY THE TIME THE TALUGARIANS CONTACTED ME, THERE WAS ONLY ONE THING LEFT TO GUARD--THE MOST INVALUABLE RESOURCE THEY HAVE:
THE ANCIENT ONE.
EXCUSE ME...?

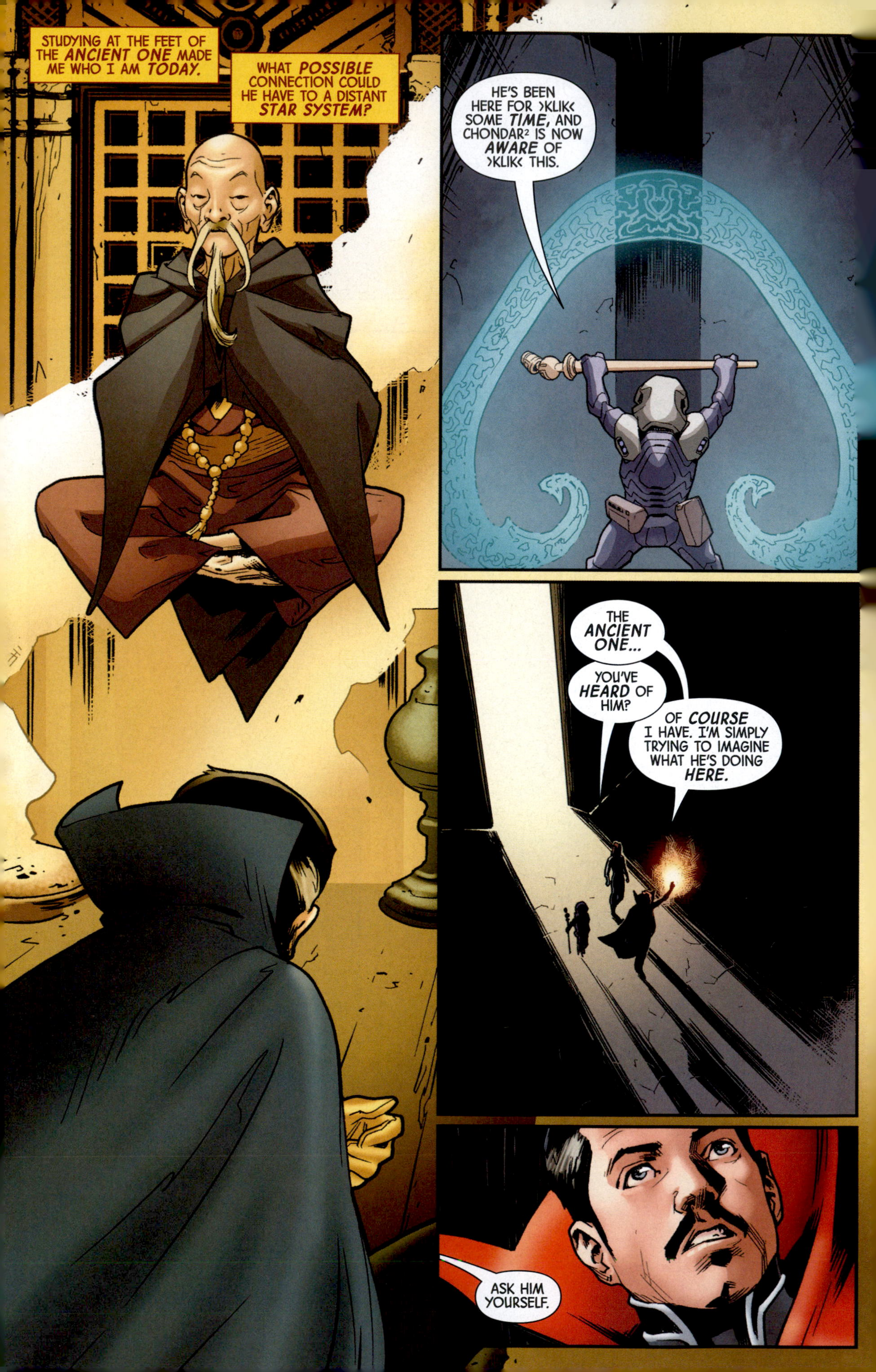
STUDYING AT THE FEET OF THE ANCIENT ONE MADE ME WHO I AM TODAY.
WHAT POSSIBLE CONNECTION COULD HE HAVE TO A DISTANT STAR SYSTEM?
HE'S BEEN HERE FOR >KLIK< SOME TIME, AND CHONDAR^{2} IS NOW AWARE OF >KLIK< THIS.
THE ANCIENT ONE...
YOU'VE HEARD OF HIM?
OF COURSE I HAVE. I'M SIMPLY TRYING TO IMAGINE WHAT HE'S DOING HERE.
ASK HIM YOURSELF.

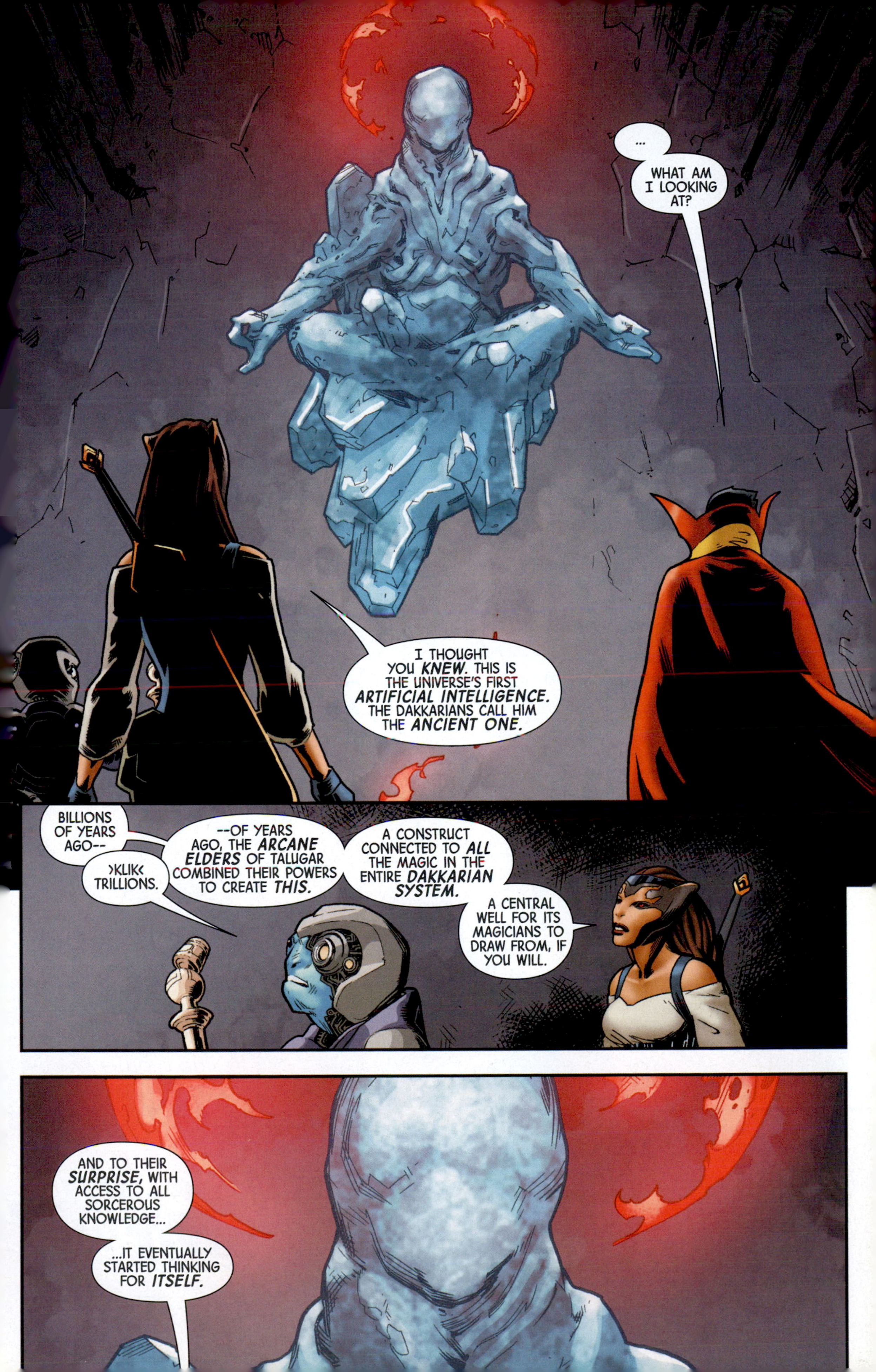
...
WHAT AM I LOOKING AT?
I THOUGHT YOU KNEW. THIS IS THE UNIVERSE'S FIRST ARTIFICIAL INTELLIGENCE. THE DAKKARIANS CALL HIM THE ANCIENT ONE.
BILLIONS OF YEARS AGO--
›KLIK‹ TRILLIONS.
--OF YEARS AGO, THE ARCANE ELDERS OF TALUGAR COMBINED THEIR POWERS TO CREATE THIS.
A CONSTRUCT CONNECTED TO ALL THE MAGIC IN THE ENTIRE DAKKARIAN SYSTEM.
A CENTRAL WELL FOR ITS MAGICIANS TO DRAW FROM, IF YOU WILL.
AND TO THEIR SURPRISE, WITH ACCESS TO ALL SORCEROUS KNOWLEDGE...
...IT EVENTUALLY STARTED THINKING FOR ITSELF.

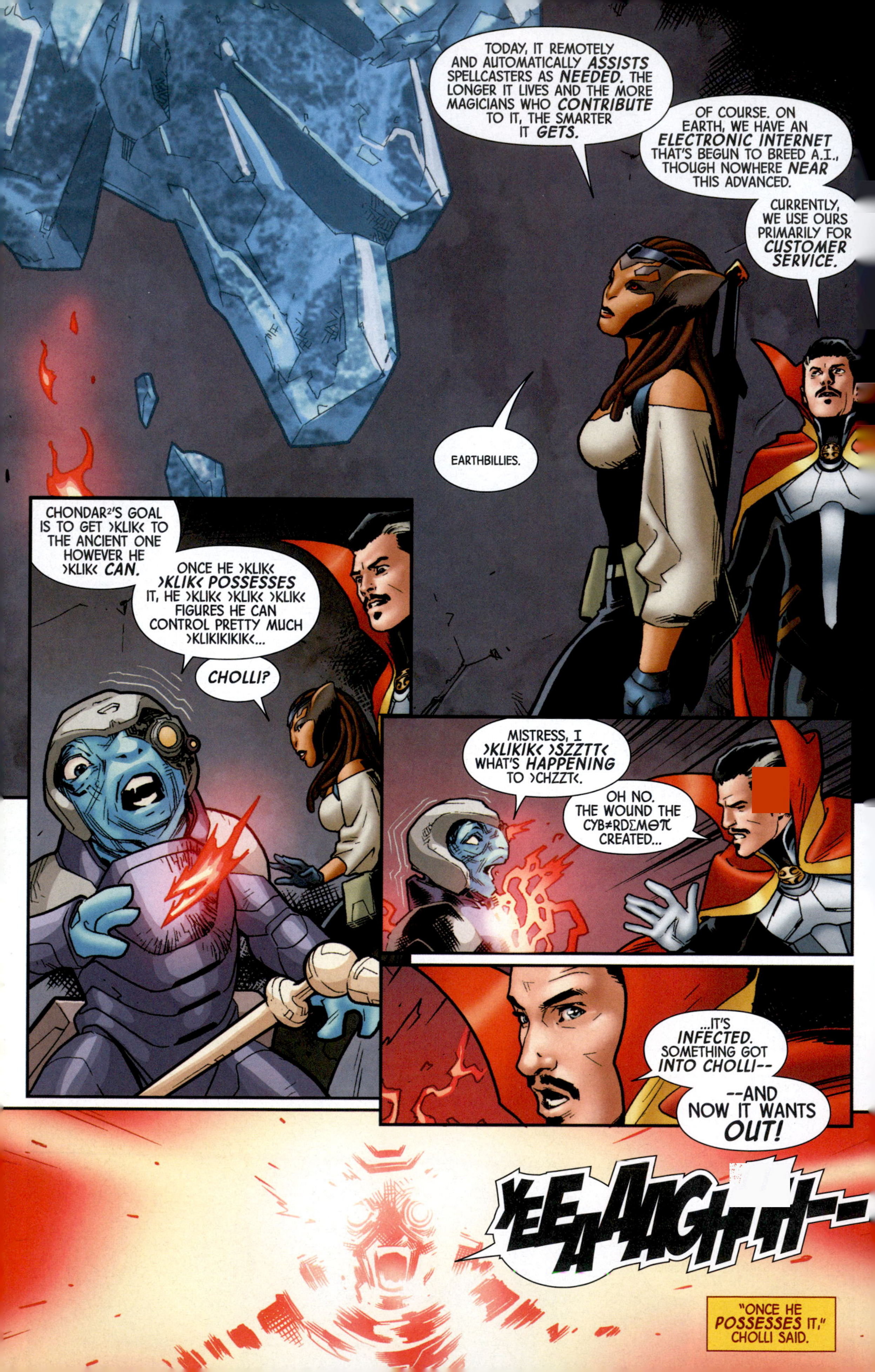
TODAY, IT REMOTELY AND AUTOMATICALLY ASSISTS SPELLCASTERS AS NEEDED. THE LONGER IT LIVES AND THE MORE MAGICIANS WHO CONTRIBUTE TO IT, THE SMARTER IT GETS.
OF COURSE, ON EARTH, WE HAVE AN ELECTRONIC INTERNET THAT'S BEGUN TO BREED A.I., THOUGH NOWHERE NEAR THIS ADVANCED.
CURRENTLY, WE USE OURS PRIMARILY FOR CUSTOMER SERVICE.
EARTHBILLIES.
CHONDAR²'S GOAL IS TO GET ›KLIK‹ TO THE ANCIENT ONE HOWEVER HE ›KLIK‹ CAN.
ONCE HE ›KLIK‹ ›KLIK‹ POSSESSES IT, HE ›KLIK‹ ›KLIK‹ ›KLIK‹ FIGURES HE CAN CONTROL PRETTY MUCH ›KLIKIKIKIK‹...
CHOLLI?
MISTRESS, I ›KLIKIK‹ ›SZZTT‹ WHAT'S HAPPENING TO ›CHZZT‹.
OH NO. THE WOUND THE CYB≠RDΣMΘπ CREATED...
...IT'S INFECTED. SOMETHING GOT INTO CHOLLI--
--AND NOW IT WANTS OUT!
YEEAAAGHHH--
"ONCE HE POSSESSES IT," CHOLLI SAID.

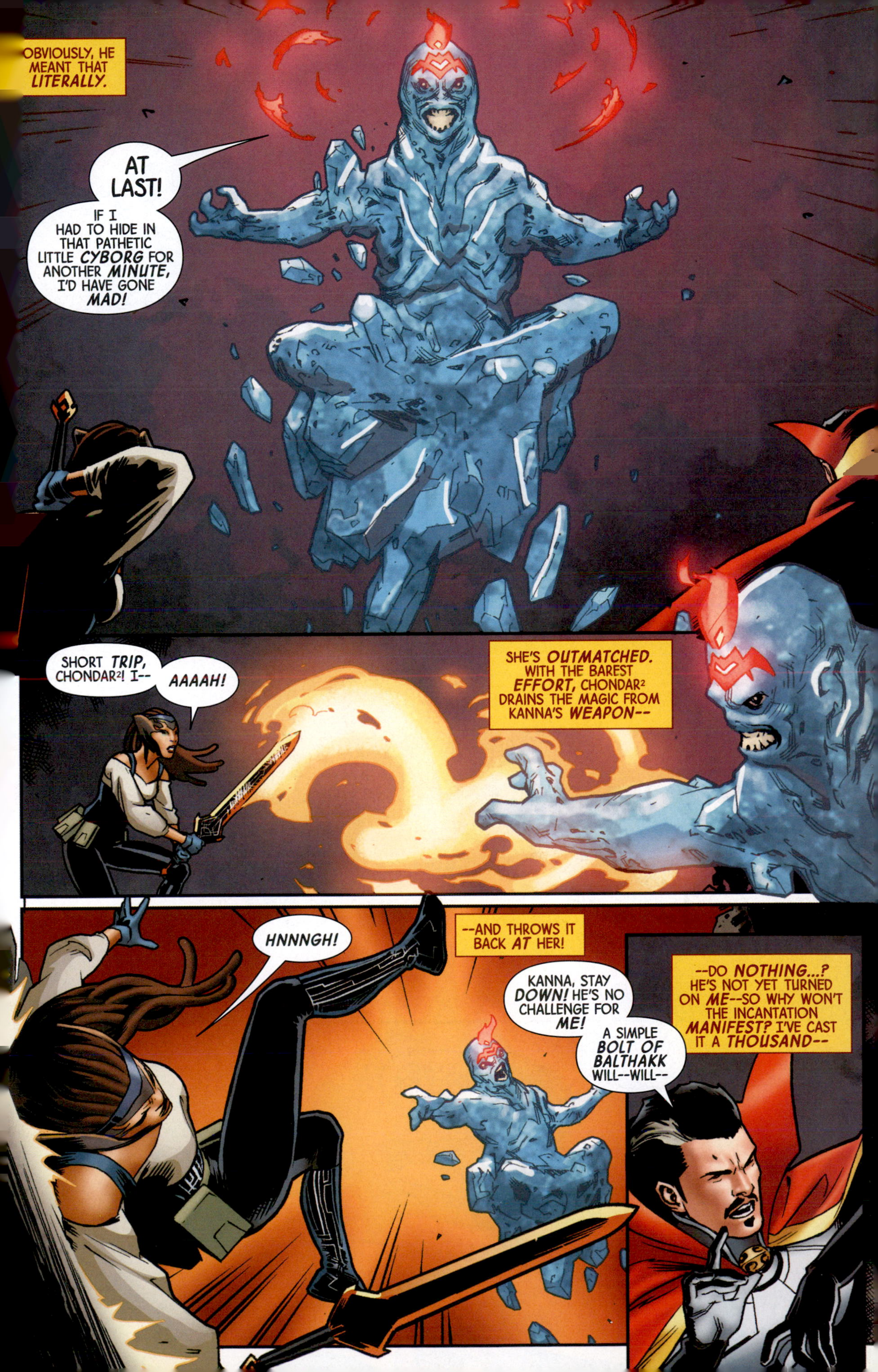
OBVIOUSLY, HE MEANT THAT LITERALLY.
AT LAST!
IF I HAD TO HIDE IN THAT PATHETIC LITTLE CYBORG FOR ANOTHER MINUTE, I'D HAVE GONE MAD!
SHORT TRIP, CHONDAR²! I--
AAAAH!
SHE'S OUTMATCHED. WITH THE BAREST EFFORT, CHONDAR² DRAINS THE MAGIC FROM KANNA'S WEAPON--
HNNNGH!
--AND THROWS IT BACK AT HER!
KANNA, STAY DOWN! HE'S NO CHALLENGE FOR ME!
A SIMPLE BOLT OF BALTHAKK WILL--WILL--
--DO NOTHING...? HE'S NOT YET TURNED ON ME--SO WHY WON'T THE INCANTATION MANIFEST? I'VE CAST IT A THOUSAND--

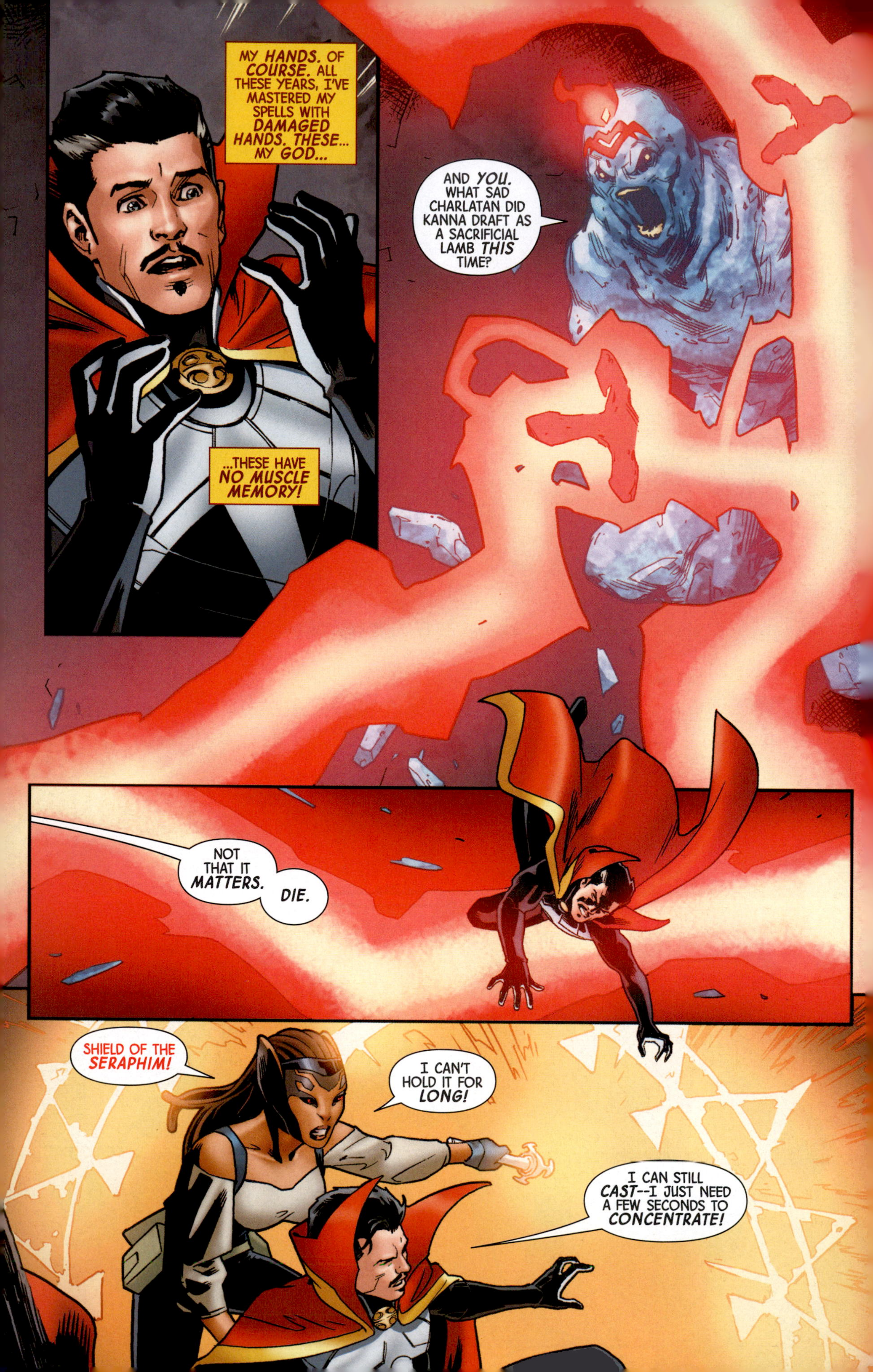
MY HANDS, OF COURSE. ALL THESE YEARS, I'VE MASTERED MY SPELLS WITH DAMAGED HANDS. THESE... MY GOD...
...THESE HAVE NO MUSCLE MEMORY!
AND YOU. WHAT SAD CHARLATAN DID KANNA DRAFT AS A SACRIFICIAL LAMB THIS TIME?
NOT THAT IT MATTERS.
DIE.
SHIELD OF THE SERAPHIM!
I CAN'T HOLD IT FOR LONG!
I CAN STILL CAST--I JUST NEED A FEW SECONDS TO CONCENTRATE!

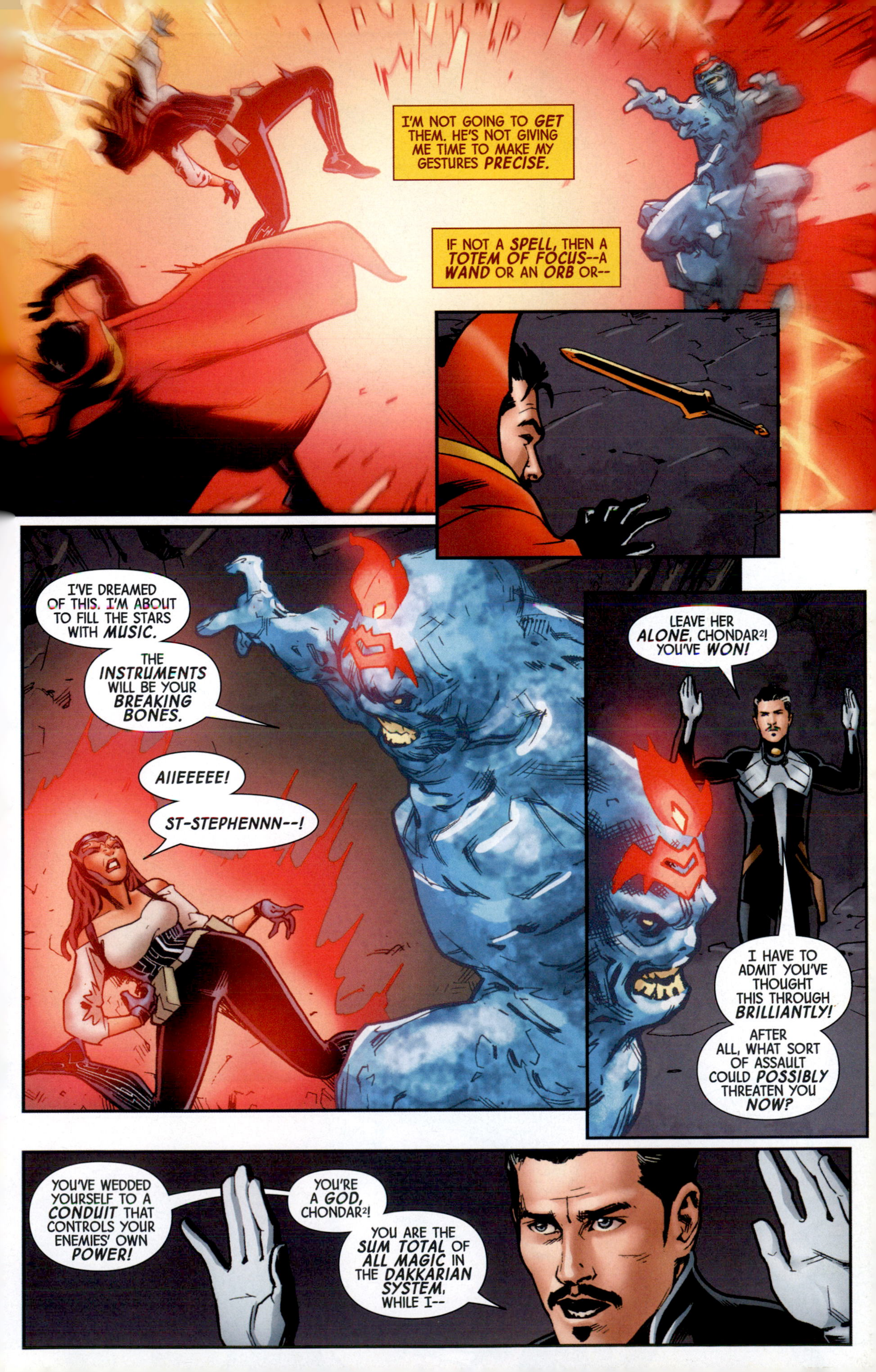
I'M NOT GOING TO GET THEM. HE'S NOT GIVING ME TIME TO MAKE MY GESTURES PRECISE.
IF NOT A SPELL, THEN A TOTEM OF FOCUS--A WAND OR AN ORB OR--
I'VE DREAMED OF THIS. I'M ABOUT TO FILL THE STARS WITH MUSIC.
THE INSTRUMENTS WILL BE YOUR BREAKING BONES.
AIIEEEEE!
ST-STEPHENNN--!
LEAVE HER ALONE, CHONDAR[2]! YOU'VE WON!
I HAVE TO ADMIT YOU'VE THOUGHT THIS THROUGH BRILLIANTLY!
AFTER ALL, WHAT SORT OF ASSAULT COULD POSSIBLY THREATEN YOU NOW?
YOU'VE WEDDED YOURSELF TO A CONDUIT THAT CONTROLS YOUR ENEMIES' OWN POWER!
YOU'RE A GOD, CHONDAR[2]!
YOU ARE THE SUM TOTAL OF ALL MAGIC IN THE DAKKARIAN SYSTEM, WHILE I--

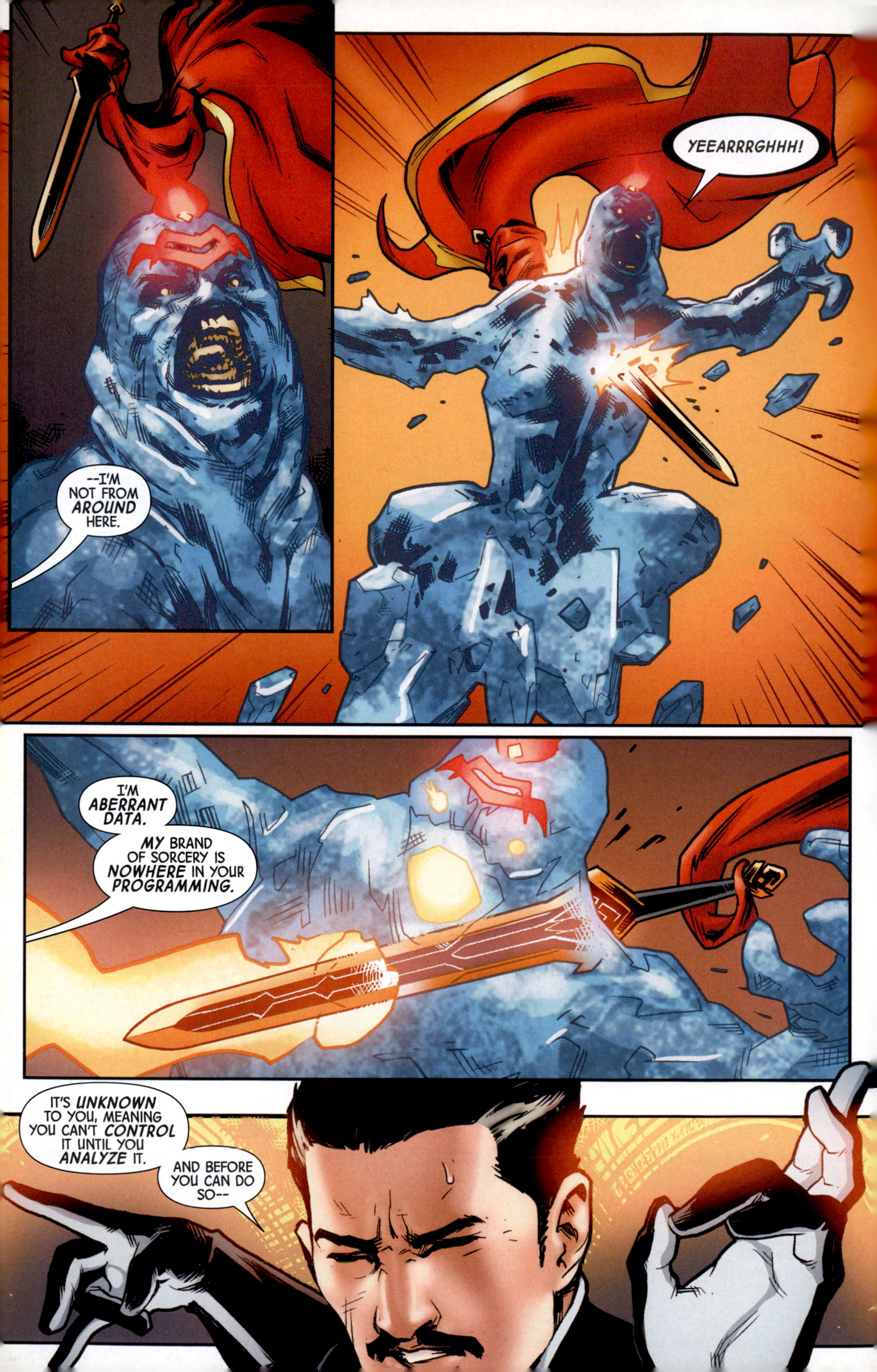
--I'M NOT FROM AROUND HERE.
YEEARRRGHHH!
I'M ABERRANT DATA.
MY BRAND OF SORCERY IS NOWHERE IN YOUR PROGRAMMING.
IT'S UNKNOWN TO YOU, MEANING YOU CAN'T CONTROL IT UNTIL YOU ANALYZE IT.
AND BEFORE YOU CAN DO SO--

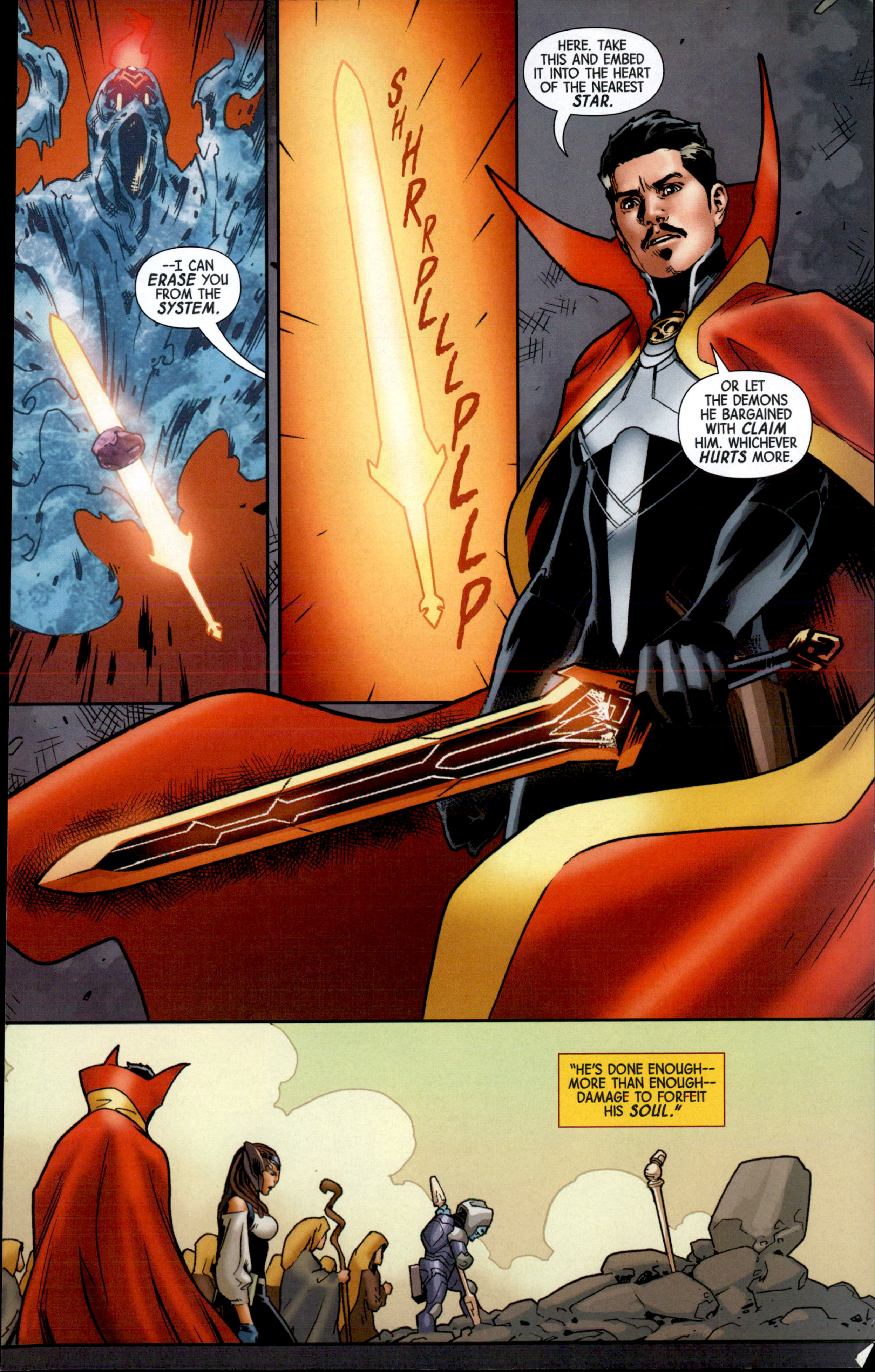
--I CAN ERASE YOU FROM THE SYSTEM.
SHHRRPLLLPLLP
HERE. TAKE THIS AND EMBED IT INTO THE HEART OF THE NEAREST STAR.
OR LET THE DEMONS HE BARGAINED WITH CLAIM HIM. WHICHEVER HURTS MORE.
"HE'S DONE ENOUGH-- MORE THAN ENOUGH-- DAMAGE TO FORFEIT HIS SOUL."

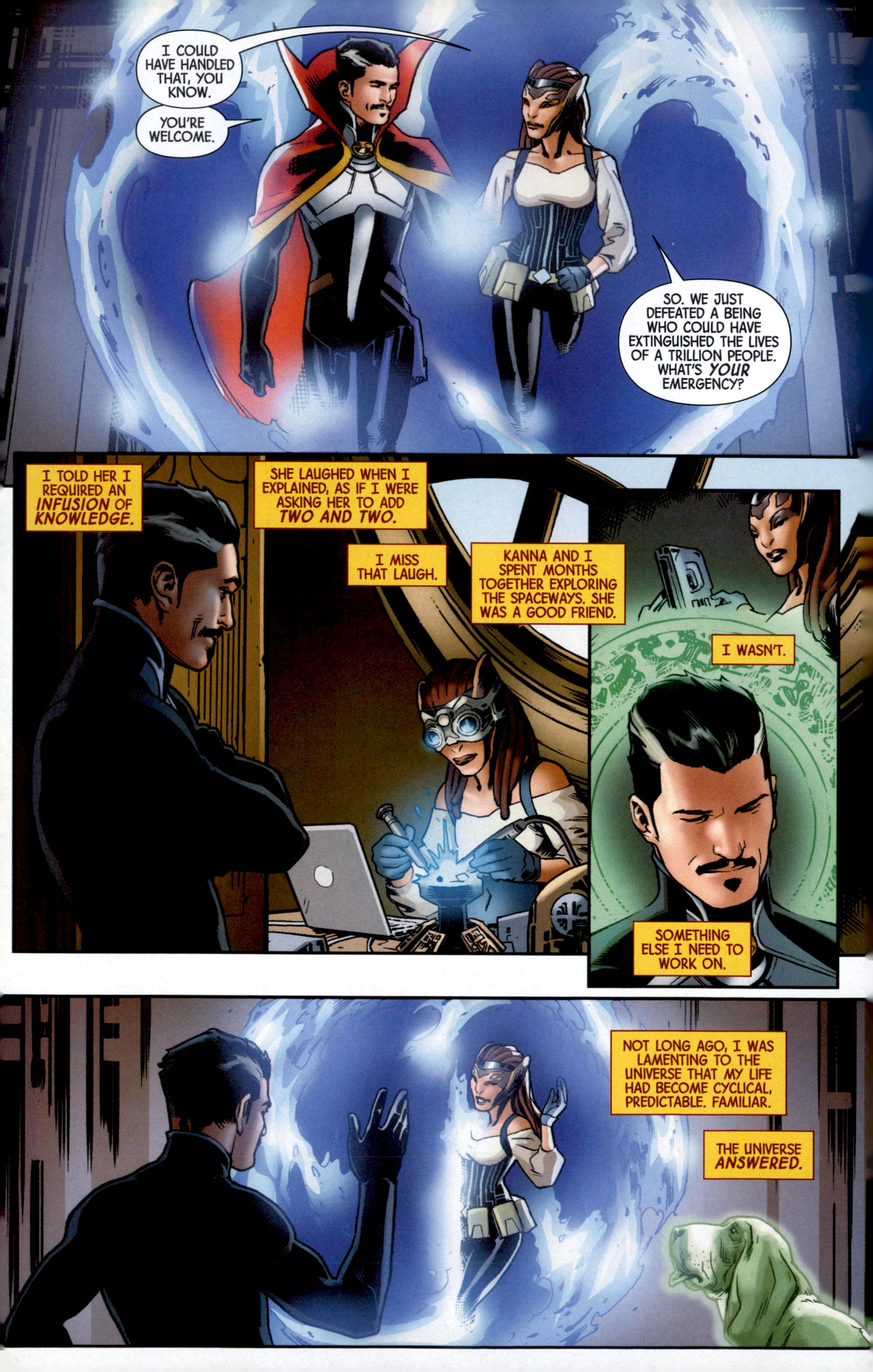

I COULD HAVE HANDLED THAT, YOU KNOW.
YOU'RE WELCOME.
SO. WE JUST DEFEATED A BEING WHO COULD HAVE EXTINGUISHED THE LIVES OF A TRILLION PEOPLE. WHAT'S YOUR EMERGENCY?
I TOLD HER I REQUIRED AN INFUSION OF KNOWLEDGE.
SHE LAUGHED WHEN I EXPLAINED, AS IF I WERE ASKING HER TO ADD TWO AND TWO.
I MISS THAT LAUGH.
KANNA AND I SPENT MONTHS TOGETHER EXPLORING THE SPACEWAYS. SHE WAS A GOOD FRIEND.
I WASN'T.
SOMETHING ELSE I NEED TO WORK ON.
NOT LONG AGO, I WAS LAMENTING TO THE UNIVERSE THAT MY LIFE HAD BECOME CYCLICAL, PREDICTABLE, FAMILIAR.
THE UNIVERSE ANSWERED.

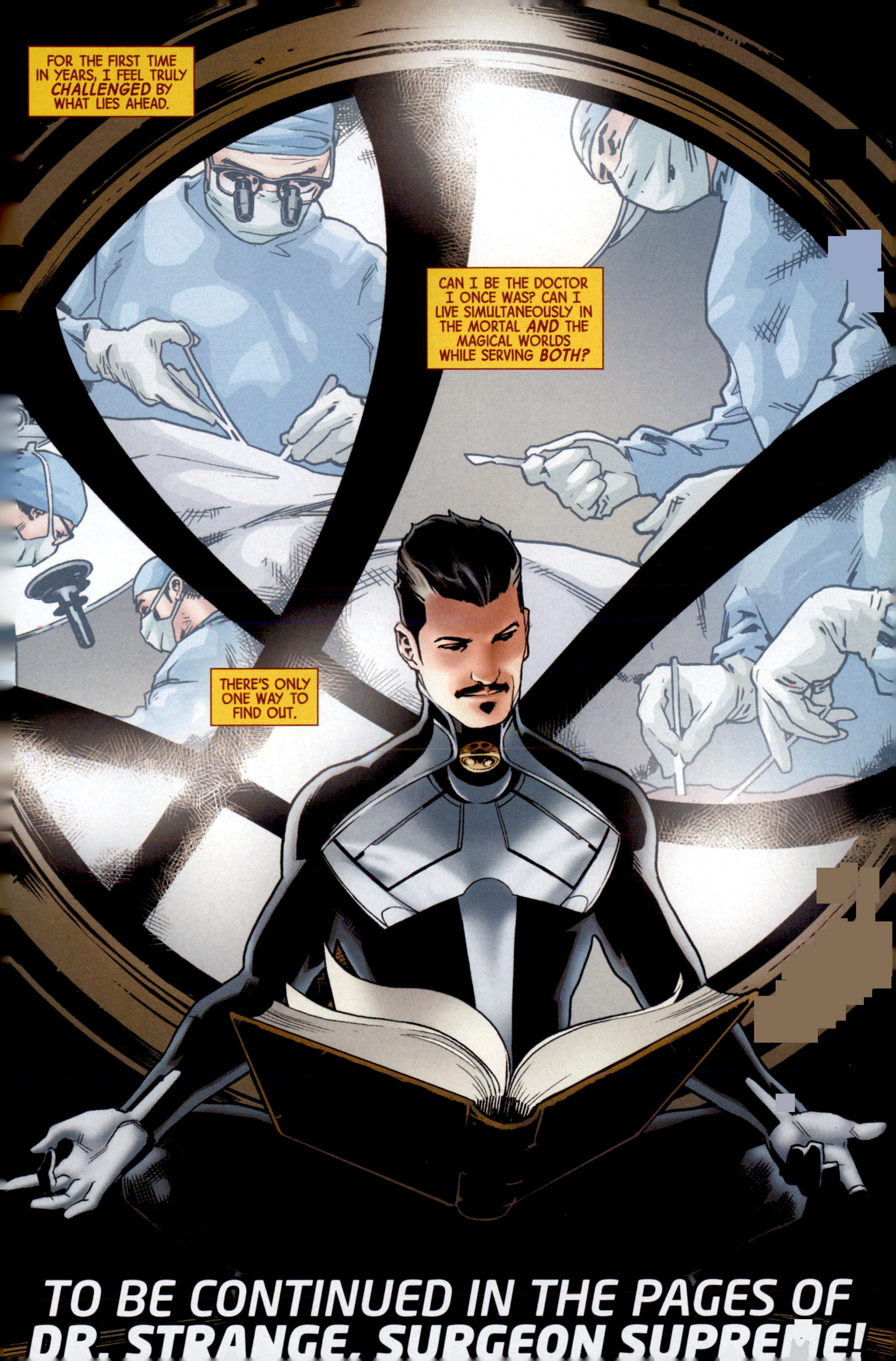
FOR THE FIRST TIME IN YEARS, I FEEL TRULY CHALLENGED BY WHAT LIES AHEAD.
CAN I BE THE DOCTOR I ONCE WAS? CAN I LIVE SIMULTANEOUSLY IN THE MORTAL AND THE MAGICAL WORLDS WHILE SERVING BOTH?
THERE'S ONLY ONE WAY TO FIND OUT.
TO BE CONTINUED IN THE PAGES OF DR. STRANGE, SURGEON SUPREME!

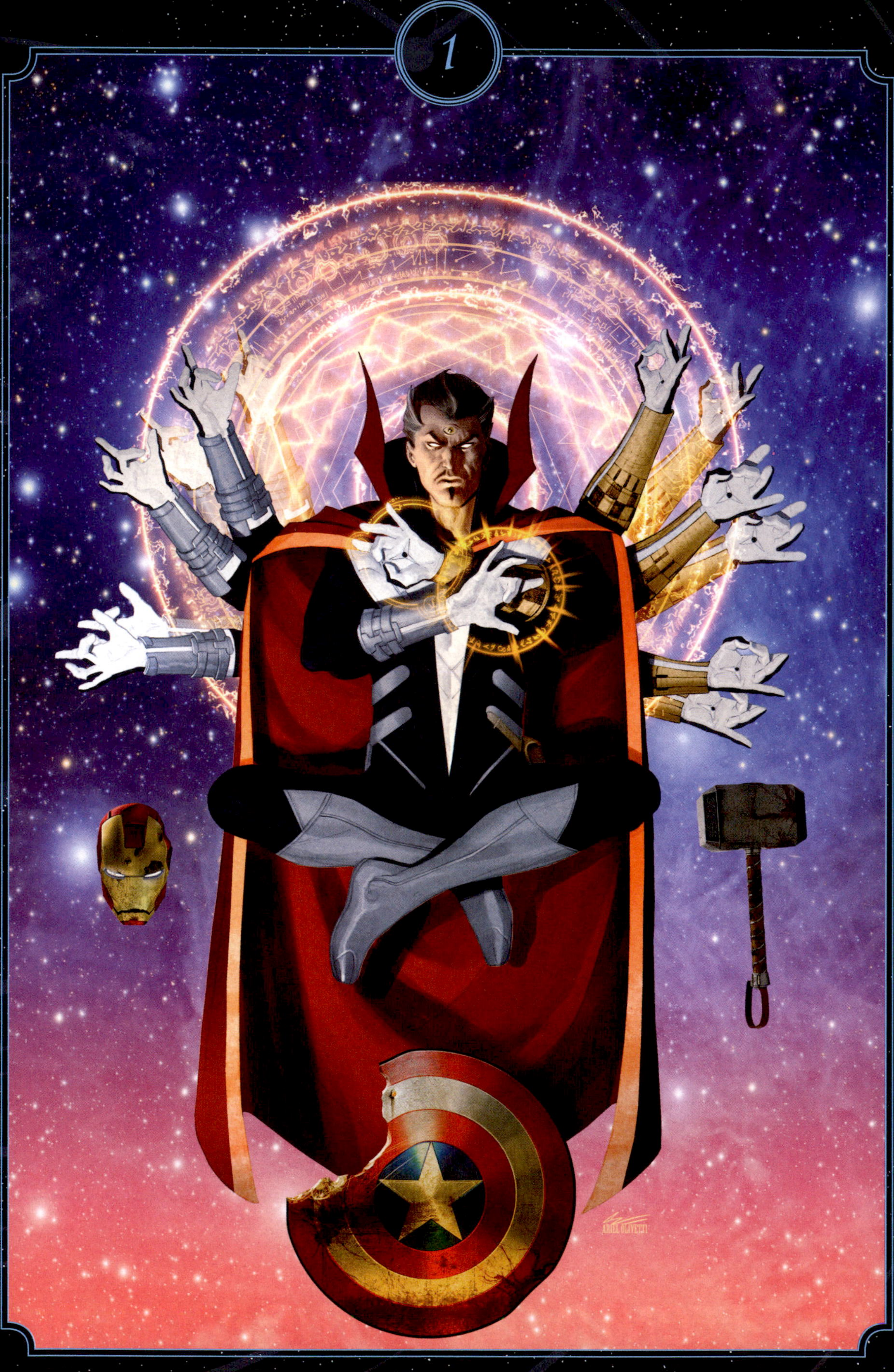
1

Doctor Strange Annual

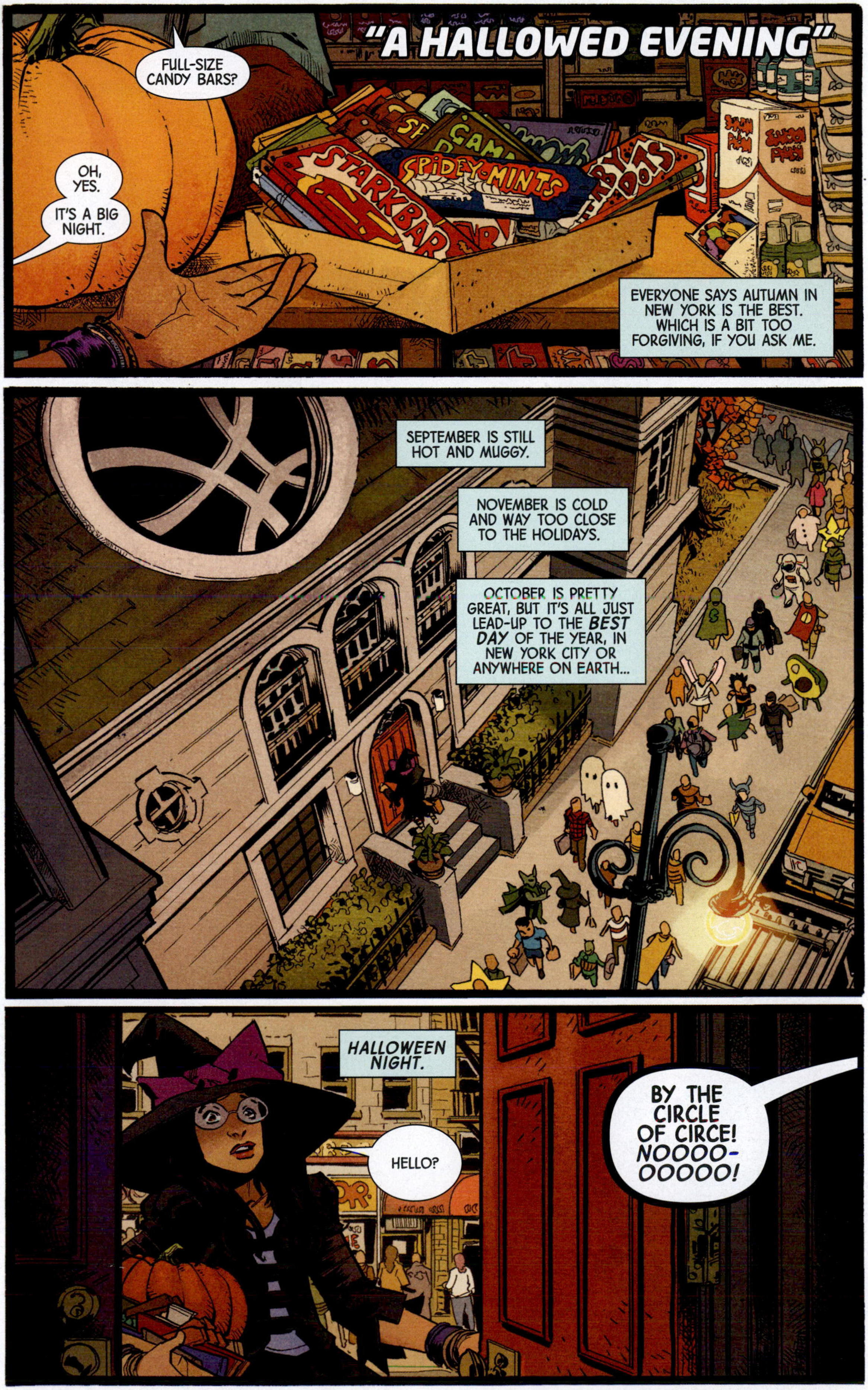
"A HALLOWED EVENING"
FULL-SIZE CANDY BARS?
OH, YES.
IT'S A BIG NIGHT.
STARKBAR
SPIDEY-MINTS
EVERYONE SAYS AUTUMN IN NEW YORK IS THE BEST. WHICH IS A BIT TOO FORGIVING, IF YOU ASK ME.
SEPTEMBER IS STILL HOT AND MUGGY.
NOVEMBER IS COLD AND WAY TOO CLOSE TO THE HOLIDAYS.
OCTOBER IS PRETTY GREAT, BUT IT'S ALL JUST LEAD-UP TO THE *BEST DAY* OF THE YEAR, IN NEW YORK CITY OR ANYWHERE ON EARTH...
HALLOWEEN NIGHT.
HELLO?
BY THE CIRCLE OF CIRCE! *NOOOO-OOOOO!*

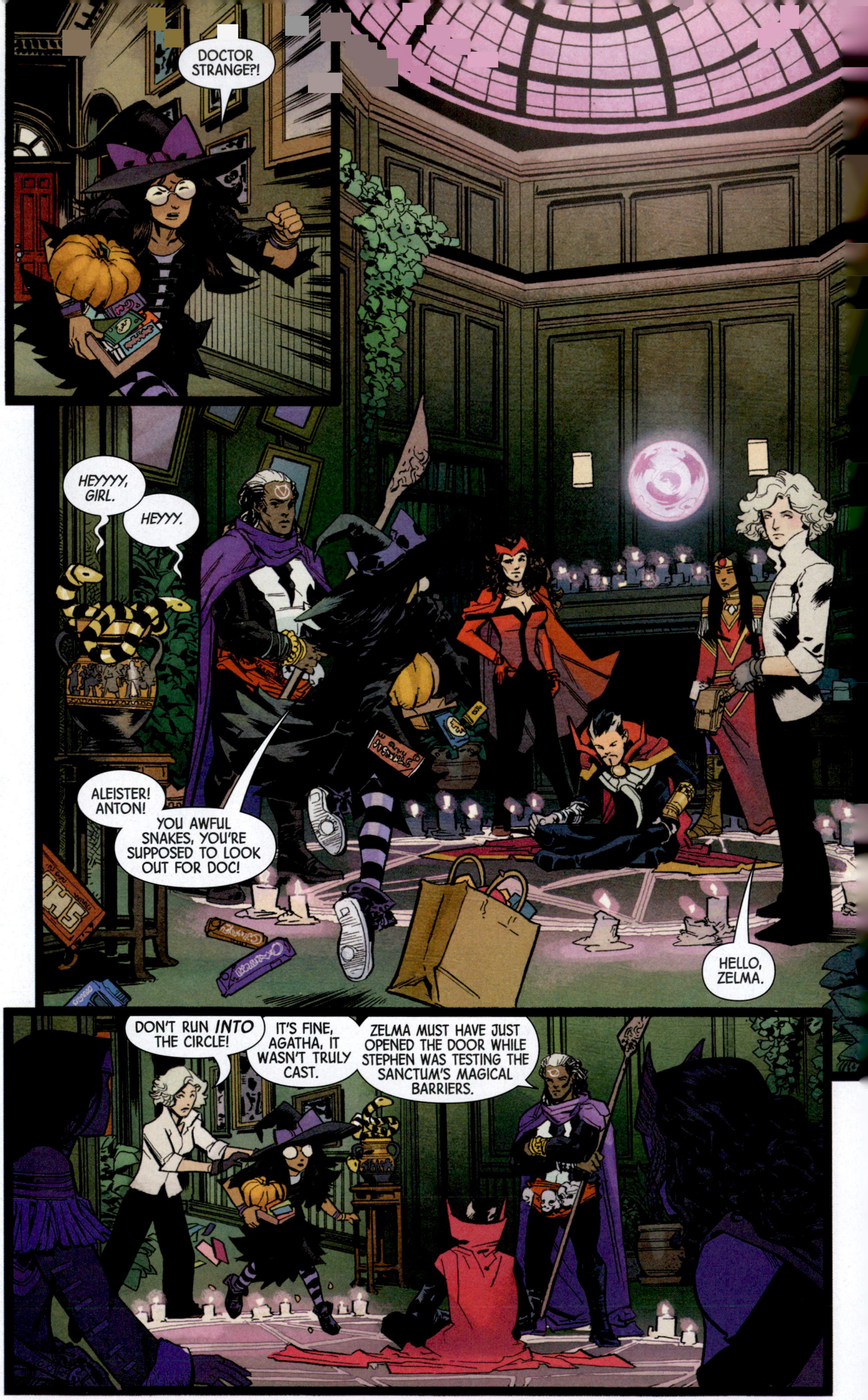
DOCTOR STRANGE?!
HEYYYY, GIRL.
HEYYY.
ALEISTER! ANTON!
YOU AWFUL SNAKES, YOU'RE SUPPOSED TO LOOK OUT FOR DOC!
HELLO, ZELMA.
DON'T RUN *INTO* THE CIRCLE!
IT'S FINE, AGATHA, IT WASN'T TRULY CAST.
ZELMA MUST HAVE JUST OPENED THE DOOR WHILE STEPHEN WAS TESTING THE SANCTUM'S MAGICAL BARRIERS.

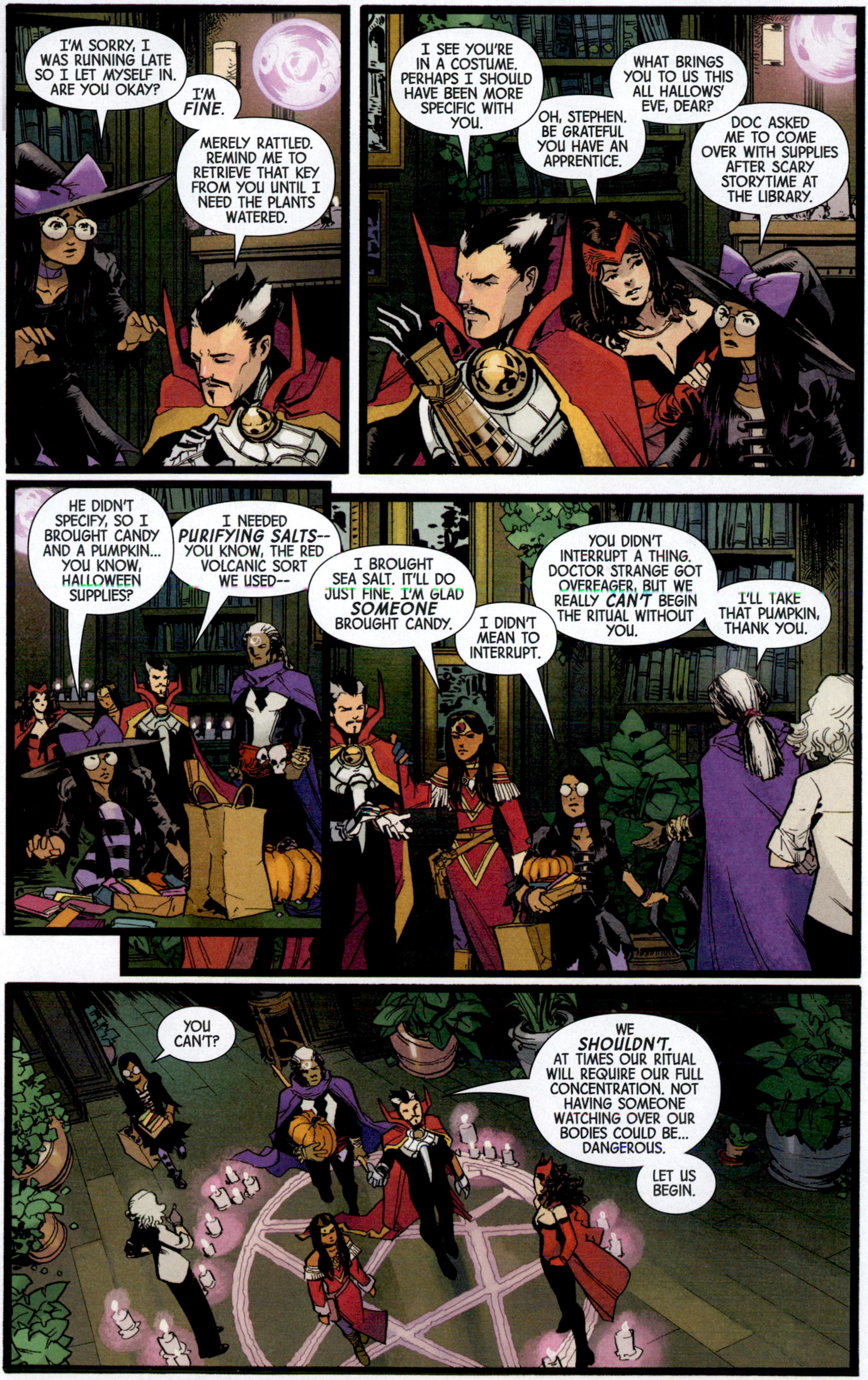

I'M SORRY, I WAS RUNNING LATE SO I LET MYSELF IN. ARE YOU OKAY?
I'M *FINE*.
MERELY RATTLED. REMIND ME TO RETRIEVE THAT KEY FROM YOU UNTIL I NEED THE PLANTS WATERED.
I SEE YOU'RE IN A COSTUME. PERHAPS I SHOULD HAVE BEEN MORE SPECIFIC WITH YOU.
OH, STEPHEN. BE GRATEFUL YOU HAVE AN APPRENTICE.
WHAT BRINGS YOU TO US THIS ALL HALLOWS' EVE, DEAR?
DOC ASKED ME TO COME OVER WITH SUPPLIES AFTER SCARY STORYTIME AT THE LIBRARY.
HE DIDN'T SPECIFY, SO I BROUGHT CANDY AND A PUMPKIN... YOU KNOW, HALLOWEEN SUPPLIES?
I NEEDED *PURIFYING SALTS*-- YOU KNOW, THE RED VOLCANIC SORT WE USED--
I BROUGHT SEA SALT. IT'LL DO JUST FINE. I'M GLAD *SOMEONE* BROUGHT CANDY.
I DIDN'T MEAN TO INTERRUPT.
YOU DIDN'T INTERRUPT A THING. DOCTOR STRANGE GOT OVEREAGER, BUT WE REALLY *CAN'T* BEGIN THE RITUAL WITHOUT YOU.
I'LL TAKE THAT PUMPKIN, THANK YOU.
YOU CAN'T?
WE *SHOULDN'T*. AT TIMES OUR RITUAL WILL REQUIRE OUR FULL CONCENTRATION. NOT HAVING SOMEONE WATCHING OVER OUR BODIES COULD BE... DANGEROUS.
LET US BEGIN.

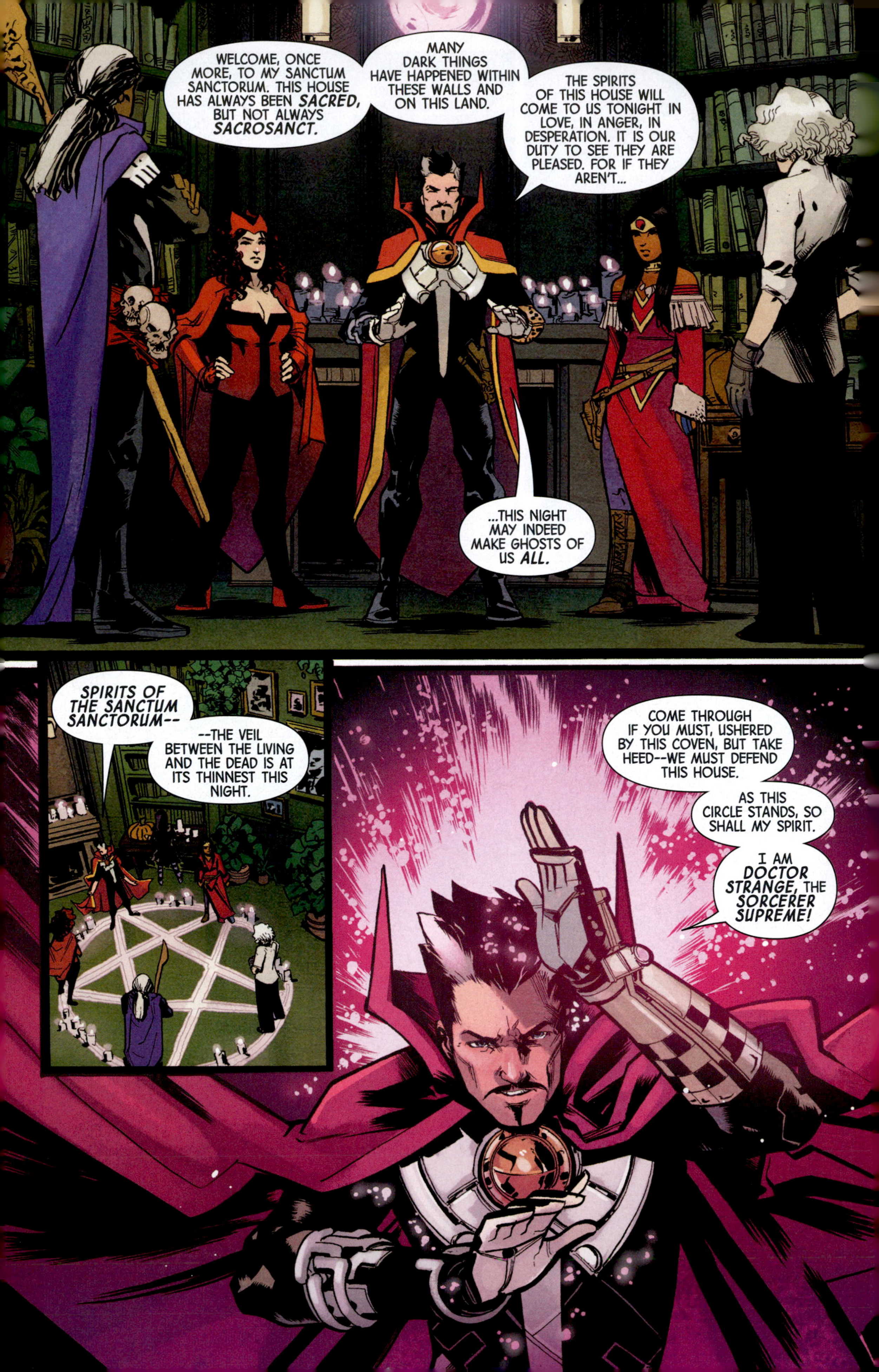
WELCOME, ONCE MORE, TO MY SANCTUM SANCTORUM. THIS HOUSE HAS ALWAYS BEEN SACRED, BUT NOT ALWAYS SACROSANCT.
MANY DARK THINGS HAVE HAPPENED WITHIN THESE WALLS AND ON THIS LAND.
THE SPIRITS OF THIS HOUSE WILL COME TO US TONIGHT IN LOVE, IN ANGER, IN DESPERATION. IT IS OUR DUTY TO SEE THEY ARE PLEASED. FOR IF THEY AREN'T...
...THIS NIGHT MAY INDEED MAKE GHOSTS OF US ALL.
SPIRITS OF THE SANCTUM SANCTORUM--
--THE VEIL BETWEEN THE LIVING AND THE DEAD IS AT ITS THINNEST THIS NIGHT.
COME THROUGH IF YOU MUST, USHERED BY THIS COVEN, BUT TAKE HEED--WE MUST DEFEND THIS HOUSE.
AS THIS CIRCLE STANDS, SO SHALL MY SPIRIT.
I AM DOCTOR STRANGE, THE SORCERER SUPREME!

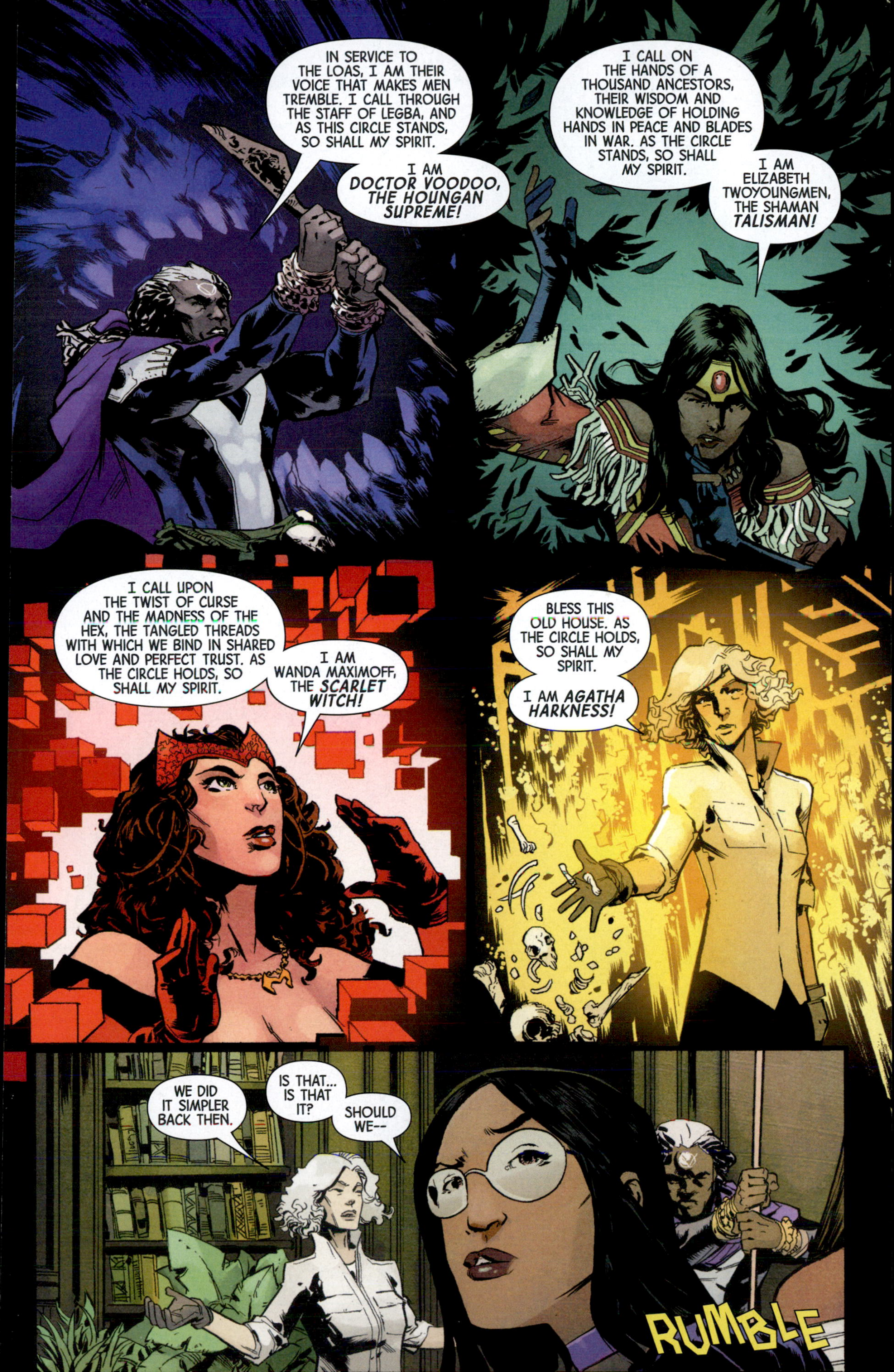

IN SERVICE TO THE LOAS, I AM THEIR VOICE THAT MAKES MEN TREMBLE. I CALL THROUGH THE STAFF OF LEGBA, AND AS THIS CIRCLE STANDS, SO SHALL MY SPIRIT.
I AM DOCTOR VOODOO, THE HOUNGAN SUPREME!
I CALL ON THE HANDS OF A THOUSAND ANCESTORS, THEIR WISDOM AND KNOWLEDGE OF HOLDING HANDS IN PEACE AND BLADES IN WAR. AS THE CIRCLE STANDS, SO SHALL MY SPIRIT.
I AM ELIZABETH TWOYOUNGMEN, THE SHAMAN TALISMAN!
I CALL UPON THE TWIST OF CURSE AND THE MADNESS OF THE HEX, THE TANGLED THREADS WITH WHICH WE BIND IN SHARED LOVE AND PERFECT TRUST. AS THE CIRCLE HOLDS, SO SHALL MY SPIRIT.
I AM WANDA MAXIMOFF, THE SCARLET WITCH!
BLESS THIS OLD HOUSE. AS THE CIRCLE HOLDS, SO SHALL MY SPIRIT.
I AM AGATHA HARKNESS!
WE DID IT SIMPLER BACK THEN.
IS THAT... IS THAT IT?
SHOULD WE--
RUMBLE

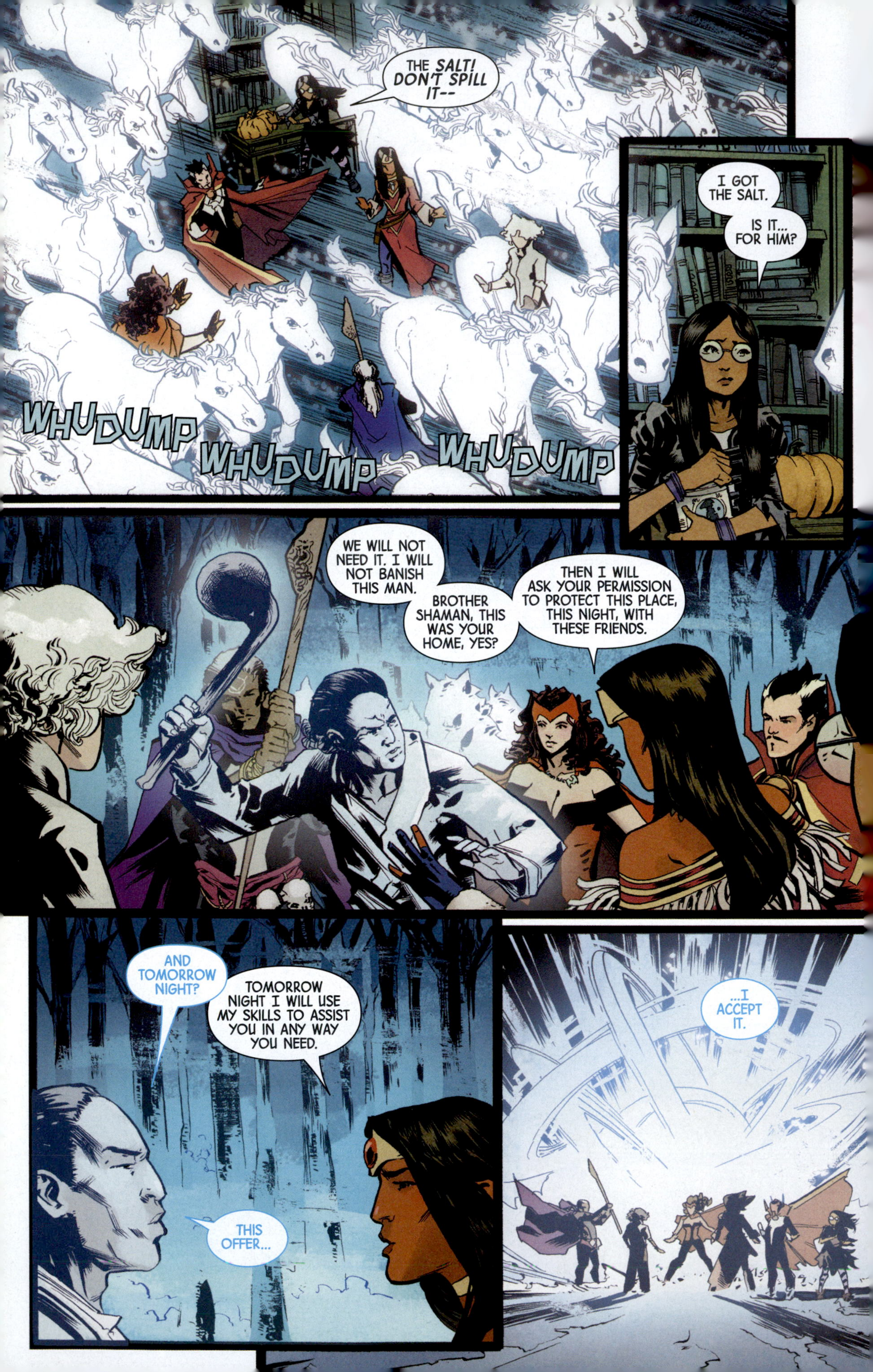
THE SALT! DON'T SPILL IT--
WHUDUMP
WHUDUMP
WHUDUMP
I GOT THE SALT.
IS IT... FOR HIM?
WE WILL NOT NEED IT. I WILL NOT BANISH THIS MAN.
BROTHER SHAMAN, THIS WAS YOUR HOME, YES?
THEN I WILL ASK YOUR PERMISSION TO PROTECT THIS PLACE, THIS NIGHT, WITH THESE FRIENDS.
AND TOMORROW NIGHT?
TOMORROW NIGHT I WILL USE MY SKILLS TO ASSIST YOU IN ANY WAY YOU NEED.
THIS OFFER...
...I ACCEPT IT.

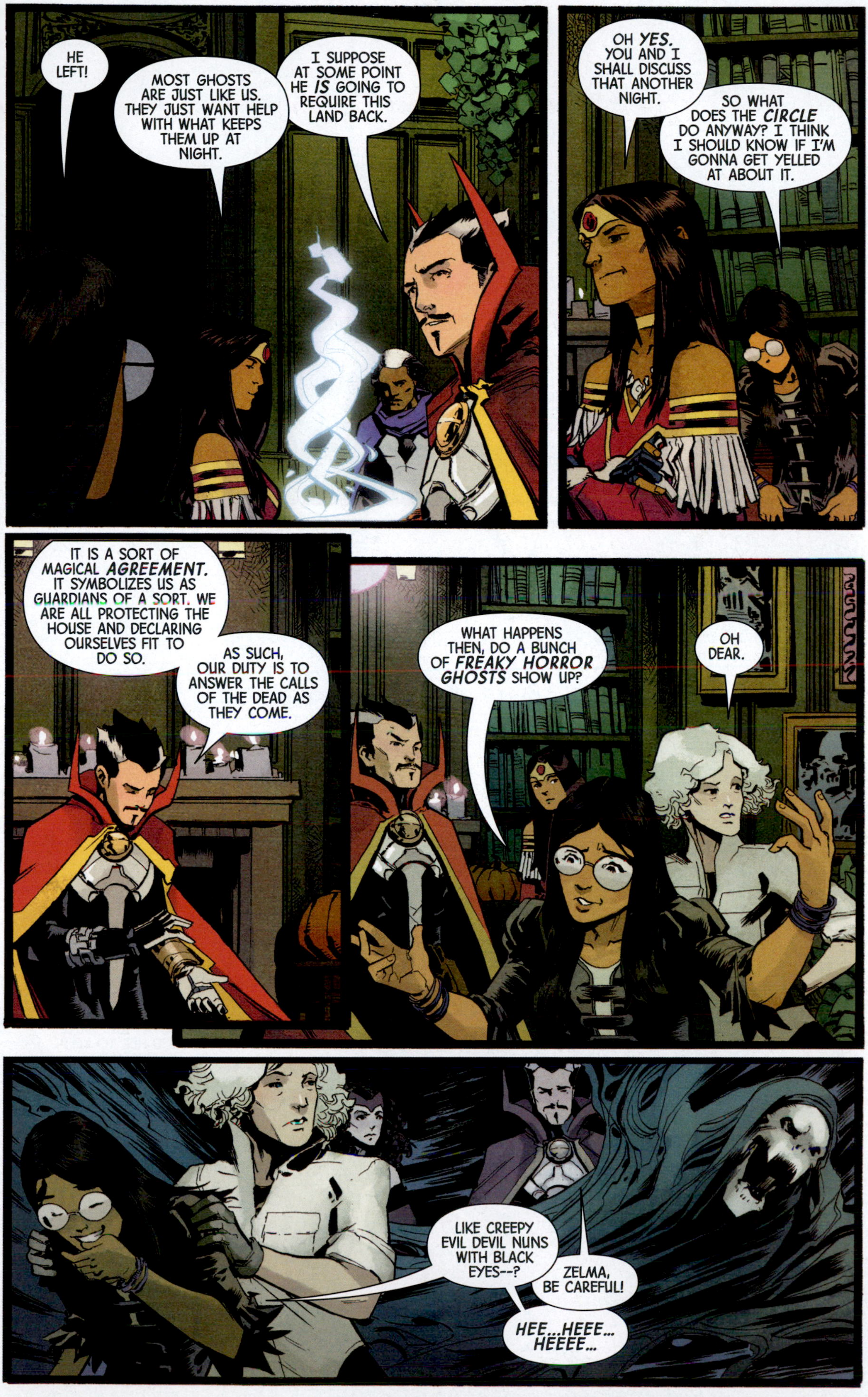
HE LEFT!
MOST GHOSTS ARE JUST LIKE US. THEY JUST WANT HELP WITH WHAT KEEPS THEM UP AT NIGHT.
I SUPPOSE AT SOME POINT HE IS GOING TO REQUIRE THIS LAND BACK.
OH YES. YOU AND I SHALL DISCUSS THAT ANOTHER NIGHT.
SO WHAT DOES THE CIRCLE DO ANYWAY? I THINK I SHOULD KNOW IF I'M GONNA GET YELLED AT ABOUT IT.
IT IS A SORT OF MAGICAL AGREEMENT. IT SYMBOLIZES US AS GUARDIANS OF A SORT. WE ARE ALL PROTECTING THE HOUSE AND DECLARING OURSELVES FIT TO DO SO.
AS SUCH, OUR DUTY IS TO ANSWER THE CALLS OF THE DEAD AS THEY COME.
WHAT HAPPENS THEN, DO A BUNCH OF FREAKY HORROR GHOSTS SHOW UP?
OH DEAR.
LIKE CREEPY EVIL DEVIL NUNS WITH BLACK EYES--?
ZELMA, BE CAREFUL!
HEE...HEEE... HEEEE...

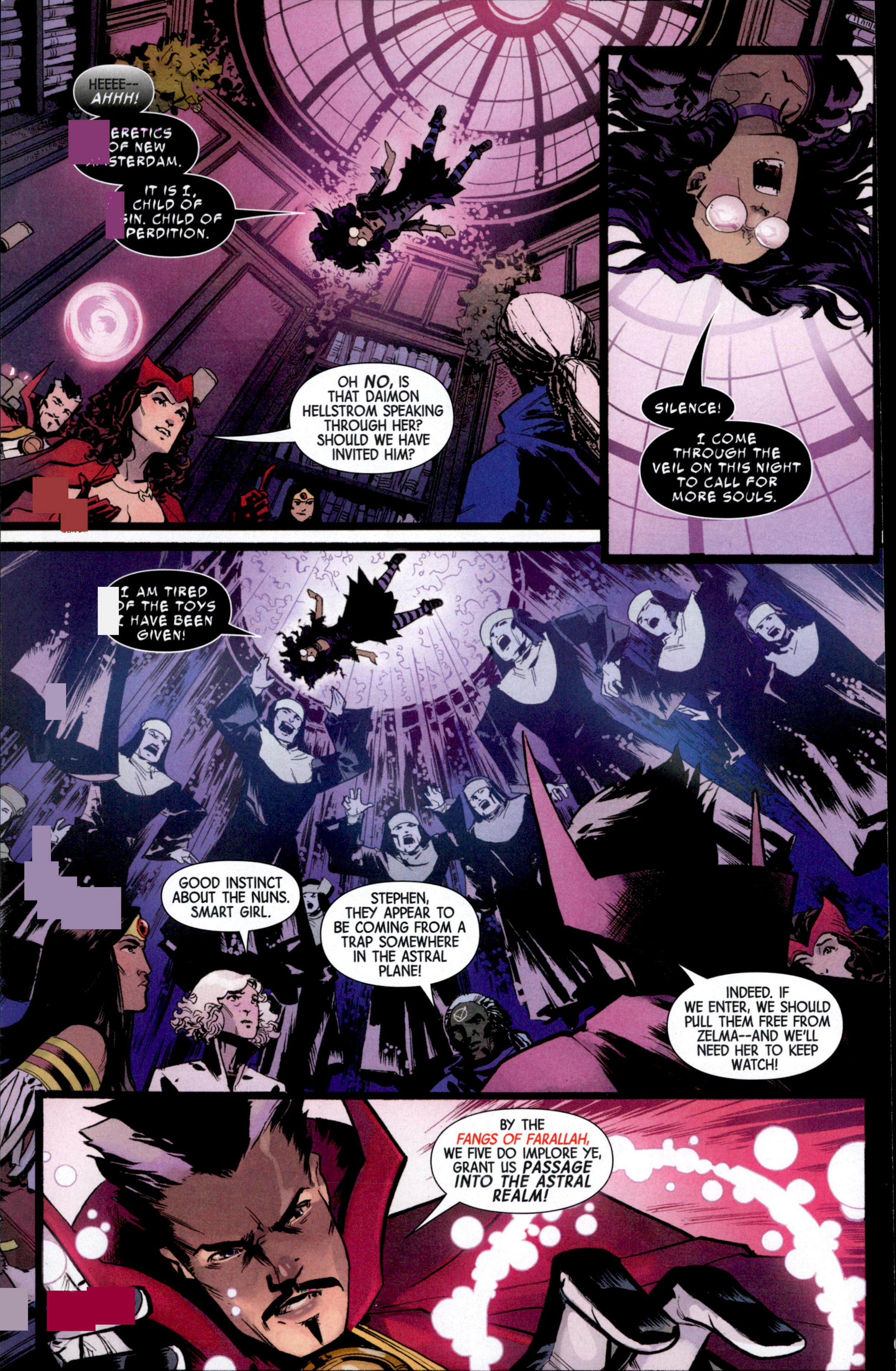

HEEEE-- AHHH!
ERETICS OF NEW STERDAM.
IT IS I, CHILD OF SIN. CHILD OF PERDITION.
OH NO, IS THAT DAIMON HELLSTROM SPEAKING THROUGH HER? SHOULD WE HAVE INVITED HIM?
SILENCE!
I COME THROUGH THE VEIL ON THIS NIGHT TO CALL FOR MORE SOULS.
I AM TIRED OF THE TOYS HAVE BEEN GIVEN!
GOOD INSTINCT ABOUT THE NUNS. SMART GIRL.
STEPHEN, THEY APPEAR TO BE COMING FROM A TRAP SOMEWHERE IN THE ASTRAL PLANE!
INDEED. IF WE ENTER, WE SHOULD PULL THEM FREE FROM ZELMA--AND WE'LL NEED HER TO KEEP WATCH!
BY THE FANGS OF FARALLAH, WE FIVE DO IMPLORE YE, GRANT US PASSAGE INTO THE ASTRAL REALM!

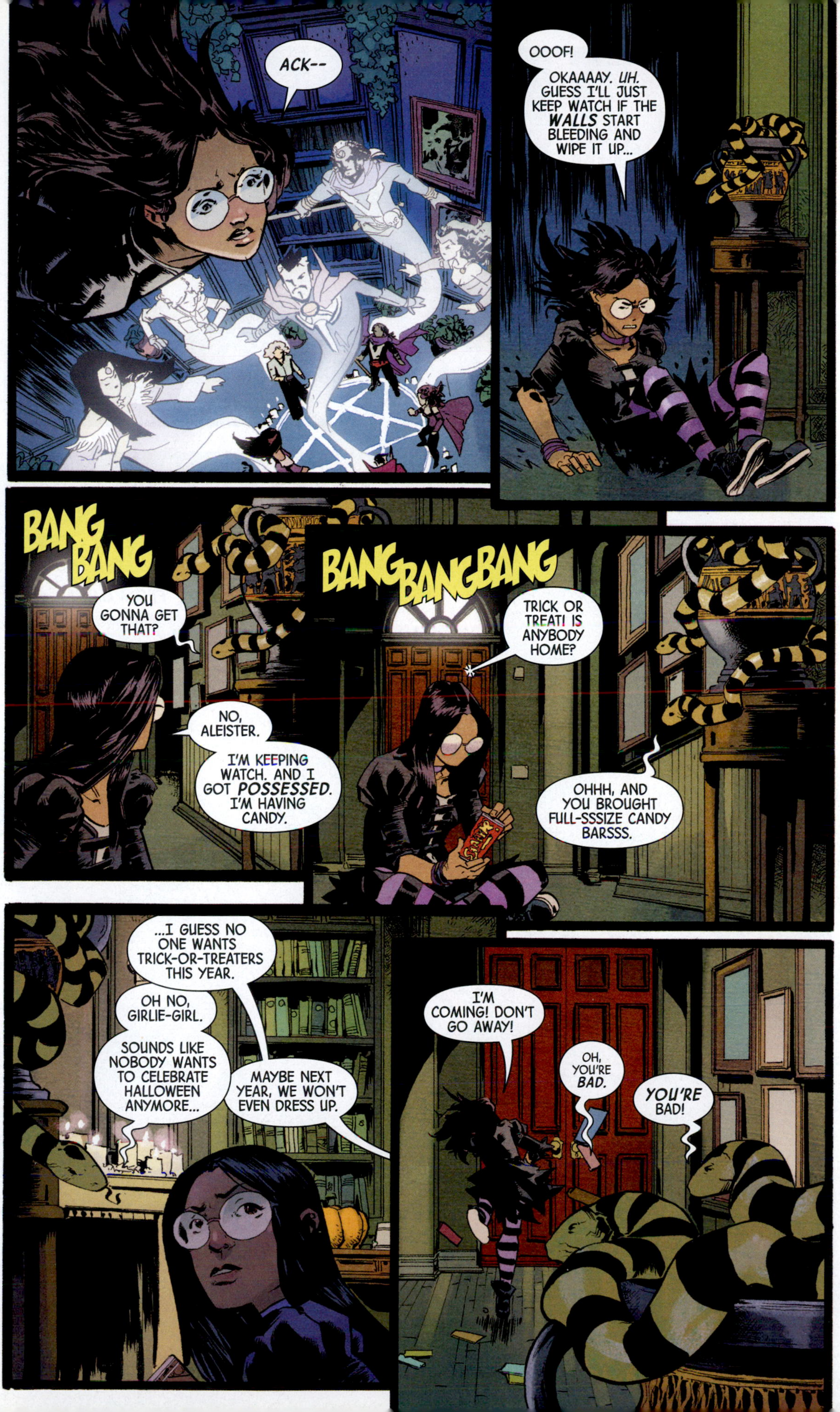
ACK--
OOOF!
OKAAAAY. UH. GUESS I'LL JUST KEEP WATCH IF THE WALLS START BLEEDING AND WIPE IT UP...
BANG BANG
YOU GONNA GET THAT?
NO, ALEISTER.
I'M KEEPING WATCH. AND I GOT POSSESSED. I'M HAVING CANDY.
BANG BANG BANG
TRICK OR TREAT! IS ANYBODY HOME?
OHHH, AND YOU BROUGHT FULL-SSSIZE CANDY BARSSS.
...I GUESS NO ONE WANTS TRICK-OR-TREATERS THIS YEAR.
OH NO, GIRLIE-GIRL.
SOUNDS LIKE NOBODY WANTS TO CELEBRATE HALLOWEEN ANYMORE...
MAYBE NEXT YEAR, WE WON'T EVEN DRESS UP.
I'M COMING! DON'T GO AWAY!
OH, YOU'RE BAD.
YOU'RE BAD!

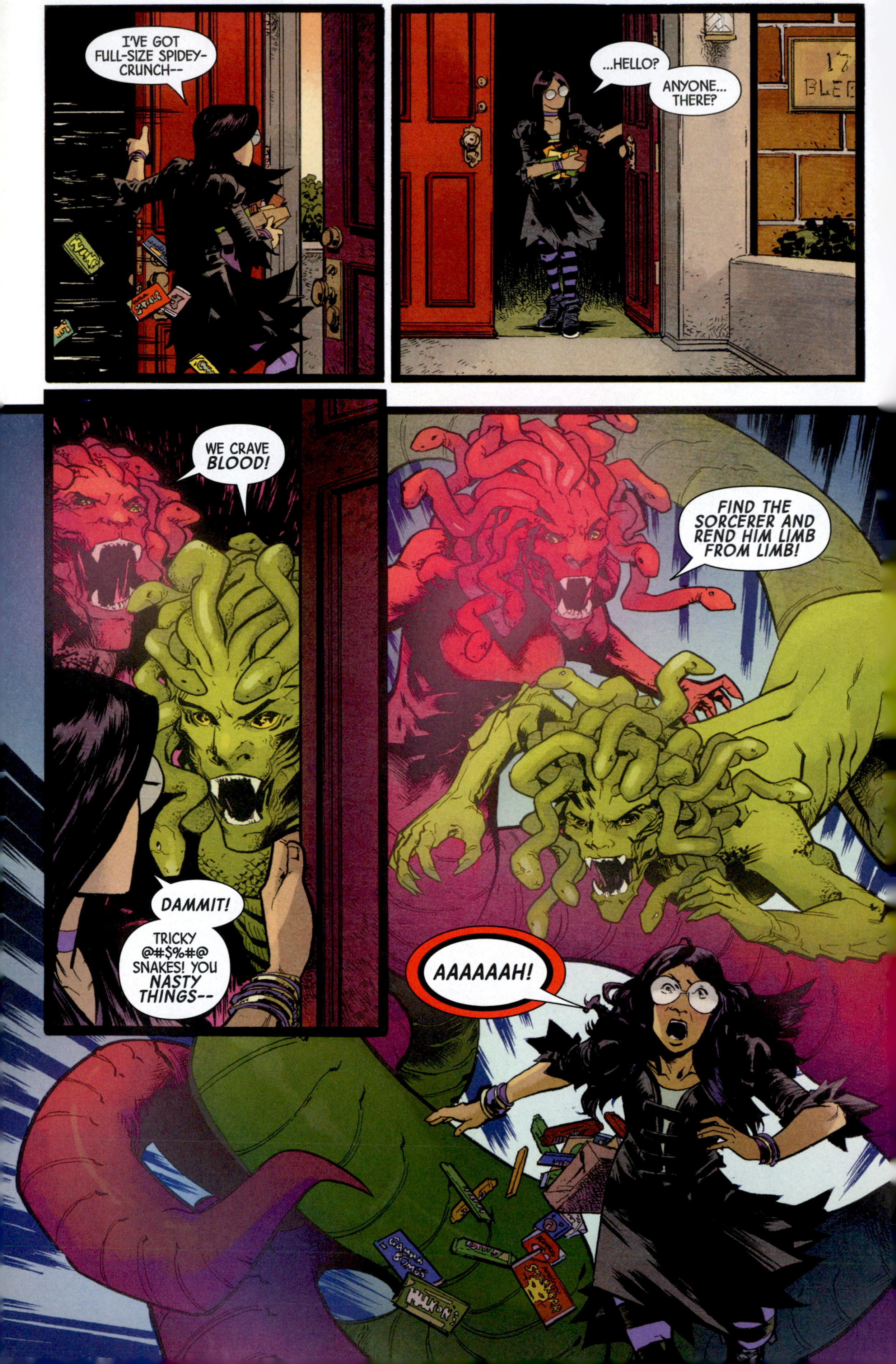
I'VE GOT FULL-SIZE SPIDEY-CRUNCH--
...HELLO?
ANYONE... THERE?
WE CRAVE BLOOD!
DAMMIT!
TRICKY @#$%#@ SNAKES! YOU NASTY THINGS--
FIND THE SORCERER AND REND HIM LIMB FROM LIMB!
AAAAAAH!

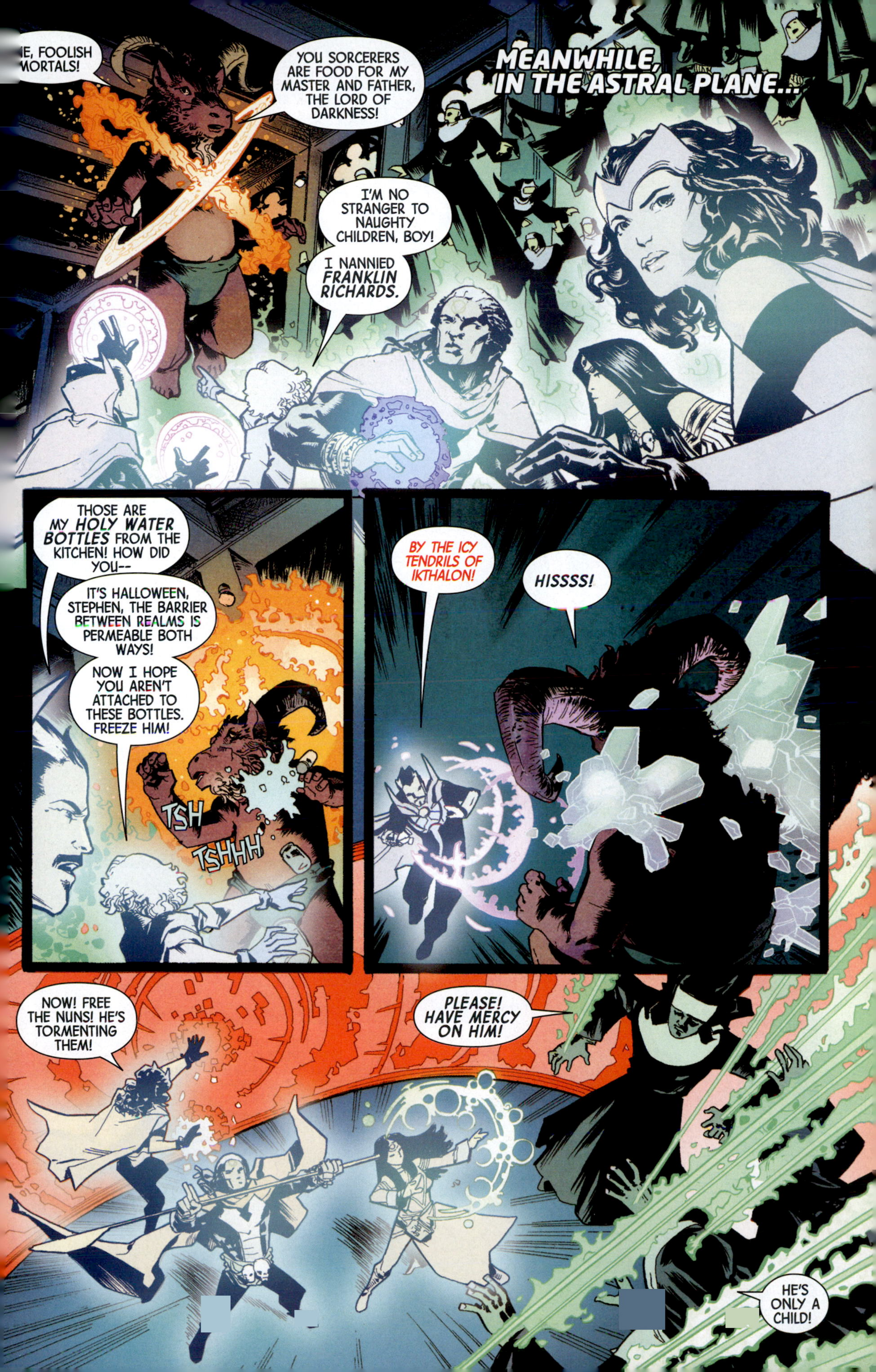

E, FOOLISH MORTALS!
YOU SORCERERS ARE FOOD FOR MY MASTER AND FATHER, THE LORD OF DARKNESS!
MEANWHILE, IN THE ASTRAL PLANE...
I'M NO STRANGER TO NAUGHTY CHILDREN, BOY!
I NANNIED FRANKLIN RICHARDS.
THOSE ARE MY HOLY WATER BOTTLES FROM THE KITCHEN! HOW DID YOU--
IT'S HALLOWEEN, STEPHEN, THE BARRIER BETWEEN REALMS IS PERMEABLE BOTH WAYS!
NOW I HOPE YOU AREN'T ATTACHED TO THESE BOTTLES. FREEZE HIM!
TSH
TSHHH
BY THE ICY TENDRILS OF IKTHALON!
HISSSS!
NOW! FREE THE NUNS! HE'S TORMENTING THEM!
PLEASE! HAVE MERCY ON HIM!
HE'S ONLY A CHILD!

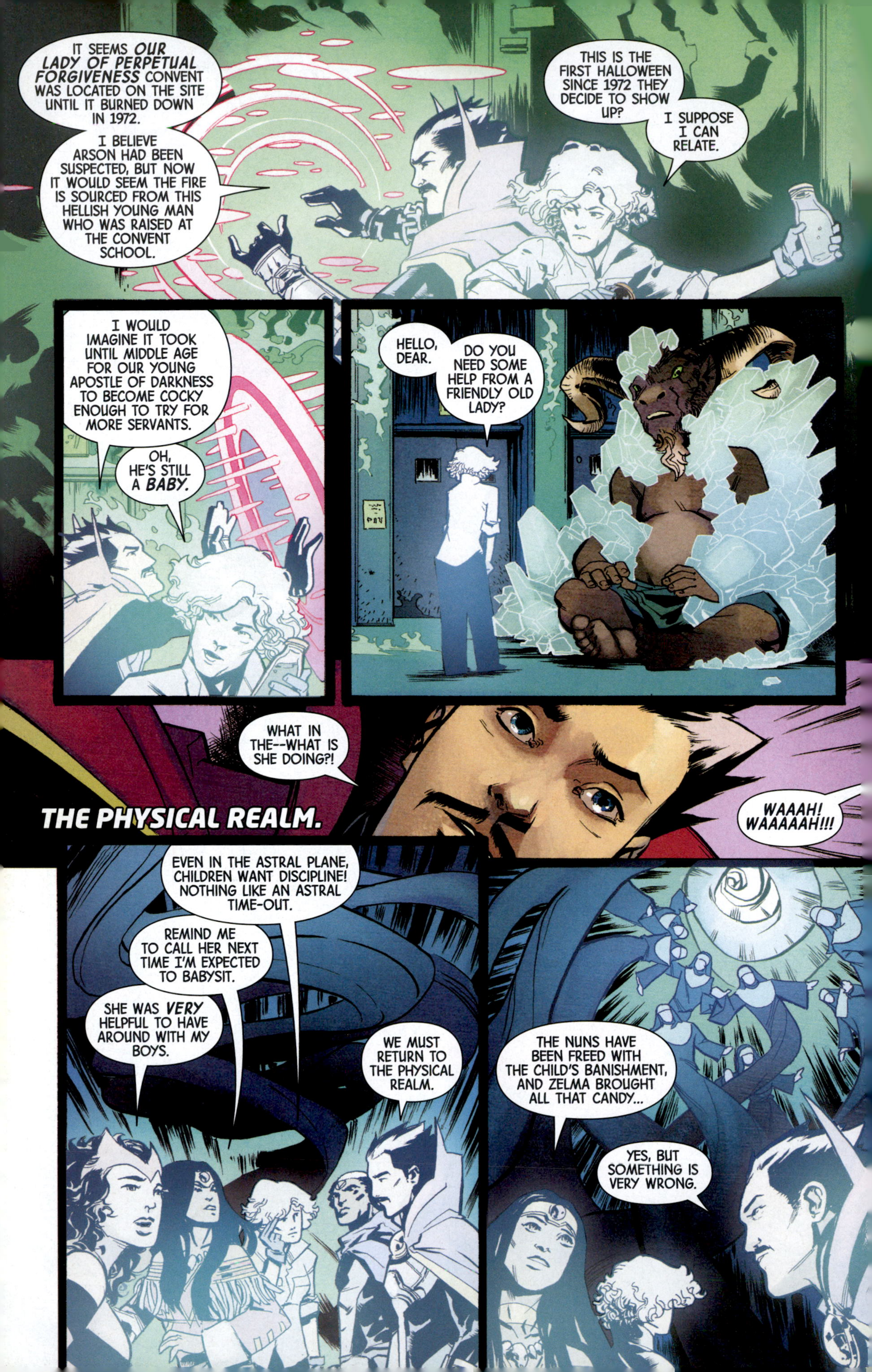
IT SEEMS OUR LADY OF PERPETUAL FORGIVENESS CONVENT WAS LOCATED ON THE SITE UNTIL IT BURNED DOWN IN 1972.
I BELIEVE ARSON HAD BEEN SUSPECTED, BUT NOW IT WOULD SEEM THE FIRE IS SOURCED FROM THIS HELLISH YOUNG MAN WHO WAS RAISED AT THE CONVENT SCHOOL.
THIS IS THE FIRST HALLOWEEN SINCE 1972 THEY DECIDE TO SHOW UP?
I SUPPOSE I CAN RELATE.
I WOULD IMAGINE IT TOOK UNTIL MIDDLE AGE FOR OUR YOUNG APOSTLE OF DARKNESS TO BECOME COCKY ENOUGH TO TRY FOR MORE SERVANTS.
OH, HE'S STILL A BABY.
HELLO, DEAR.
DO YOU NEED SOME HELP FROM A FRIENDLY OLD LADY?
WHAT IN THE--WHAT IS SHE DOING?!
WAAAH! WAAAAAH!!!
THE PHYSICAL REALM.
EVEN IN THE ASTRAL PLANE, CHILDREN WANT DISCIPLINE! NOTHING LIKE AN ASTRAL TIME-OUT.
REMIND ME TO CALL HER NEXT TIME I'M EXPECTED TO BABYSIT.
SHE WAS VERY HELPFUL TO HAVE AROUND WITH MY BOYS.
WE MUST RETURN TO THE PHYSICAL REALM.
THE NUNS HAVE BEEN FREED WITH THE CHILD'S BANISHMENT, AND ZELMA BROUGHT ALL THAT CANDY...
YES, BUT SOMETHING IS VERY WRONG.

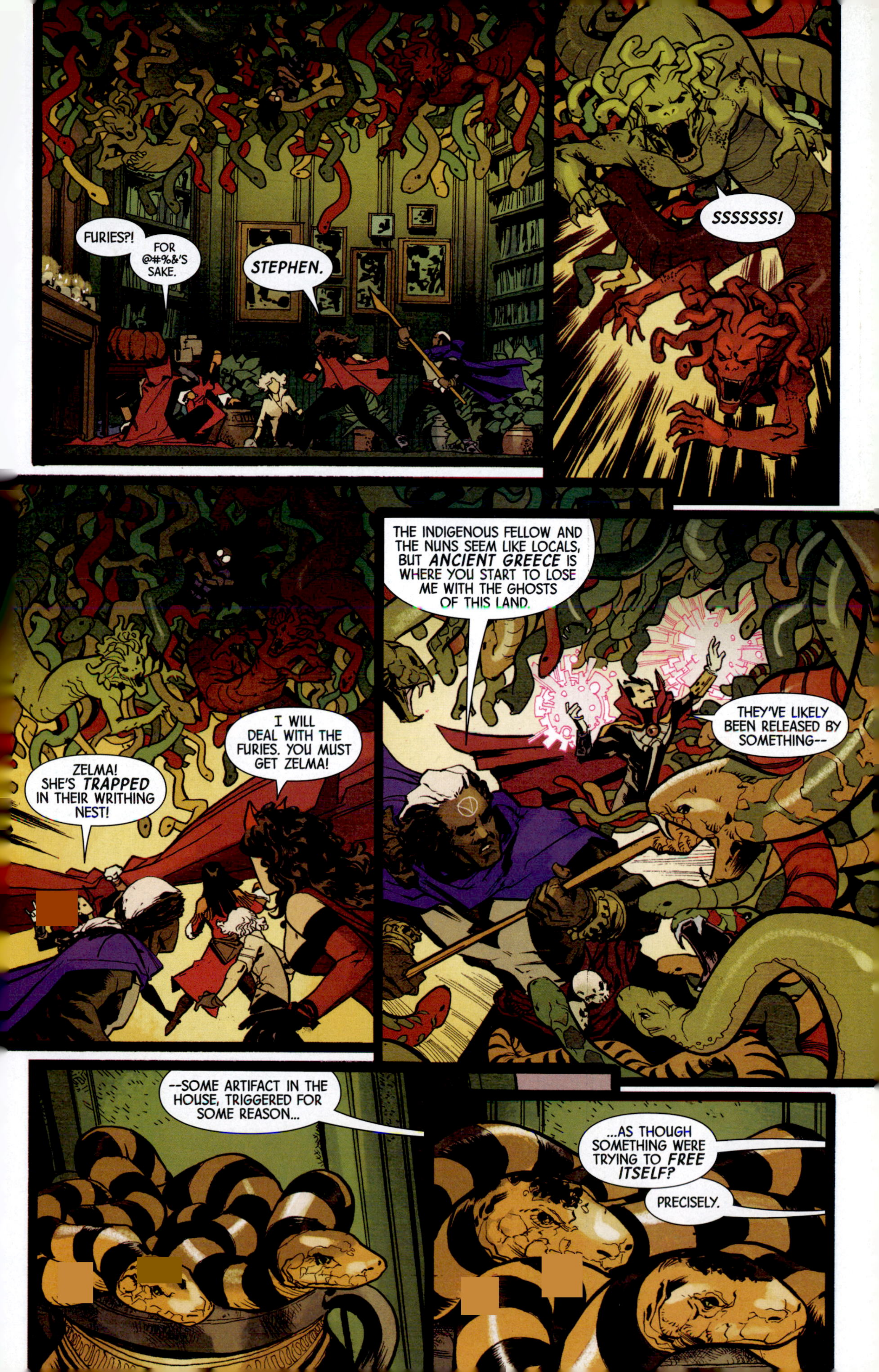
FURIES?!
FOR @#%&'S SAKE.
STEPHEN.
SSSSSSS!
ZELMA! SHE'S TRAPPED IN THEIR WRITHING NEST!
I WILL DEAL WITH THE FURIES. YOU MUST GET ZELMA!
THE INDIGENOUS FELLOW AND THE NUNS SEEM LIKE LOCALS, BUT ANCIENT GREECE IS WHERE YOU START TO LOSE ME WITH THE GHOSTS OF THIS LAND.
THEY'VE LIKELY BEEN RELEASED BY SOMETHING--
--SOME ARTIFACT IN THE HOUSE, TRIGGERED FOR SOME REASON...
...AS THOUGH SOMETHING WERE TRYING TO FREE ITSELF?
PRECISELY.

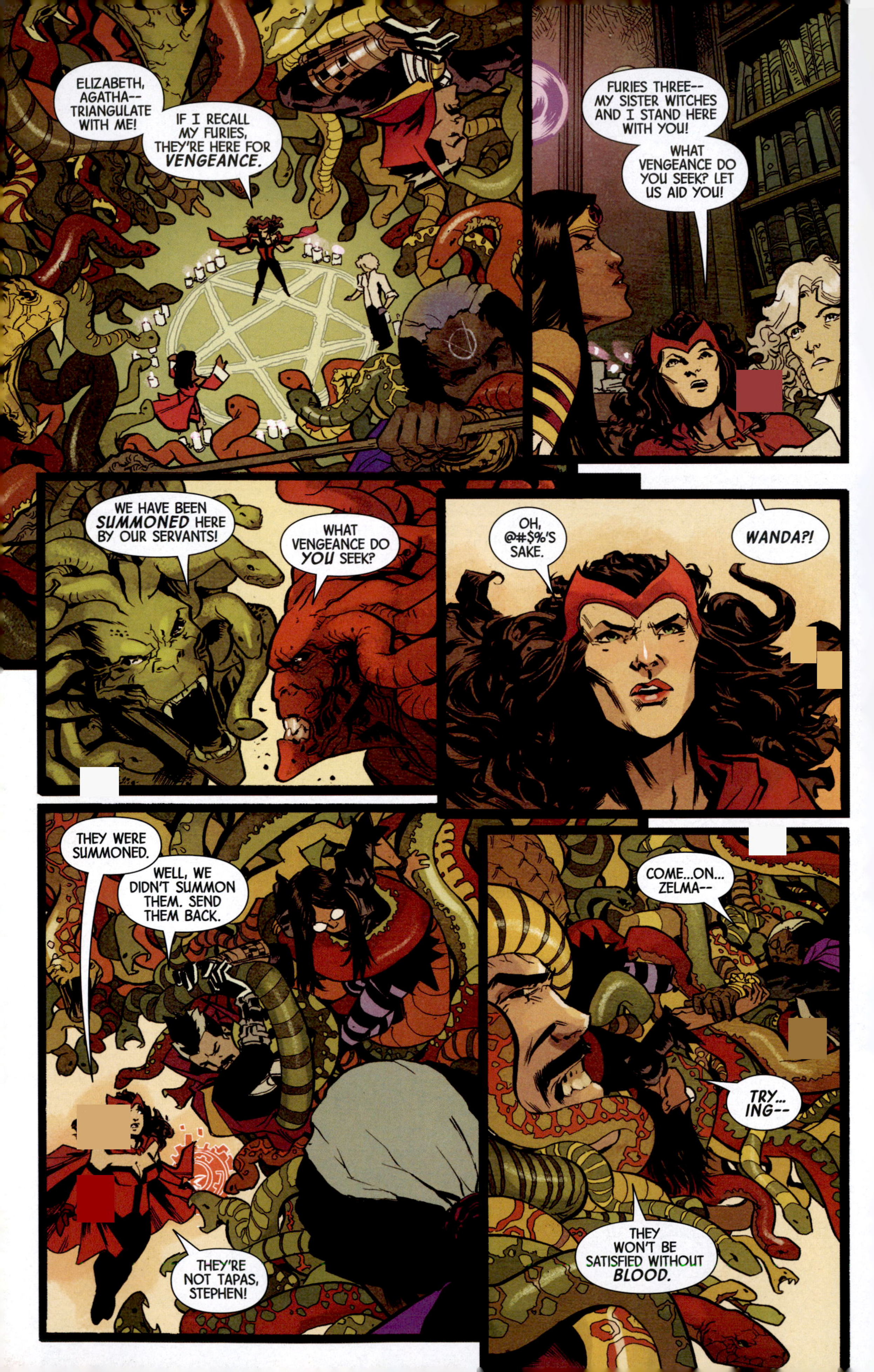

ELIZABETH, AGATHA-- TRIANGULATE WITH ME!
IF I RECALL MY FURIES, THEY'RE HERE FOR VENGEANCE.
FURIES THREE-- MY SISTER WITCHES AND I STAND HERE WITH YOU!
WHAT VENGEANCE DO YOU SEEK? LET US AID YOU!
WE HAVE BEEN SUMMONED HERE BY OUR SERVANTS!
WHAT VENGEANCE DO YOU SEEK?
OH, @#$%'S SAKE.
WANDA?!
THEY WERE SUMMONED.
WELL, WE DIDN'T SUMMON THEM. SEND THEM BACK.
THEY'RE NOT TAPAS, STEPHEN!
COME...ON... ZELMA--
TRY... ING--
THEY WON'T BE SATISFIED WITHOUT BLOOD.

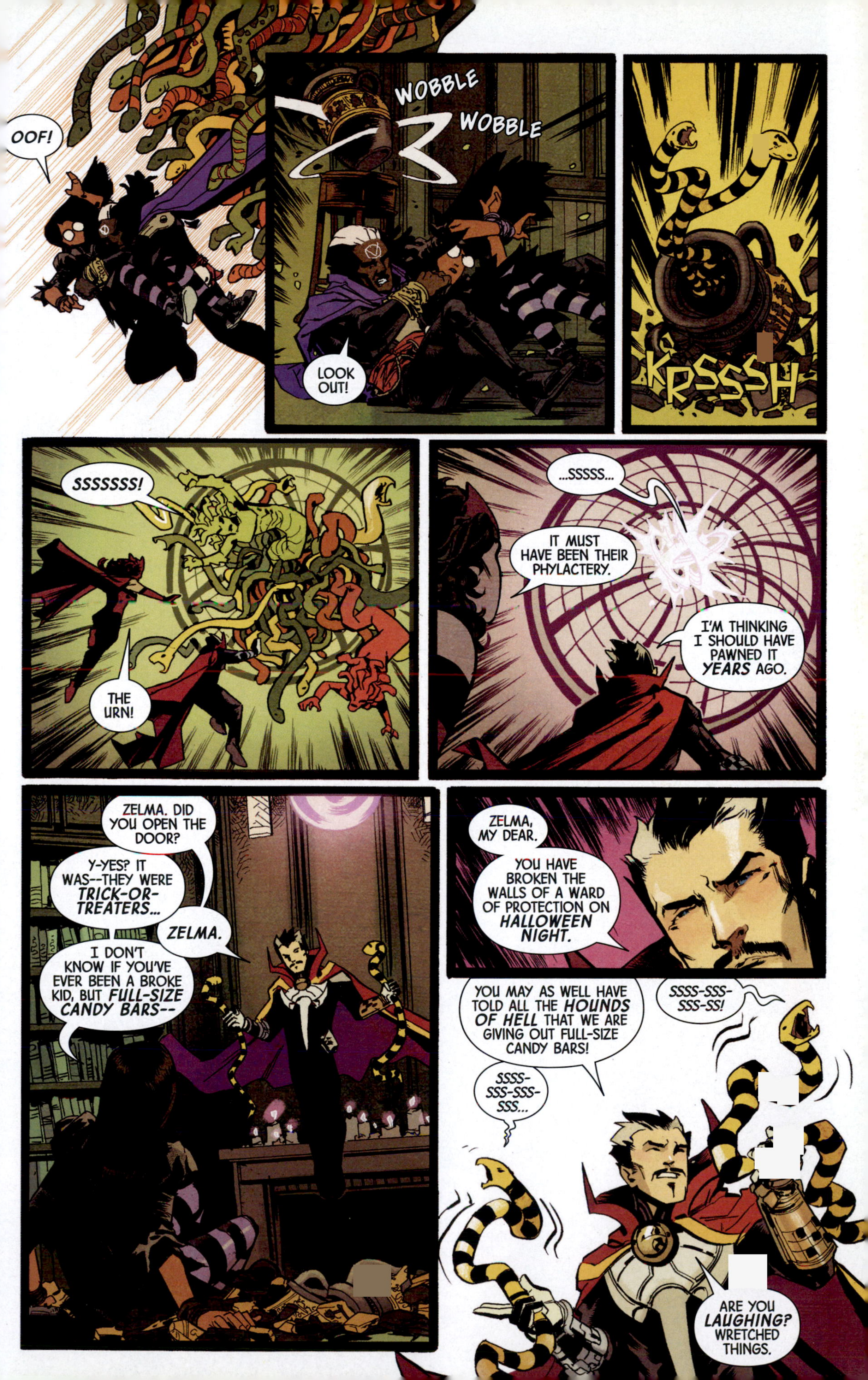
OOF!
WOBBLE
WOBBLE
LOOK OUT!
KRSSSH
SSSSSSS!
THE URN!
...SSSSS...
IT MUST HAVE BEEN THEIR PHYLACTERY.
I'M THINKING I SHOULD HAVE PAWNED IT YEARS AGO.
ZELMA. DID YOU OPEN THE DOOR?
Y-YES? IT WAS--THEY WERE TRICK-OR-TREATERS...
ZELMA.
I DON'T KNOW IF YOU'VE EVER BEEN A BROKE KID, BUT FULL-SIZE CANDY BARS--
ZELMA, MY DEAR.
YOU HAVE BROKEN THE WALLS OF A WARD OF PROTECTION ON HALLOWEEN NIGHT.
YOU MAY AS WELL HAVE TOLD ALL THE HOUNDS OF HELL THAT WE ARE GIVING OUT FULL-SIZE CANDY BARS!
SSSS-SSS-SSS-SS!
SSSS-SSS-SSS-SSS...
ARE YOU LAUGHING? WRETCHED THINGS.

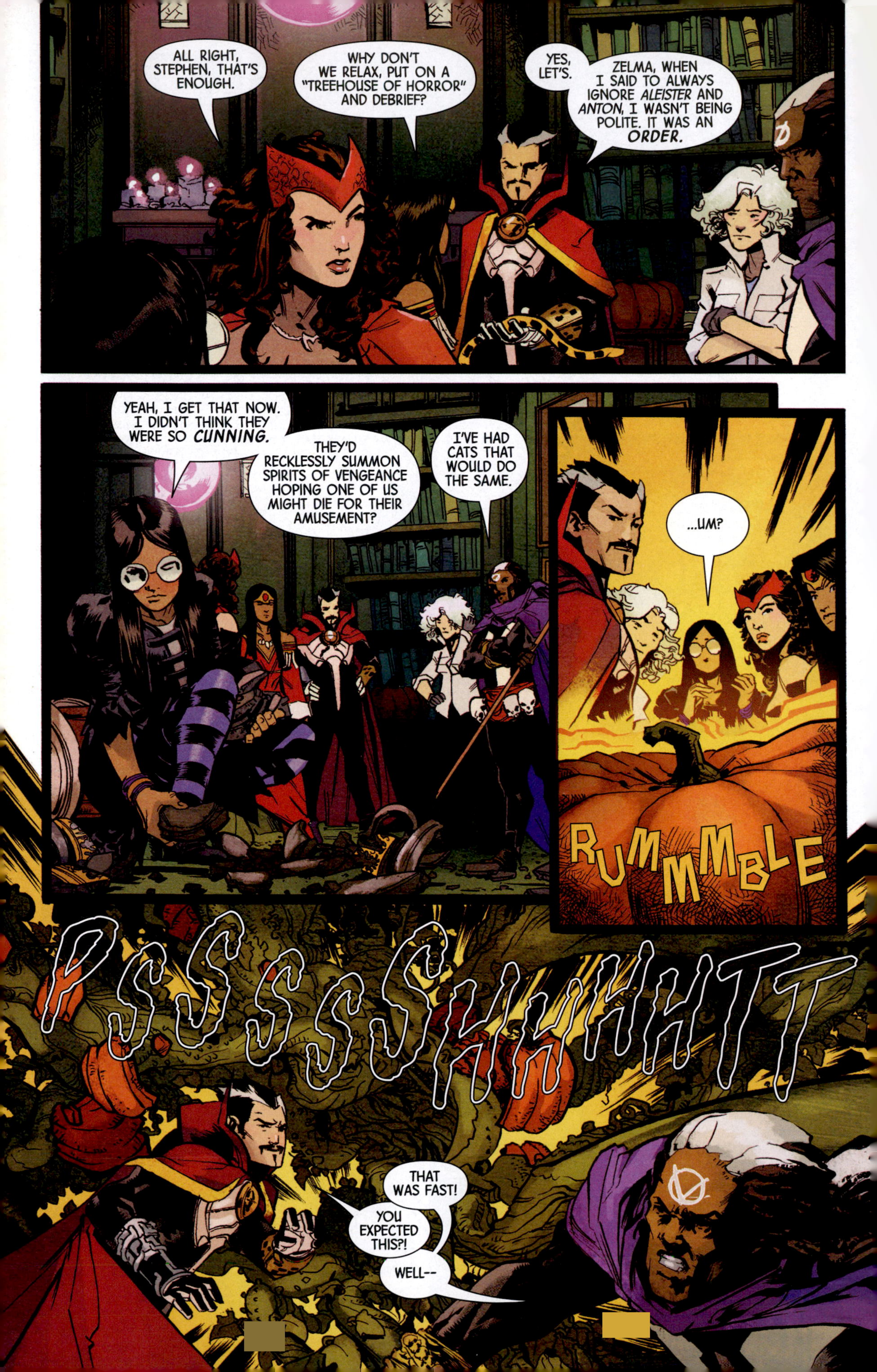

ALL RIGHT, STEPHEN, THAT'S ENOUGH.
WHY DON'T WE RELAX, PUT ON A "TREEHOUSE OF HORROR" AND DEBRIEF?
YES, LET'S.
ZELMA, WHEN I SAID TO ALWAYS IGNORE *ALEISTER* AND *ANTON*, I WASN'T BEING POLITE. IT WAS AN **ORDER.**
YEAH, I GET THAT NOW. I DIDN'T THINK THEY WERE SO **CUNNING.**
THEY'D RECKLESSLY SUMMON SPIRITS OF VENGEANCE HOPING ONE OF US MIGHT DIE FOR THEIR AMUSEMENT?
I'VE HAD CATS THAT WOULD DO THE SAME.
...UM?
RUMMMBLE
PSSSSSHHHHTT
THAT WAS FAST!
YOU EXPECTED THIS?!
WELL--

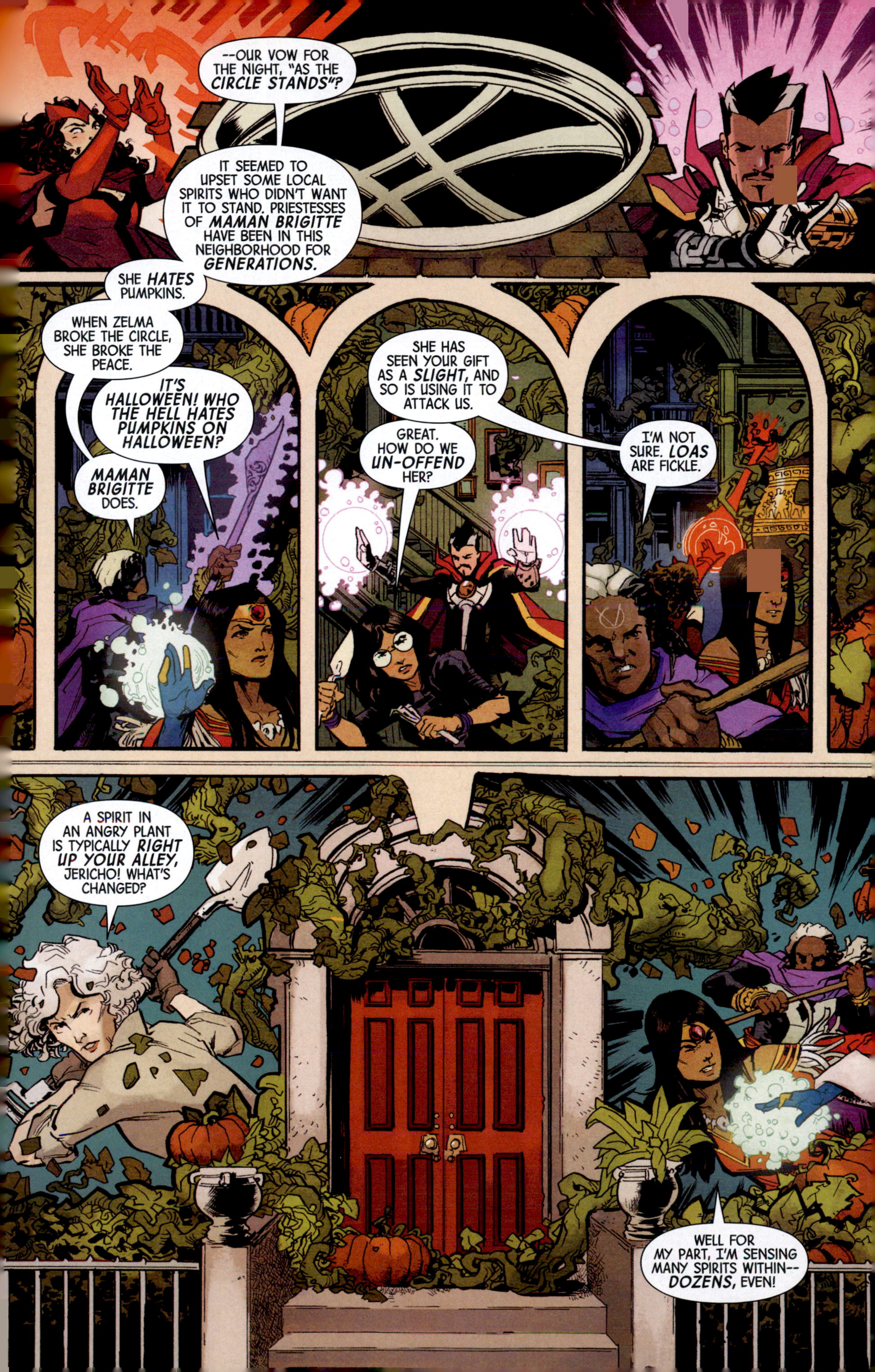
--OUR VOW FOR THE NIGHT, "AS THE CIRCLE STANDS"?
IT SEEMED TO UPSET SOME LOCAL SPIRITS WHO DIDN'T WANT IT TO STAND. PRIESTESSES OF MAMAN BRIGITTE HAVE BEEN IN THIS NEIGHBORHOOD FOR GENERATIONS.
SHE HATES PUMPKINS.
WHEN ZELMA BROKE THE CIRCLE, SHE BROKE THE PEACE.
IT'S HALLOWEEN! WHO THE HELL HATES PUMPKINS ON HALLOWEEN?
MAMAN BRIGITTE DOES.
SHE HAS SEEN YOUR GIFT AS A SLIGHT, AND SO IS USING IT TO ATTACK US.
GREAT. HOW DO WE UN-OFFEND HER?
I'M NOT SURE. LOAS ARE FICKLE.
A SPIRIT IN AN ANGRY PLANT IS TYPICALLY RIGHT UP YOUR ALLEY, JERICHO! WHAT'S CHANGED?
WELL FOR MY PART, I'M SENSING MANY SPIRITS WITHIN-- DOZENS, EVEN!

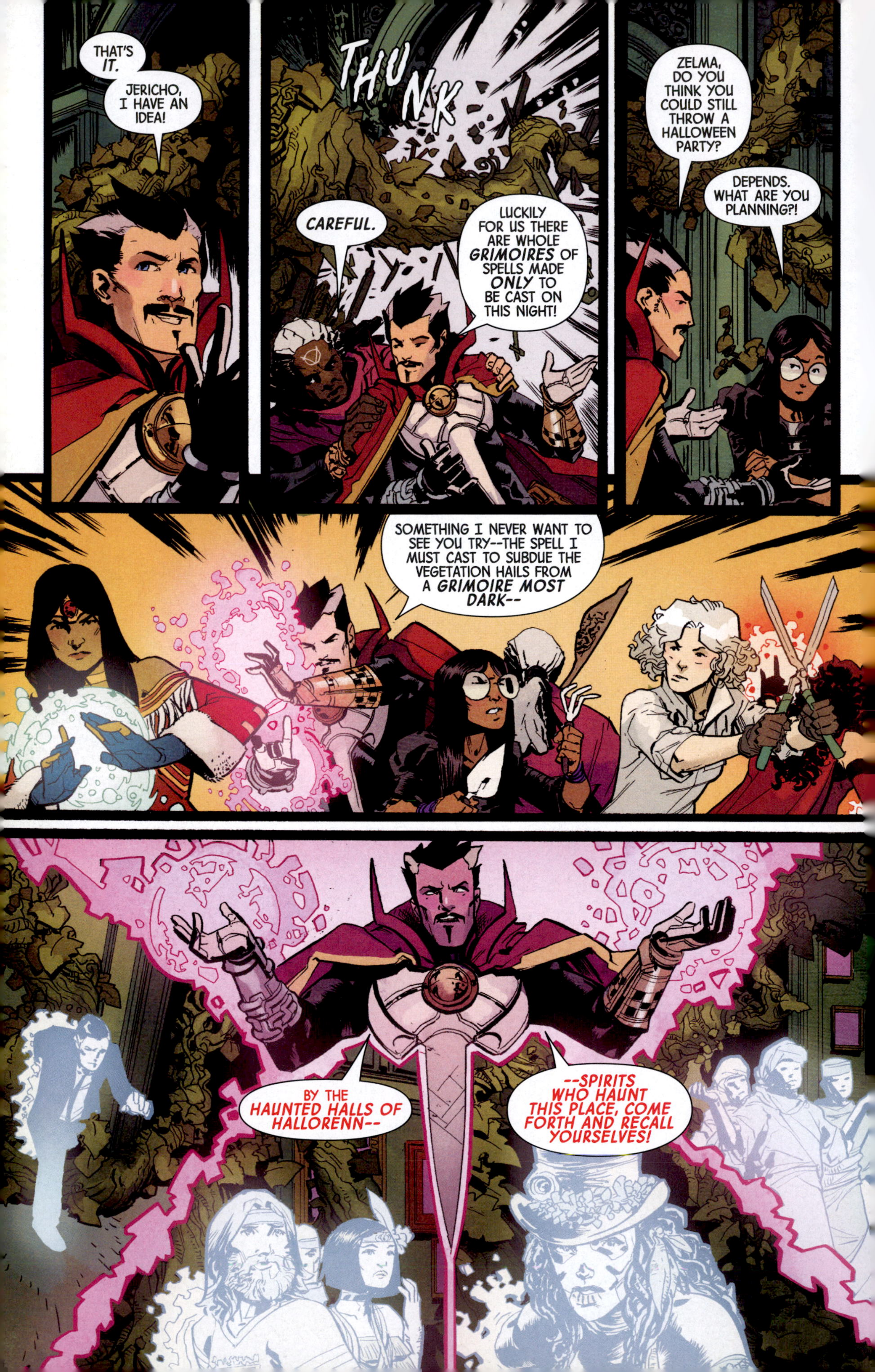
THAT'S *IT.*
JERICHO, I HAVE AN IDEA!
THUNK
CAREFUL.
LUCKILY FOR US THERE ARE WHOLE *GRIMOIRES* OF SPELLS MADE *ONLY* TO BE CAST ON THIS NIGHT!
ZELMA, DO YOU THINK YOU COULD STILL THROW A HALLOWEEN PARTY?
DEPENDS. WHAT ARE YOU PLANNING?!
SOMETHING I NEVER WANT TO SEE YOU TRY--THE SPELL I MUST CAST TO SUBDUE THE VEGETATION HAILS FROM A *GRIMOIRE MOST DARK*--
BY THE HAUNTED HALLS OF HALLORENN--
--SPIRITS WHO HAUNT THIS PLACE, COME FORTH AND RECALL YOURSELVES!

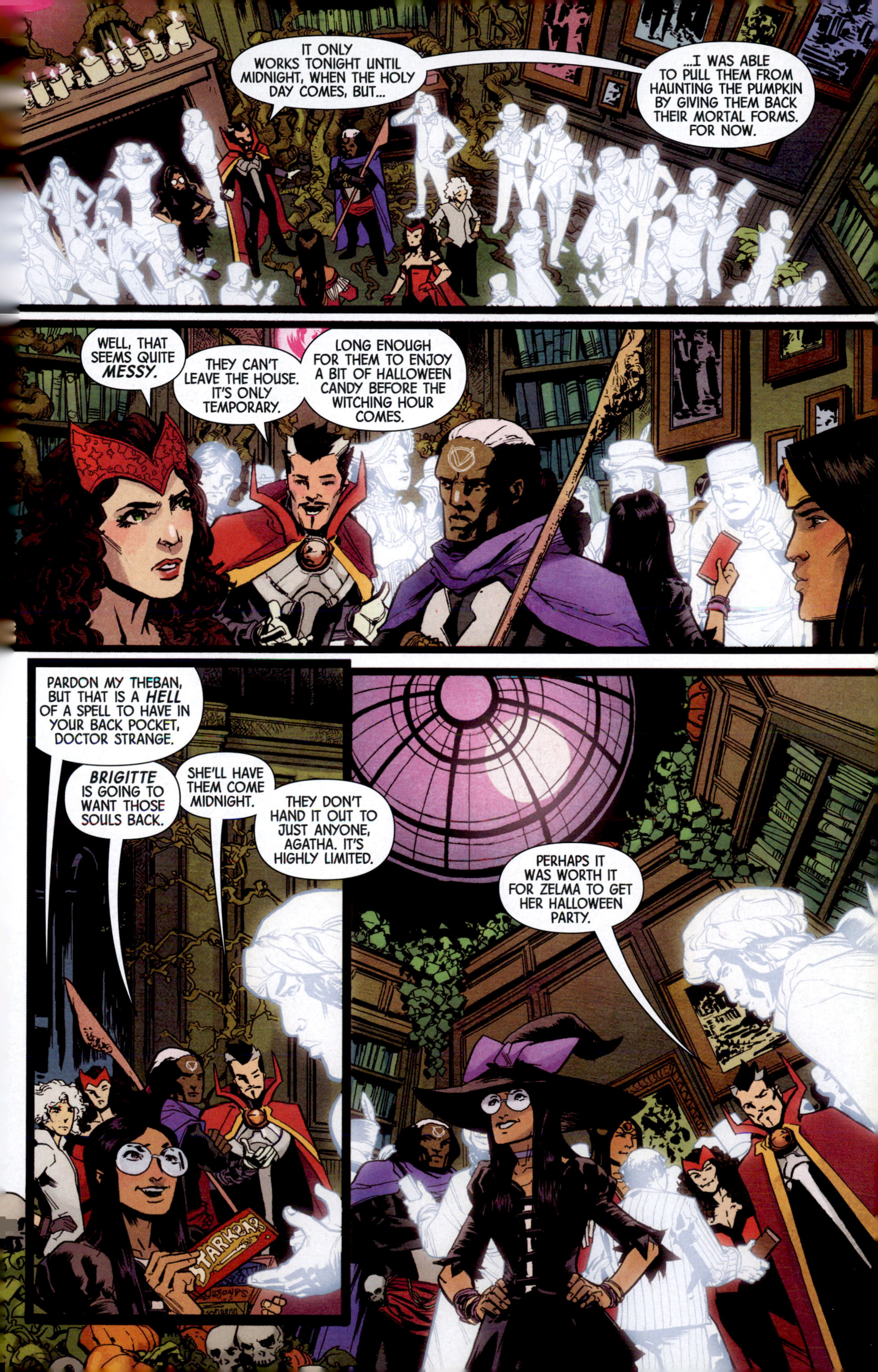
IT ONLY WORKS TONIGHT UNTIL MIDNIGHT, WHEN THE HOLY DAY COMES, BUT...
...I WAS ABLE TO PULL THEM FROM HAUNTING THE PUMPKIN BY GIVING THEM BACK THEIR MORTAL FORMS. FOR NOW.
WELL, THAT SEEMS QUITE *MESSY.*
THEY CAN'T LEAVE THE HOUSE. IT'S ONLY TEMPORARY.
LONG ENOUGH FOR THEM TO ENJOY A BIT OF HALLOWEEN CANDY BEFORE THE WITCHING HOUR COMES.
PARDON MY THEBAN, BUT THAT IS A *HELL* OF A SPELL TO HAVE IN YOUR BACK POCKET, DOCTOR STRANGE.
BRIGITTE IS GOING TO WANT THOSE SOULS BACK.
SHE'LL HAVE THEM COME MIDNIGHT.
THEY DON'T HAND IT OUT TO JUST ANYONE, AGATHA. IT'S HIGHLY LIMITED.
PERHAPS IT WAS WORTH IT FOR ZELMA TO GET HER HALLOWEEN PARTY.
STARKBAR

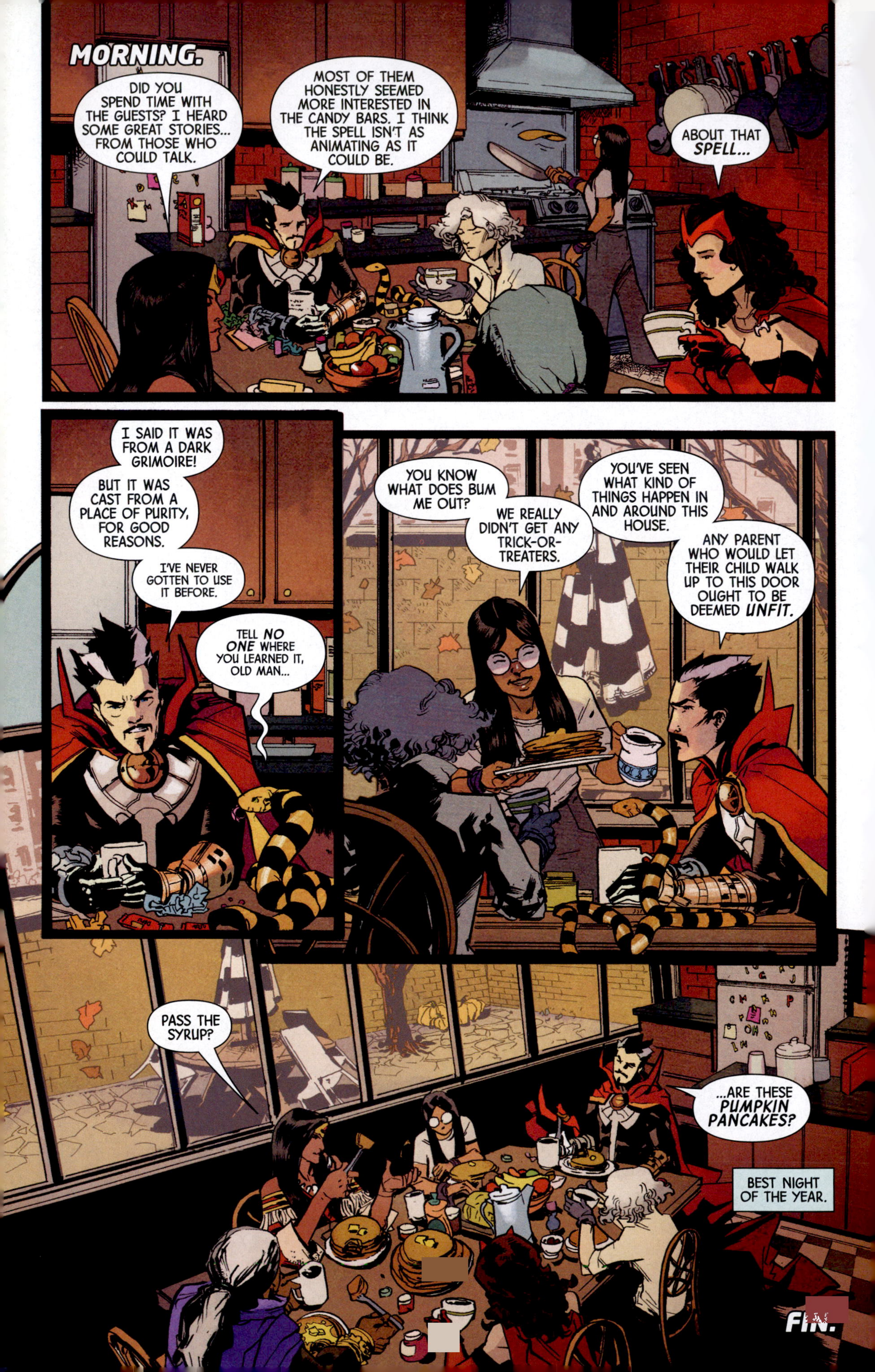
MORNING.
DID YOU SPEND TIME WITH THE GUESTS? I HEARD SOME GREAT STORIES... FROM THOSE WHO COULD TALK.
MOST OF THEM HONESTLY SEEMED MORE INTERESTED IN THE CANDY BARS. I THINK THE SPELL ISN'T AS ANIMATING AS IT COULD BE.
ABOUT THAT SPELL...
I SAID IT WAS FROM A DARK GRIMOIRE!
BUT IT WAS CAST FROM A PLACE OF PURITY, FOR GOOD REASONS.
I'VE NEVER GOTTEN TO USE IT BEFORE.
TELL NO ONE WHERE YOU LEARNED IT, OLD MAN...
YOU KNOW WHAT DOES BUM ME OUT?
WE REALLY DIDN'T GET ANY TRICK-OR-TREATERS.
YOU'VE SEEN WHAT KIND OF THINGS HAPPEN IN AND AROUND THIS HOUSE.
ANY PARENT WHO WOULD LET THEIR CHILD WALK UP TO THIS DOOR OUGHT TO BE DEEMED UNFIT.
PASS THE SYRUP?
...ARE THESE PUMPKIN PANCAKES?
BEST NIGHT OF THE YEAR.
FIN.

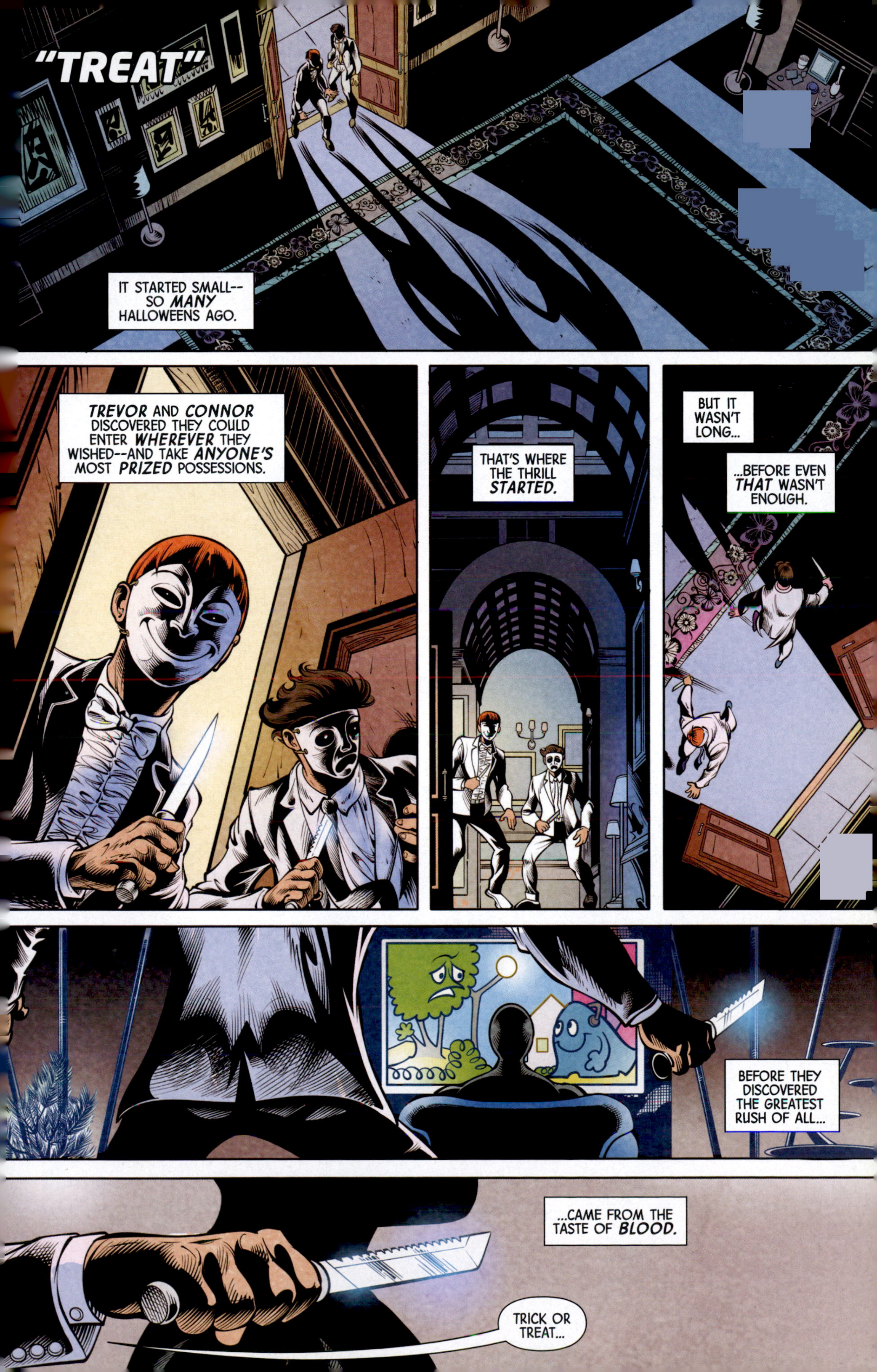
"TREAT"
IT STARTED SMALL-- SO MANY HALLOWEENS AGO.
TREVOR AND CONNOR DISCOVERED THEY COULD ENTER WHEREVER THEY WISHED--AND TAKE ANYONE'S MOST PRIZED POSSESSIONS.
THAT'S WHERE THE THRILL STARTED.
BUT IT WASN'T LONG...
...BEFORE EVEN THAT WASN'T ENOUGH.
BEFORE THEY DISCOVERED THE GREATEST RUSH OF ALL...
...CAME FROM THE TASTE OF BLOOD.
TRICK OR TREAT...

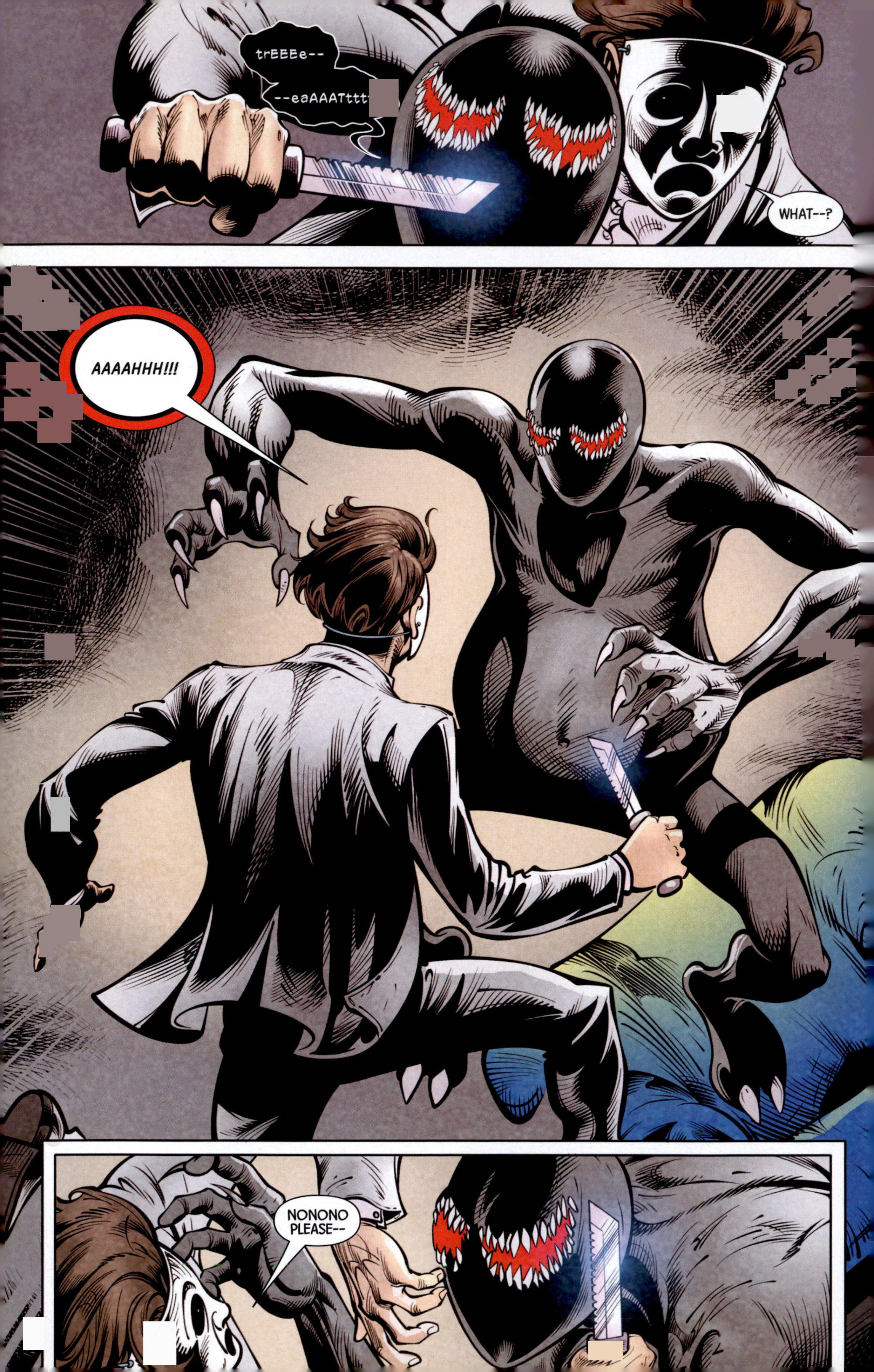
trEEEe--
--eaAAATttt
WHAT--?
AAAAHHH!!!
NONONO PLEASE--

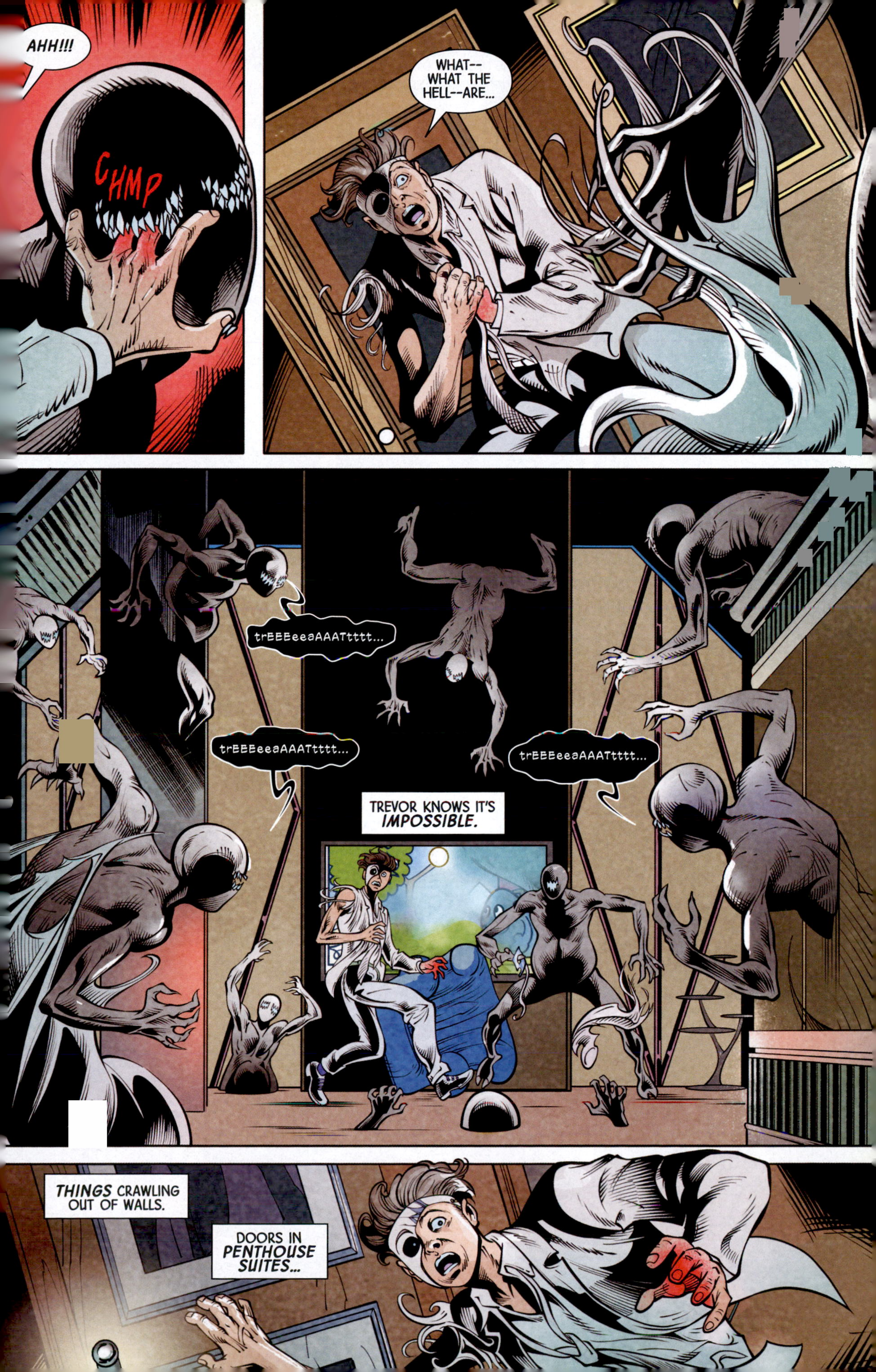
AHH!!!
CHMP
WHAT-- WHAT THE HELL--ARE...
trEBBeeaAAATtttt...
trEBBeeaAAATtttt...
trEBBeeaAAATtttt...
TREVOR KNOWS IT'S IMPOSSIBLE.
THINGS CRAWLING OUT OF WALLS.
DOORS IN PENTHOUSE SUITES...

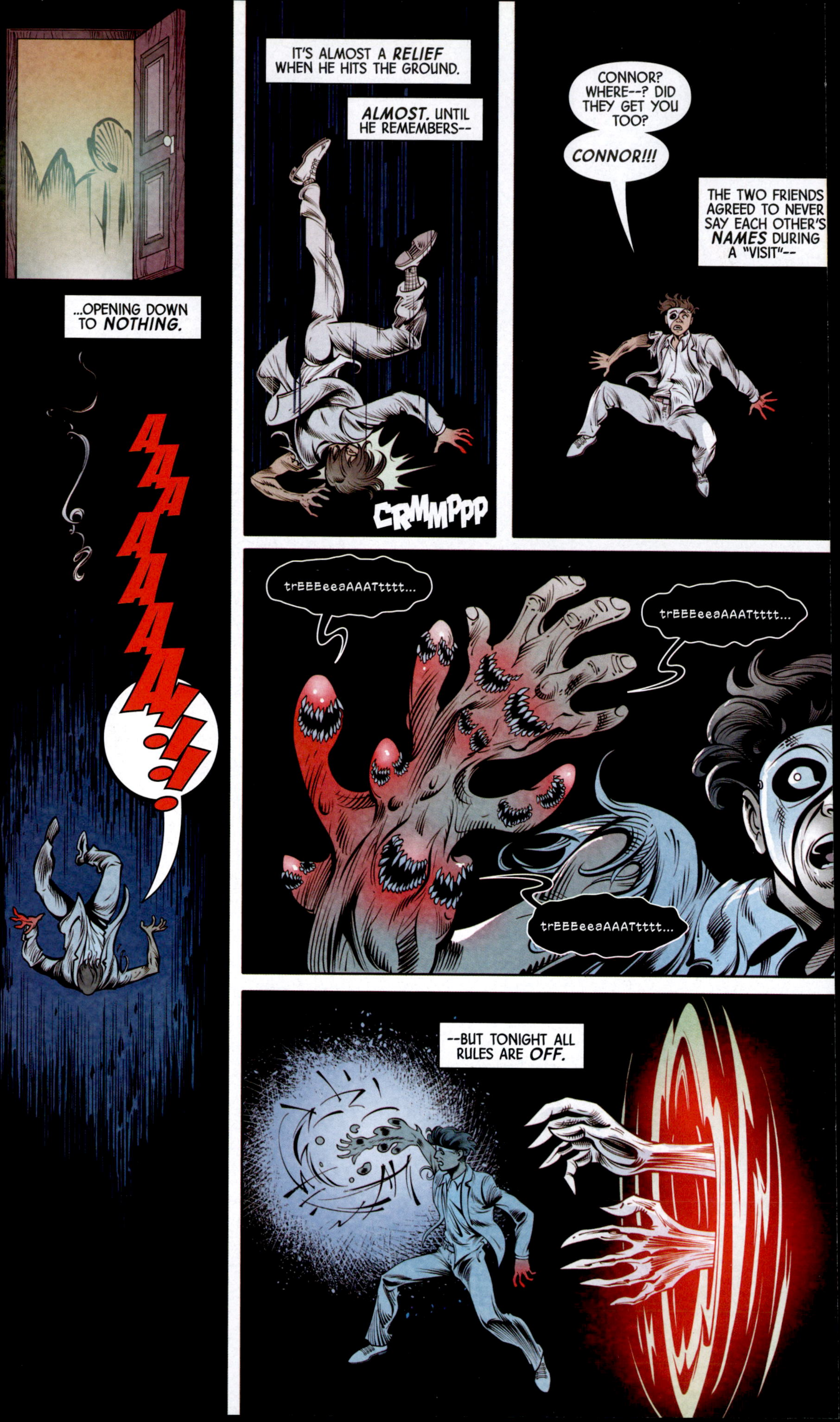
...OPENING DOWN TO NOTHING.
AAAAAAAAAA!!
IT'S ALMOST A RELIEF WHEN HE HITS THE GROUND.
ALMOST. UNTIL HE REMEMBERS--
CRMMPPP
CONNOR? WHERE--? DID THEY GET YOU TOO?
CONNOR!!!
THE TWO FRIENDS AGREED TO NEVER SAY EACH OTHER'S NAMES DURING A "VISIT"--
trEEEeeaAAATtttt...
trEEEeeaAAATtttt...
trEEEeeaAAATtttt...
--BUT TONIGHT ALL RULES ARE OFF.

ONCE UPON A TIME, TREVOR AND CONNOR WERE *ORDINARY*.

DIRECTIONLESS.

AH--

AH!!!

UNTIL THE FOSTER BROTHERS *MET*, AND THEY *BOTH* FELT IT.

AN ABILITY SUDDENLY UNLOCKED IN *BOTH* OF THEM...

OKAY, THEN...

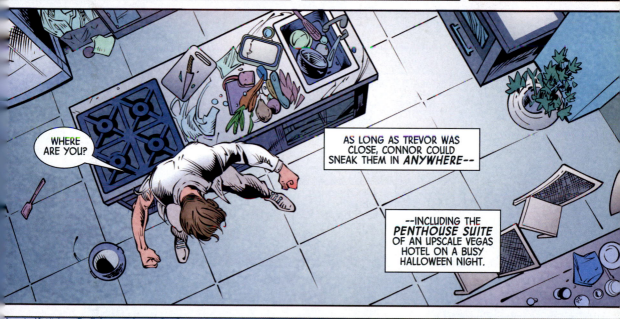

WHERE ARE YOU?

AS LONG AS TREVOR WAS CLOSE, CONNOR COULD SNEAK THEM IN *ANYWHERE*--

--INCLUDING THE *PENTHOUSE SUITE* OF AN UPSCALE VEGAS HOTEL ON A BUSY HALLOWEEN NIGHT.

AND TREVOR-- IN RETURN...

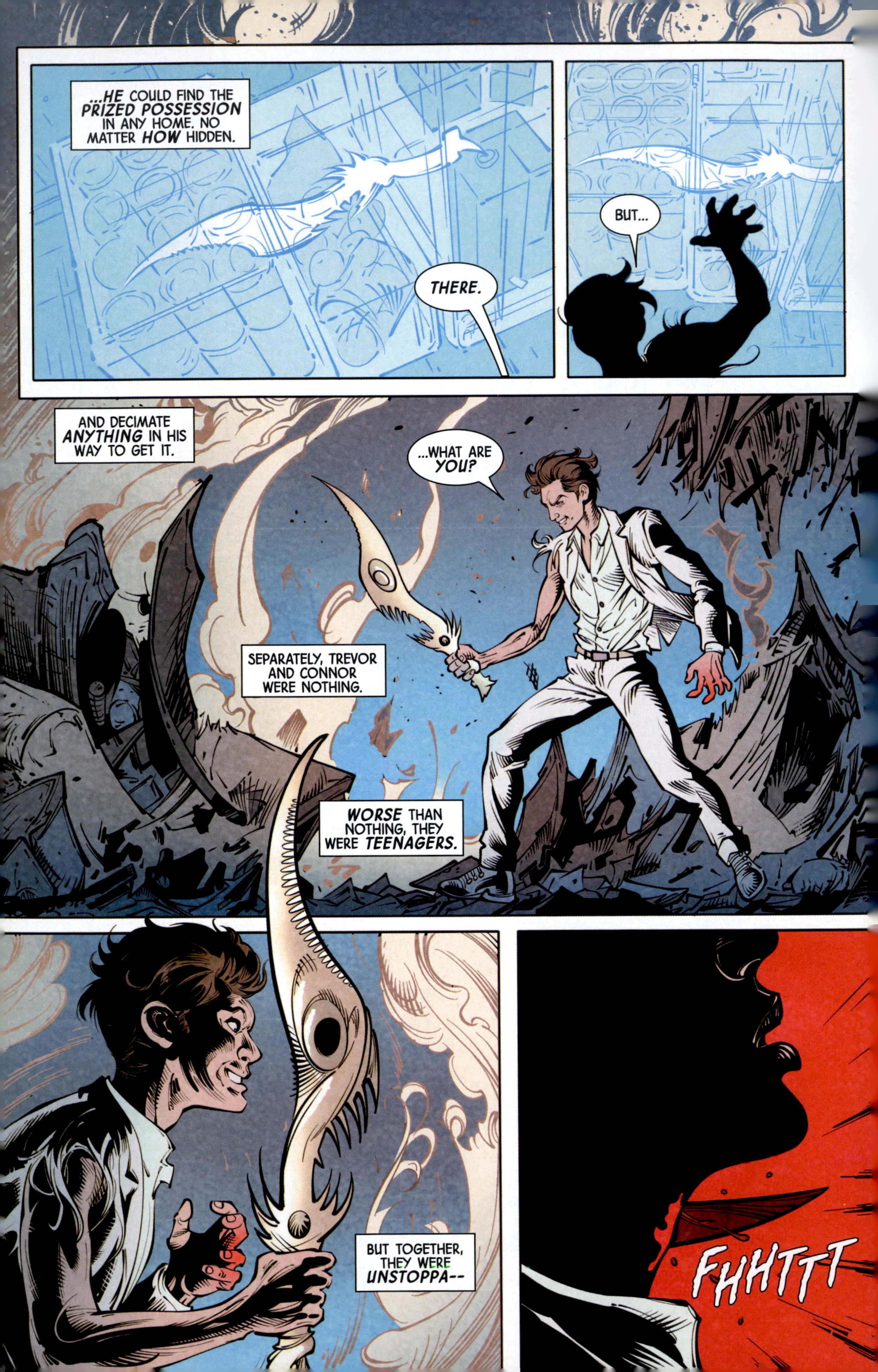

...HE COULD FIND THE PRIZED POSSESSION IN ANY HOME. NO MATTER HOW HIDDEN.
THERE.
BUT...
AND DECIMATE ANYTHING IN HIS WAY TO GET IT.
...WHAT ARE YOU?
SEPARATELY, TREVOR AND CONNOR WERE NOTHING.
WORSE THAN NOTHING, THEY WERE TEENAGERS.
BUT TOGETHER, THEY WERE UNSTOPPA--
FHHTTT

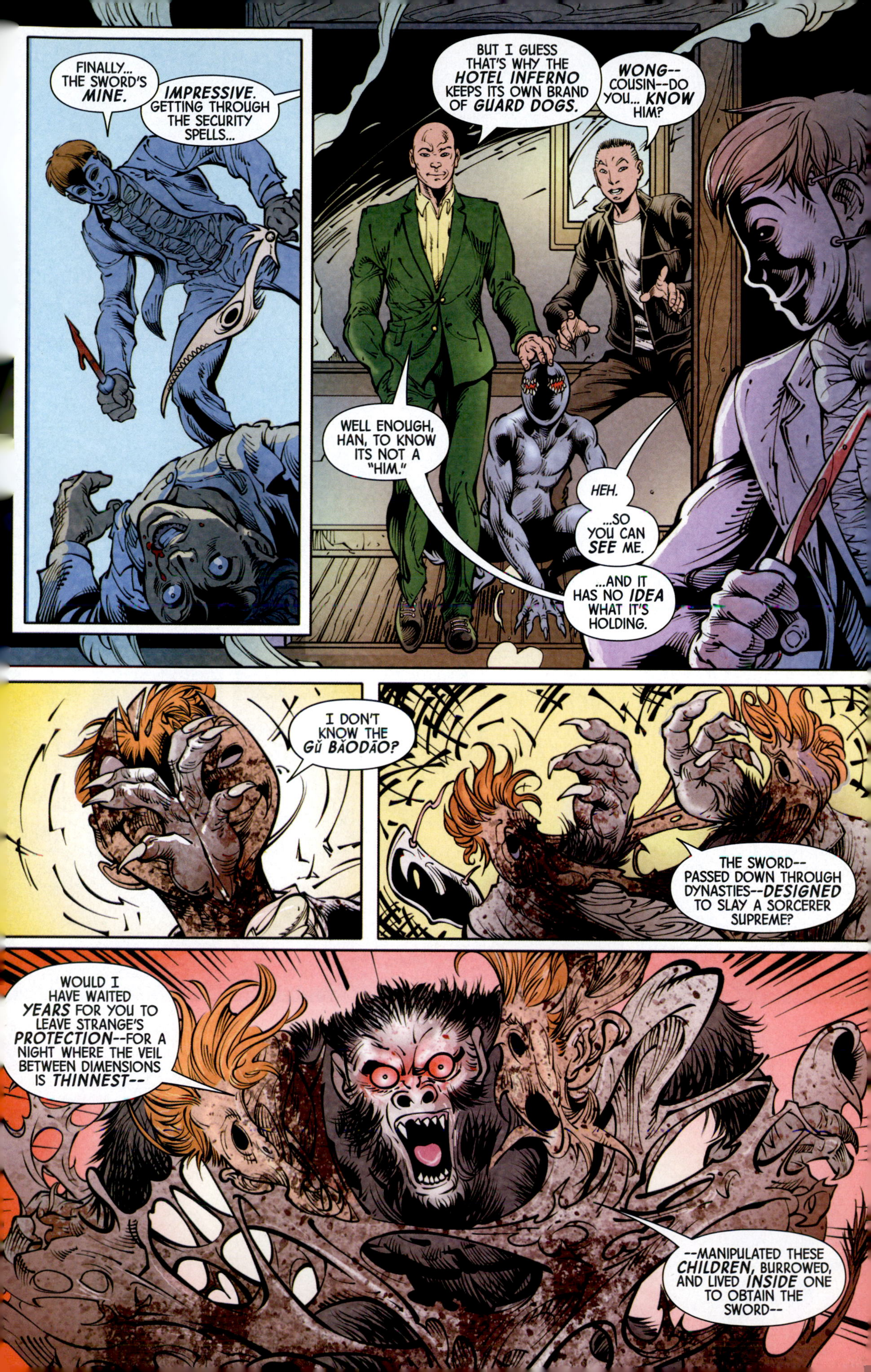
FINALLY... THE SWORD'S MINE.
IMPRESSIVE. GETTING THROUGH THE SECURITY SPELLS...
BUT I GUESS THAT'S WHY THE HOTEL INFERNO KEEPS ITS OWN BRAND OF GUARD DOGS.
WONG--COUSIN--DO YOU... KNOW HIM?
WELL ENOUGH, HAN, TO KNOW ITS NOT A "HIM."
HEH.
...SO YOU CAN SEE ME.
...AND IT HAS NO IDEA WHAT IT'S HOLDING.
I DON'T KNOW THE GǓ BǍODĀO?
THE SWORD--PASSED DOWN THROUGH DYNASTIES--DESIGNED TO SLAY A SORCERER SUPREME?
WOULD I HAVE WAITED YEARS FOR YOU TO LEAVE STRANGE'S PROTECTION--FOR A NIGHT WHERE THE VEIL BETWEEN DIMENSIONS IS THINNEST--
--MANIPULATED THESE CHILDREN, BURROWED, AND LIVED INSIDE ONE TO OBTAIN THE SWORD--

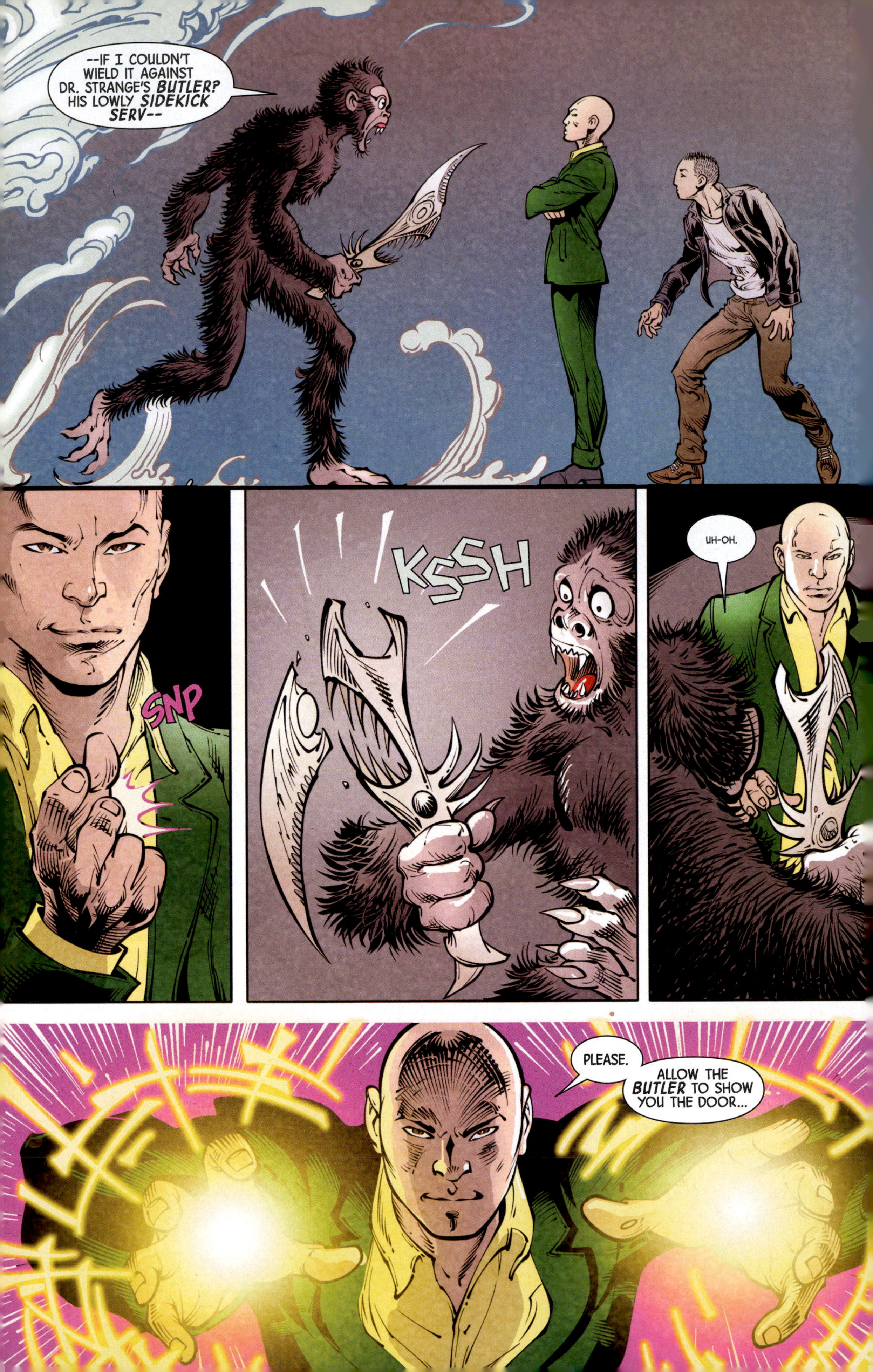
--IF I COULDN'T WIELD IT AGAINST DR. STRANGE'S BUTLER? HIS LOWLY SIDEKICK SERV--
SNP
KSSH
UH-OH.
PLEASE.
ALLOW THE BUTLER TO SHOW YOU THE DOOR...

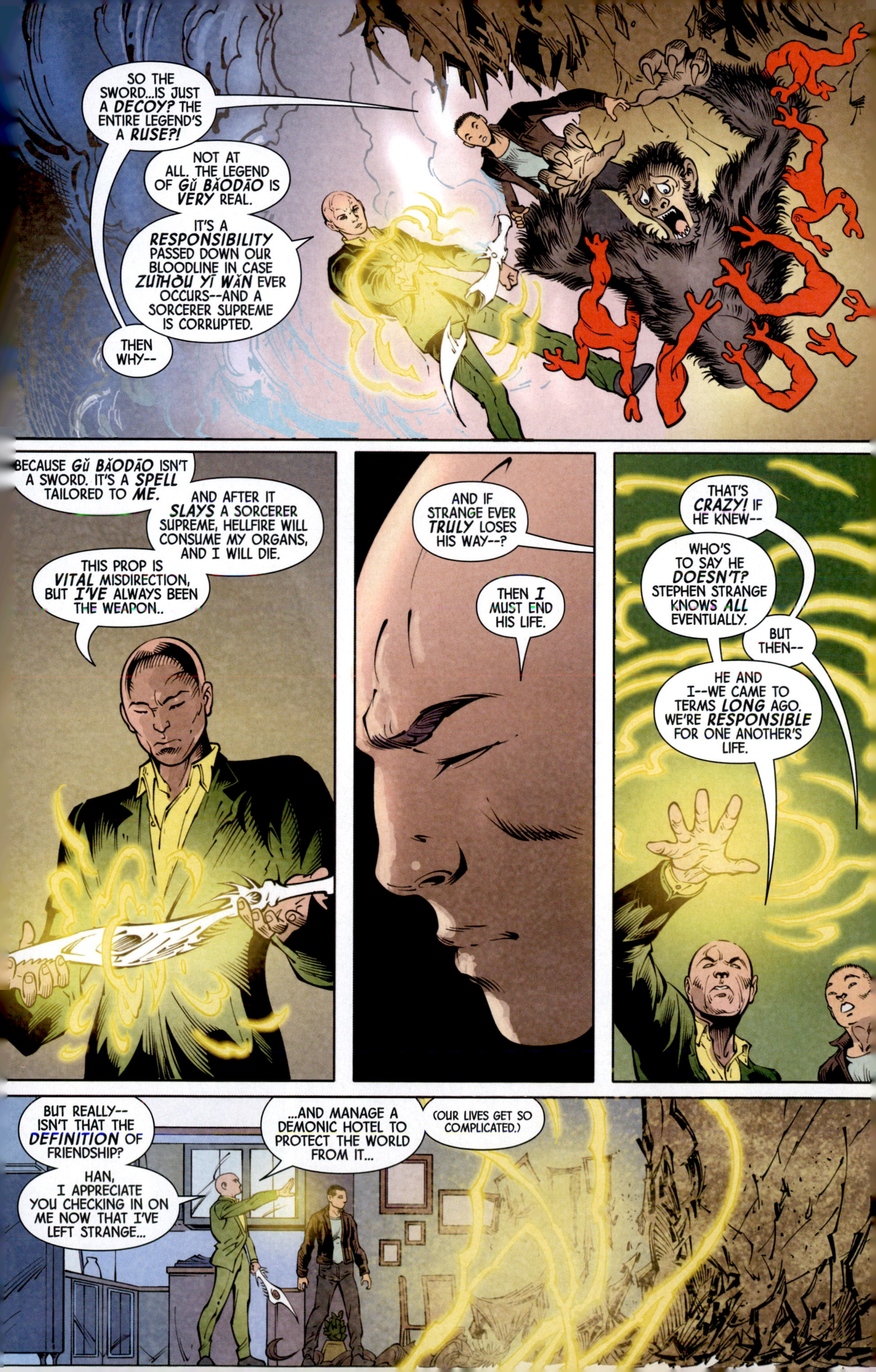
SO THE SWORD...IS JUST A DECOY? THE ENTIRE LEGEND'S A RUSE?!
NOT AT ALL. THE LEGEND OF GǓ BǍODĀO IS VERY REAL.
IT'S A RESPONSIBILITY PASSED DOWN OUR BLOODLINE IN CASE ZUTHŌU YĪ WǍN EVER OCCURS--AND A SORCERER SUPREME IS CORRUPTED.
THEN WHY--
BECAUSE GǓ BǍODĀO ISN'T A SWORD. IT'S A SPELL TAILORED TO ME.
AND AFTER IT SLAYS A SORCERER SUPREME, HELLFIRE WILL CONSUME MY ORGANS, AND I WILL DIE.
THIS PROP IS VITAL MISDIRECTION, BUT I'VE ALWAYS BEEN THE WEAPON..
AND IF STRANGE EVER TRULY LOSES HIS WAY--?
THEN I MUST END HIS LIFE.
THAT'S CRAZY! IF HE KNEW--
WHO'S TO SAY HE DOESN'T? STEPHEN STRANGE KNOWS ALL EVENTUALLY.
BUT THEN--
HE AND I--WE CAME TO TERMS LONG AGO. WE'RE RESPONSIBLE FOR ONE ANOTHER'S LIFE.
BUT REALLY--ISN'T THAT THE DEFINITION OF FRIENDSHIP?
HAN, I APPRECIATE YOU CHECKING IN ON ME NOW THAT I'VE LEFT STRANGE...
...AND MANAGE A DEMONIC HOTEL TO PROTECT THE WORLD FROM IT...
(OUR LIVES GET SO COMPLICATED.)

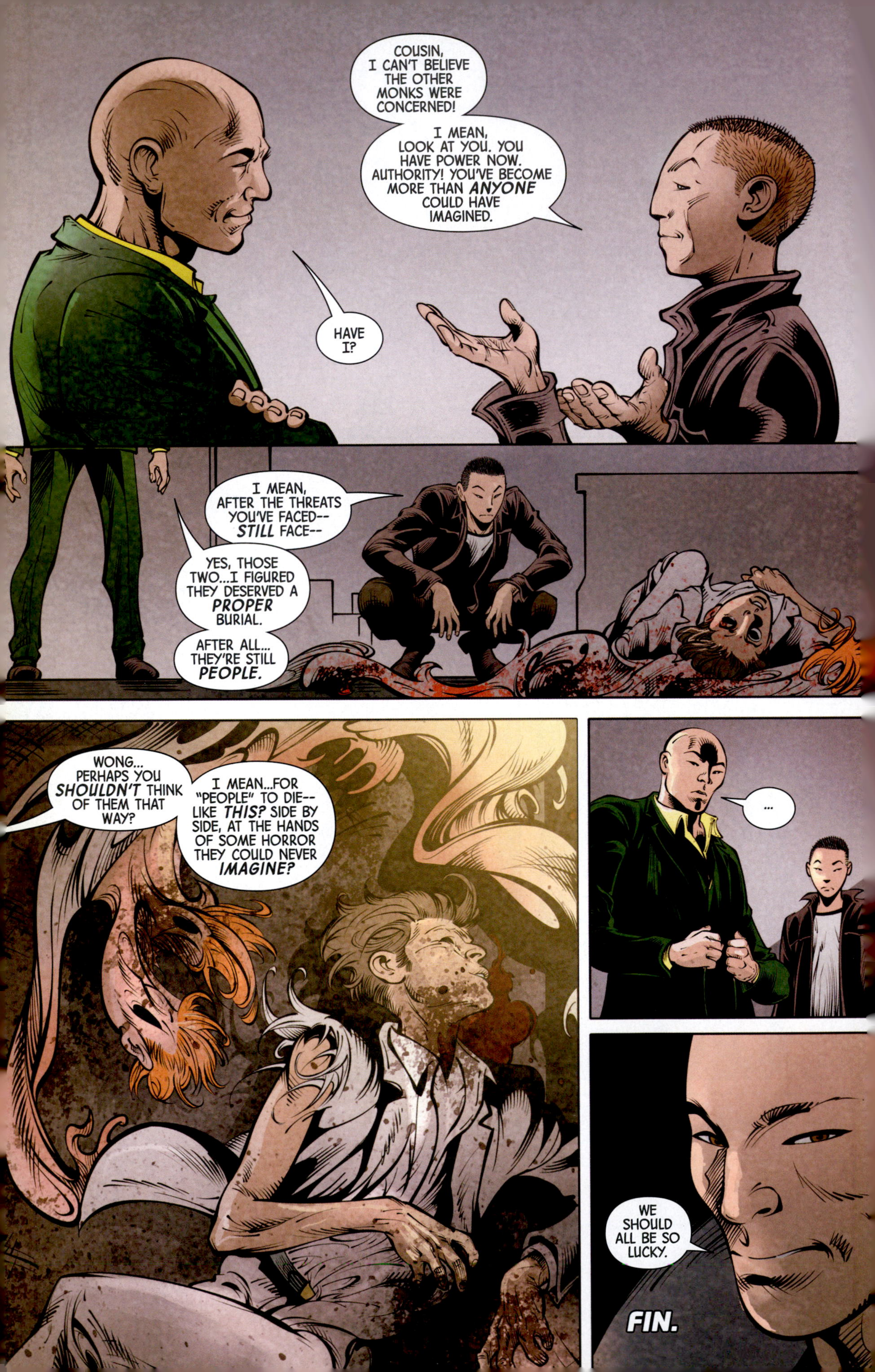
COUSIN, I CAN'T BELIEVE THE OTHER MONKS WERE CONCERNED!
I MEAN, LOOK AT YOU. YOU HAVE POWER NOW. AUTHORITY! YOU'VE BECOME MORE THAN ANYONE COULD HAVE IMAGINED.
HAVE I?
I MEAN, AFTER THE THREATS YOU'VE FACED-- STILL FACE--
YES, THOSE TWO...I FIGURED THEY DESERVED A PROPER BURIAL.
AFTER ALL... THEY'RE STILL PEOPLE.
WONG... PERHAPS YOU SHOULDN'T THINK OF THEM THAT WAY?
I MEAN...FOR "PEOPLE" TO DIE-- LIKE THIS? SIDE BY SIDE, AT THE HANDS OF SOME HORROR THEY COULD NEVER IMAGINE?
...
WE SHOULD ALL BE SO LUCKY.
FIN.

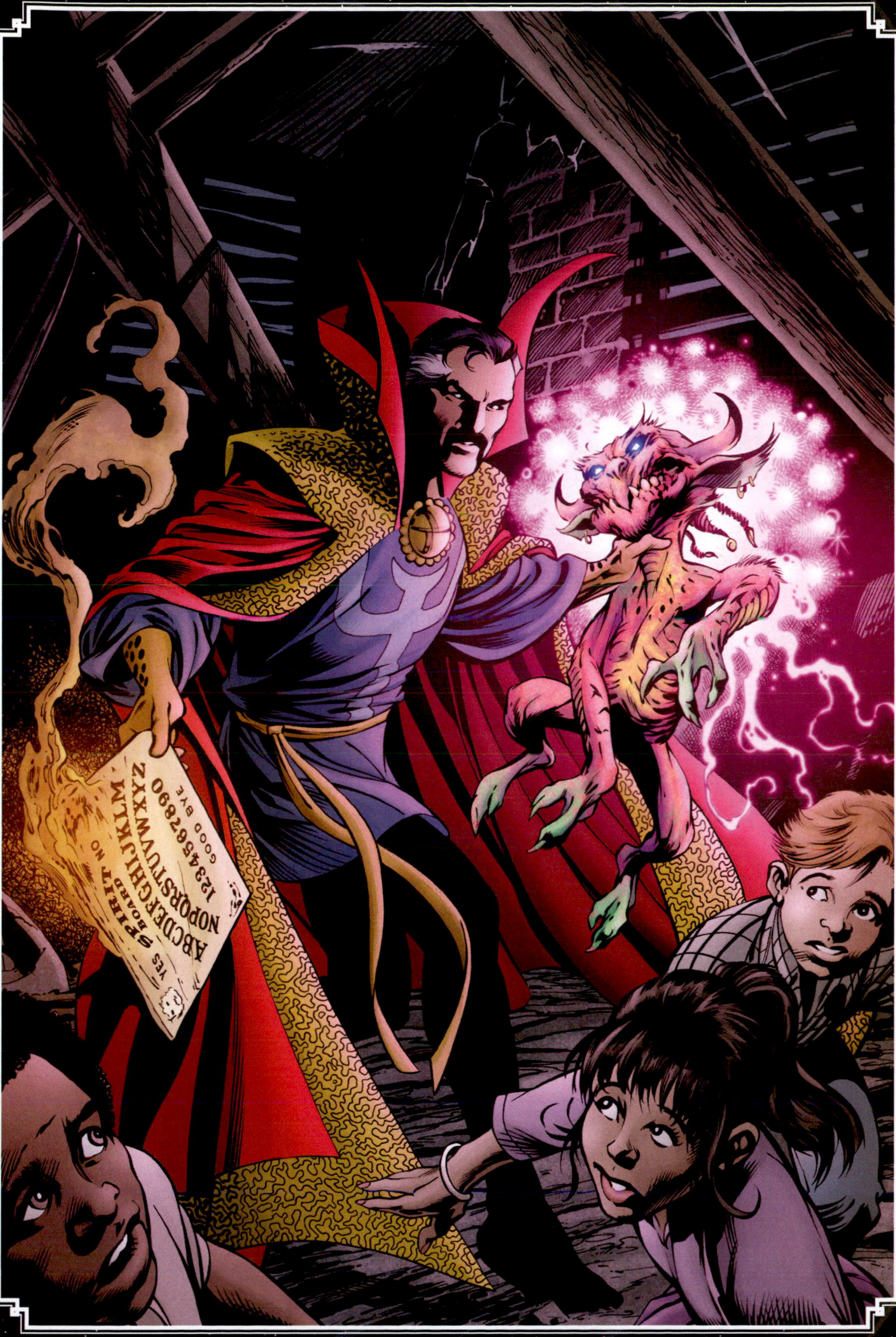
YES
SPIRIT BOARD
NO
1234567890
GOOD BYE

Alan Davis, Mark Farmer & Matt Hollingsworth

#18 MARVELS 25TH TRIBUTE VARIANT

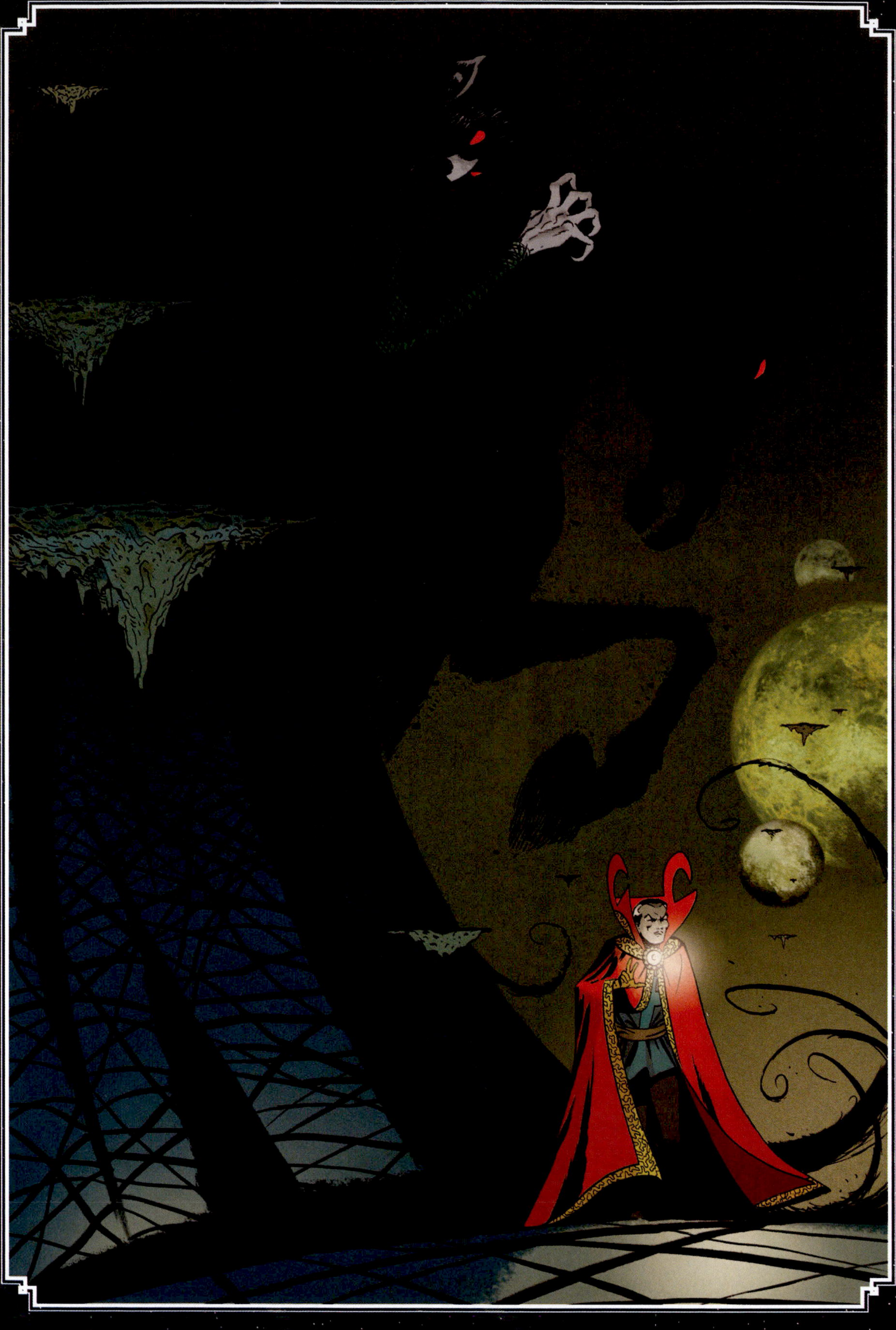

Marcos Martin

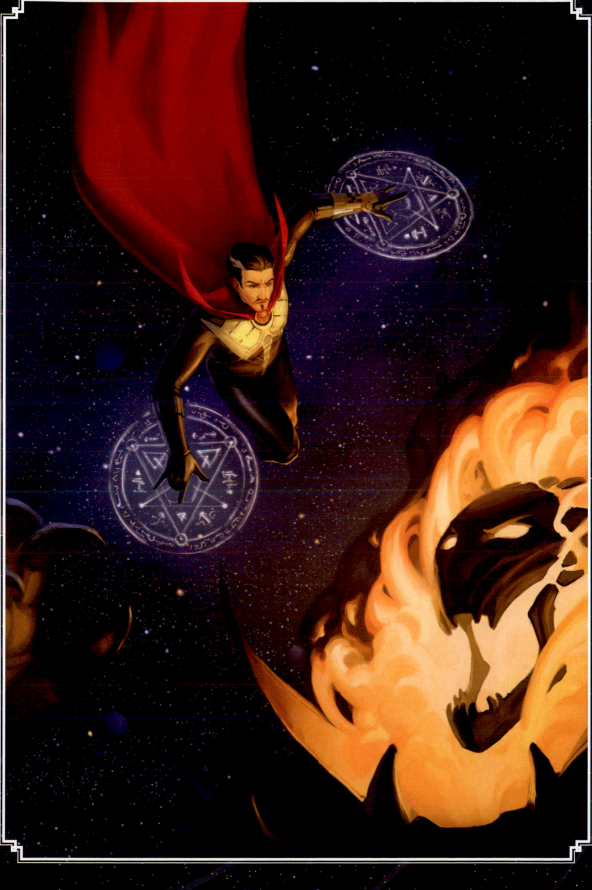

Irina Nordsol

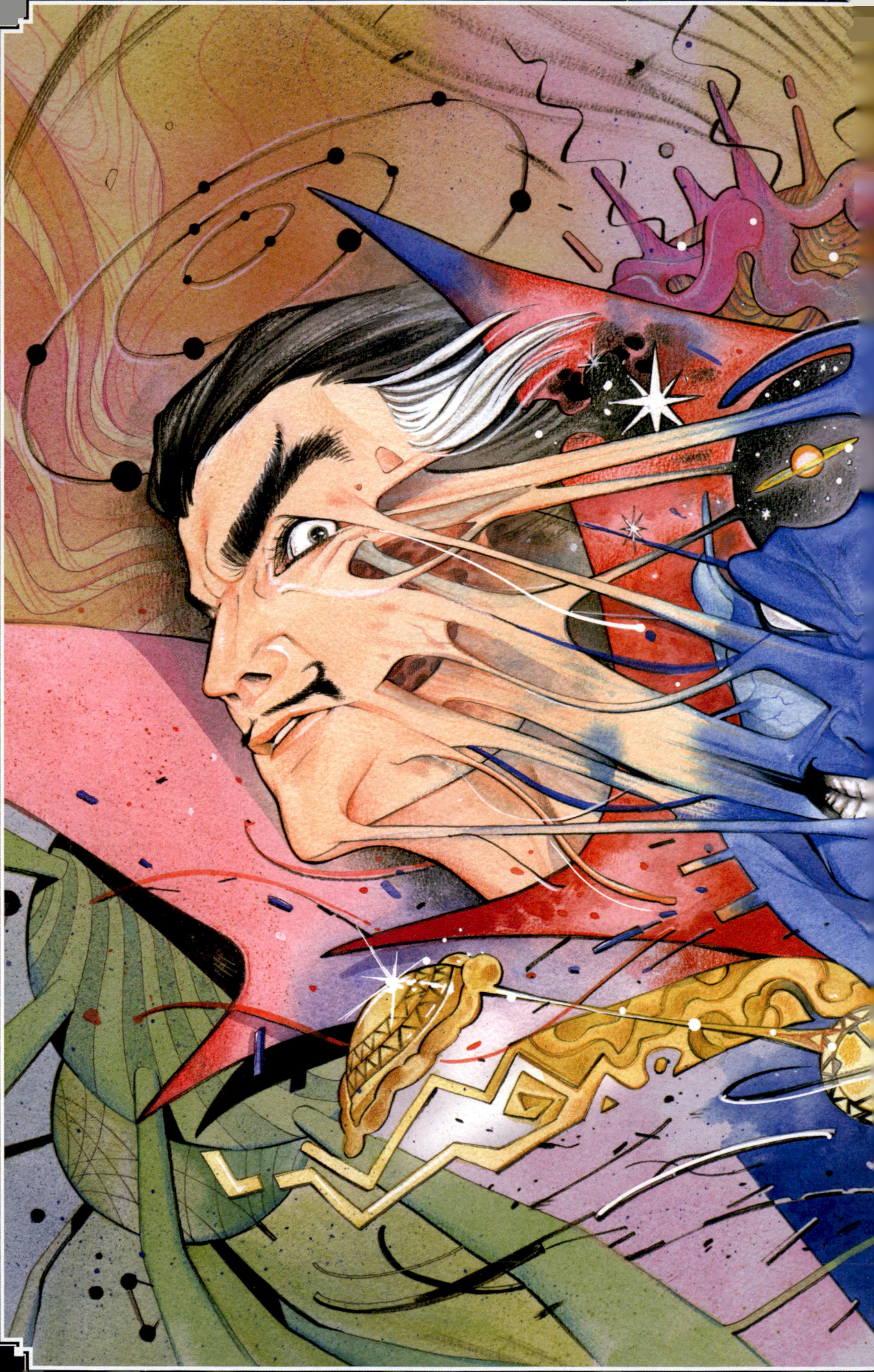

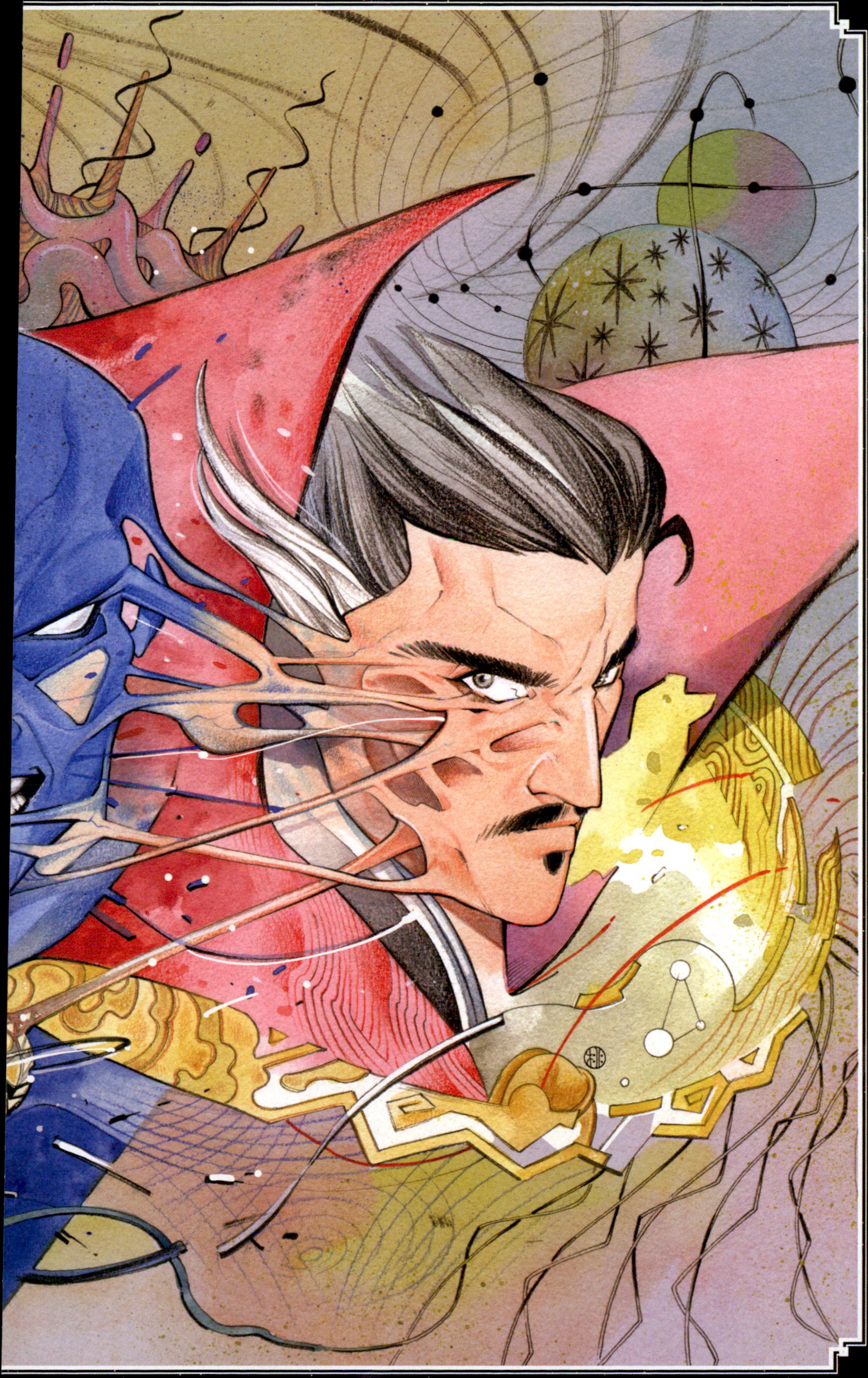

Peach Momoko
#20 IMMORTAL VARIANT

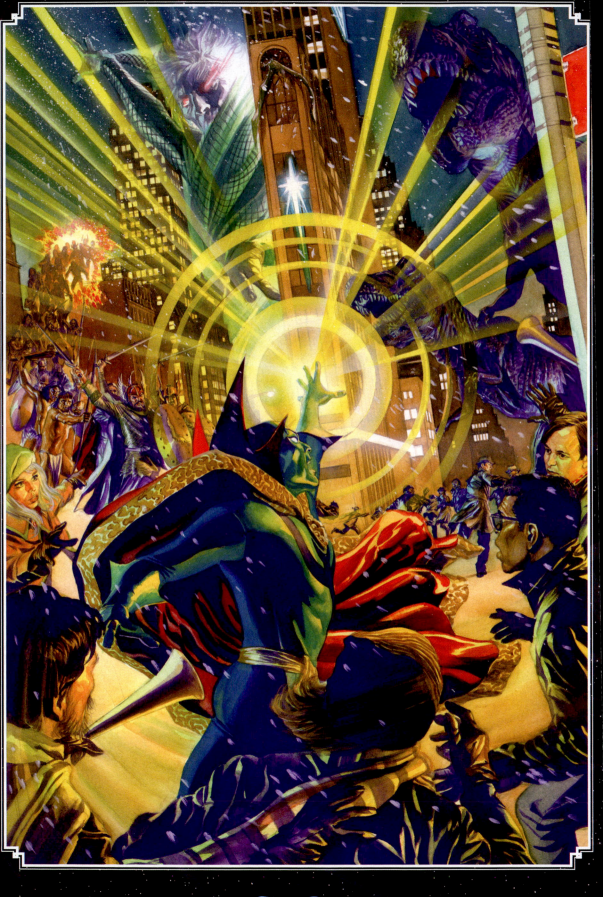

Alex Ross

#20 MARVELS 25TH TRIBUTE VARIANT

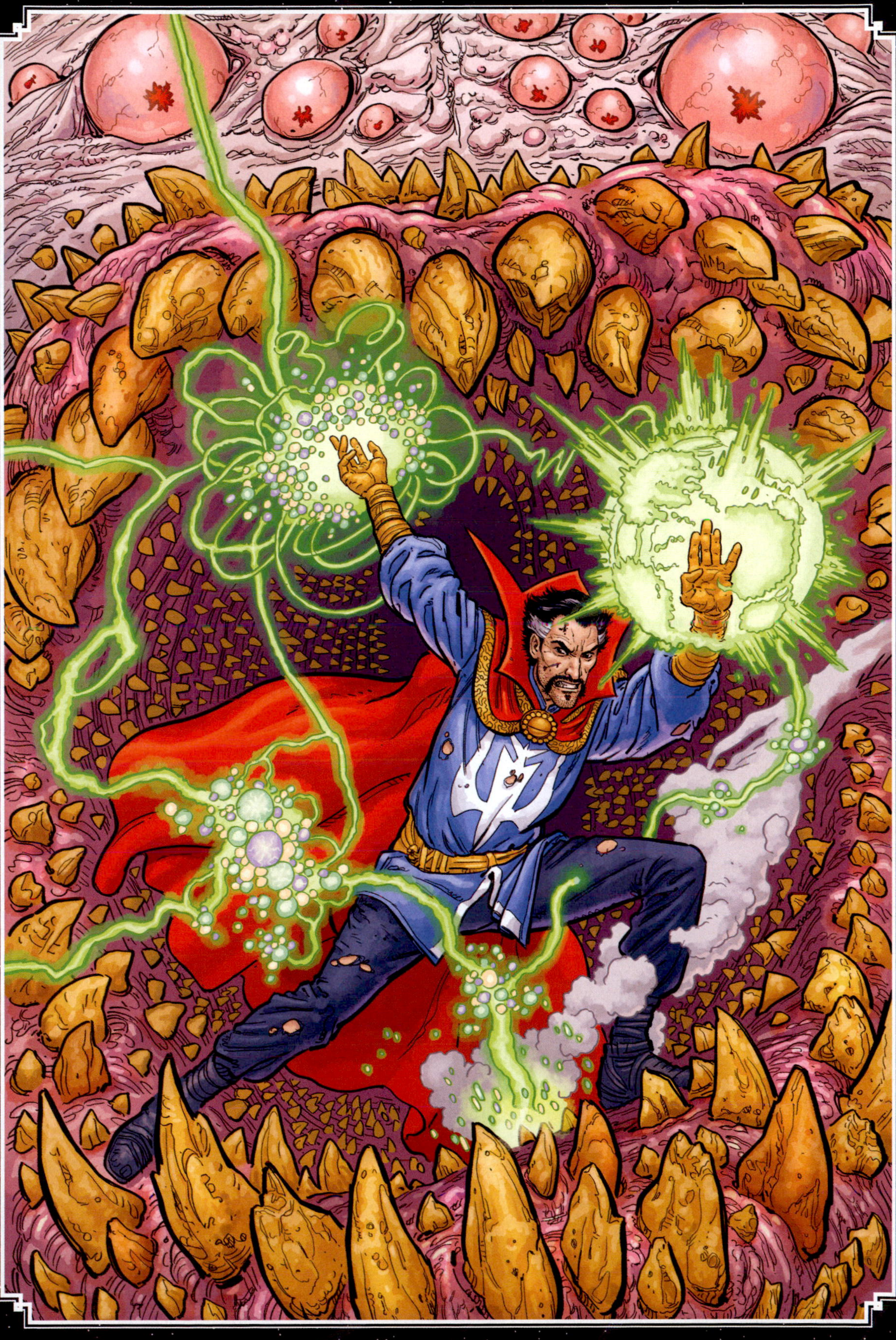

Steve Skroce & Dave Stewart
DOCTOR STRANGE ANNUAL #1 VARIANT

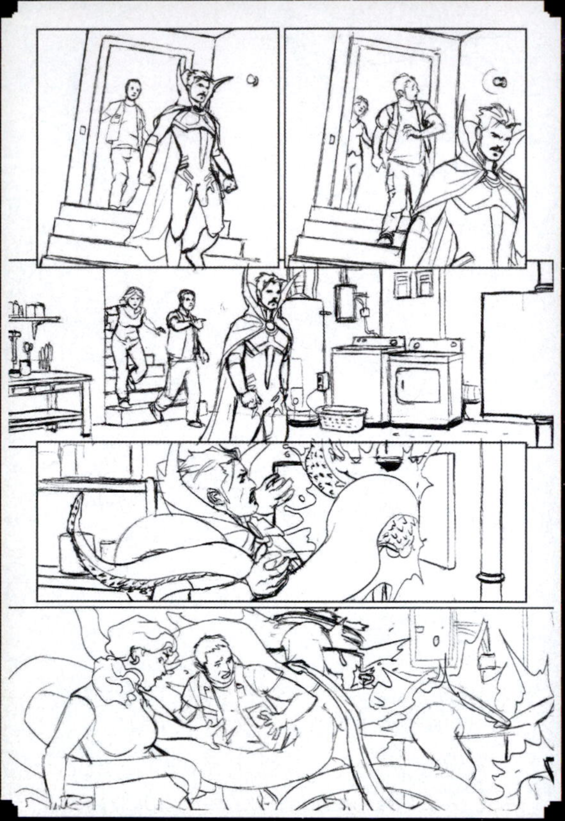

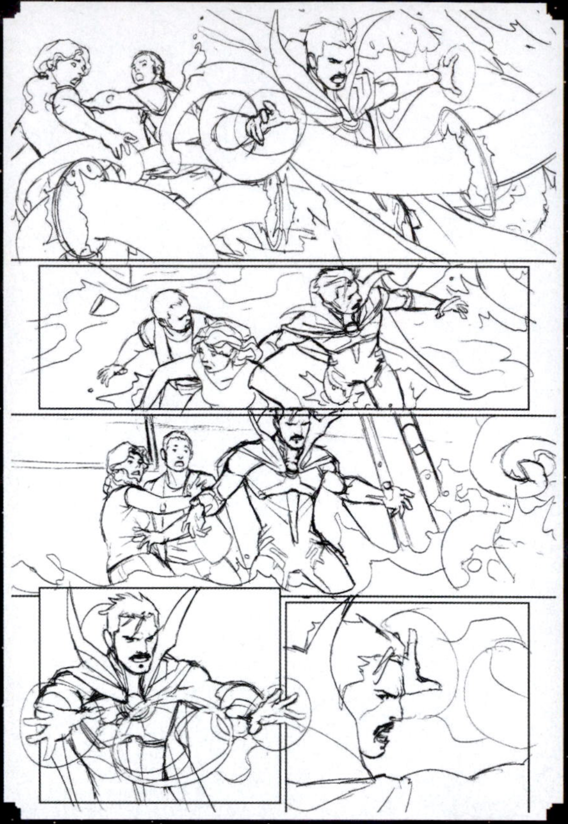

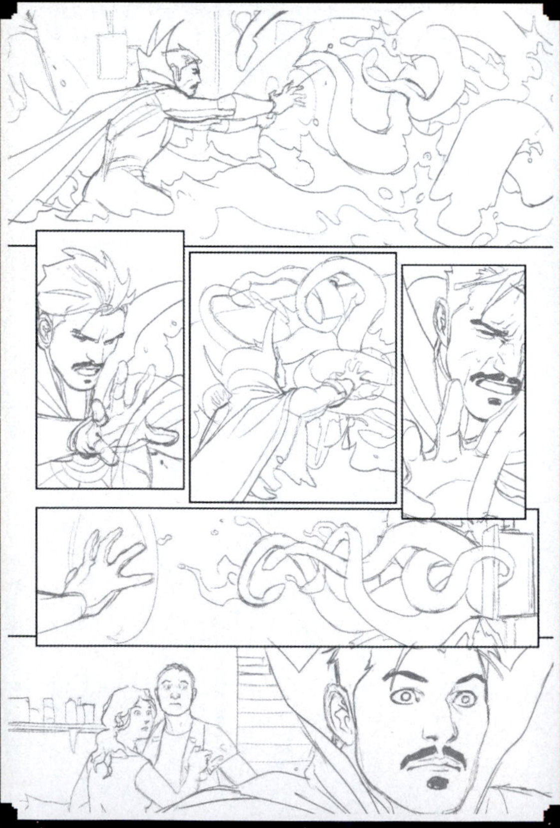

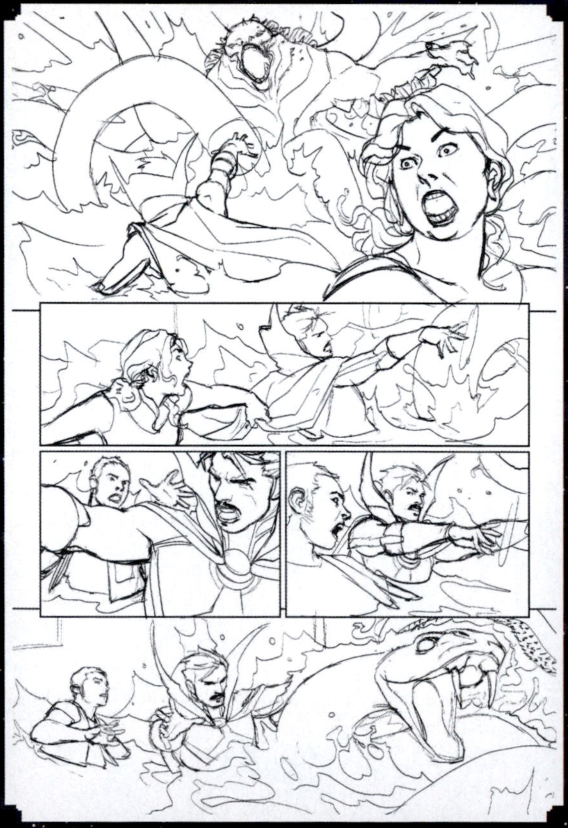

#18, PAGES 13-16 LAYOUTS BY

Jesús Saiz

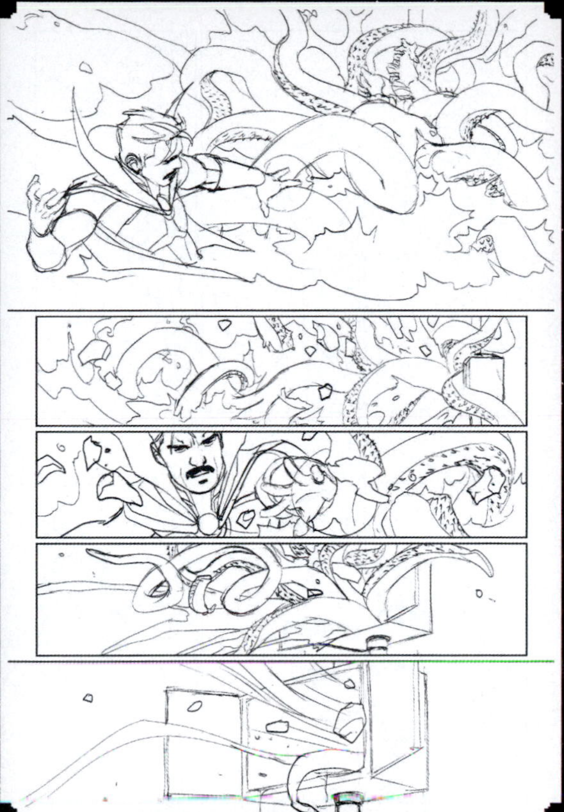

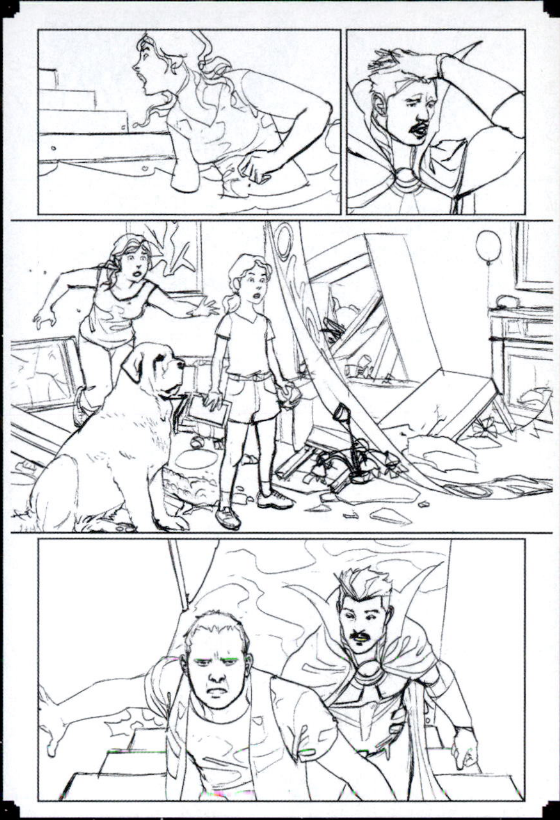

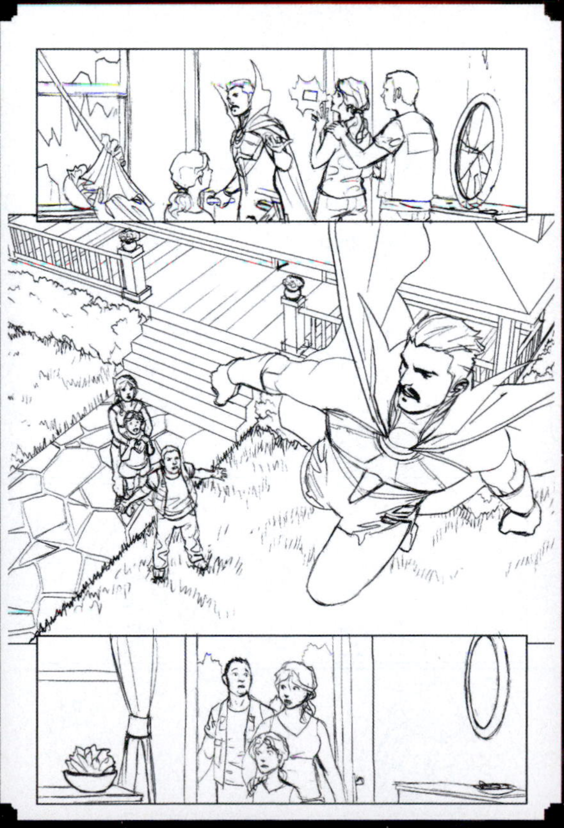

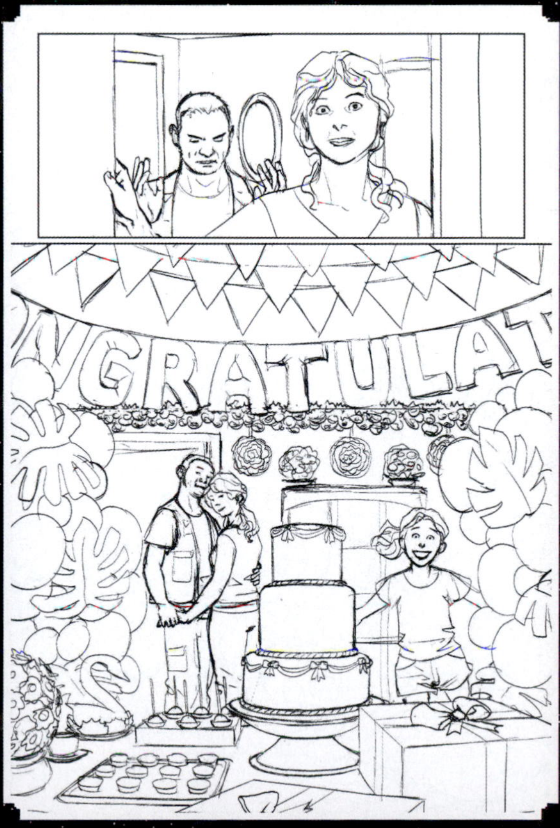
NGRATULAT

#18 , PAGES 17-20 LAYOUTS BY

Jesús Saiz

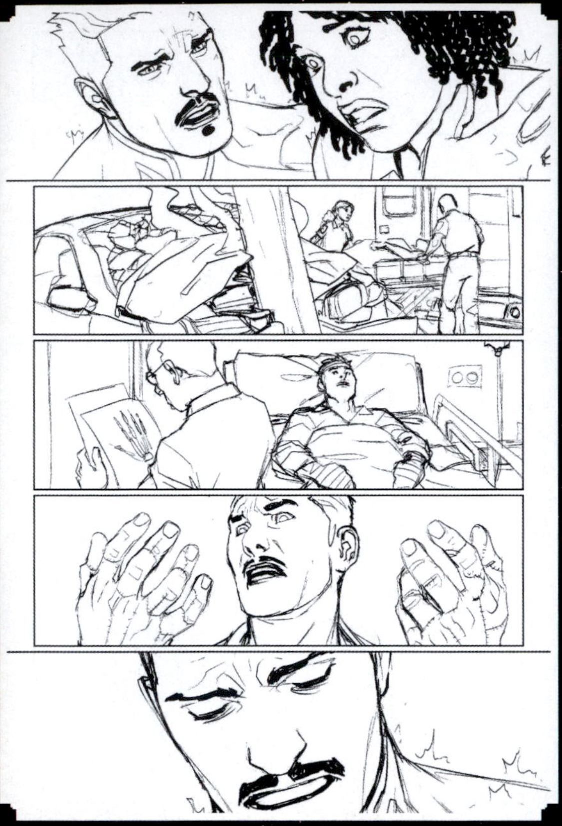
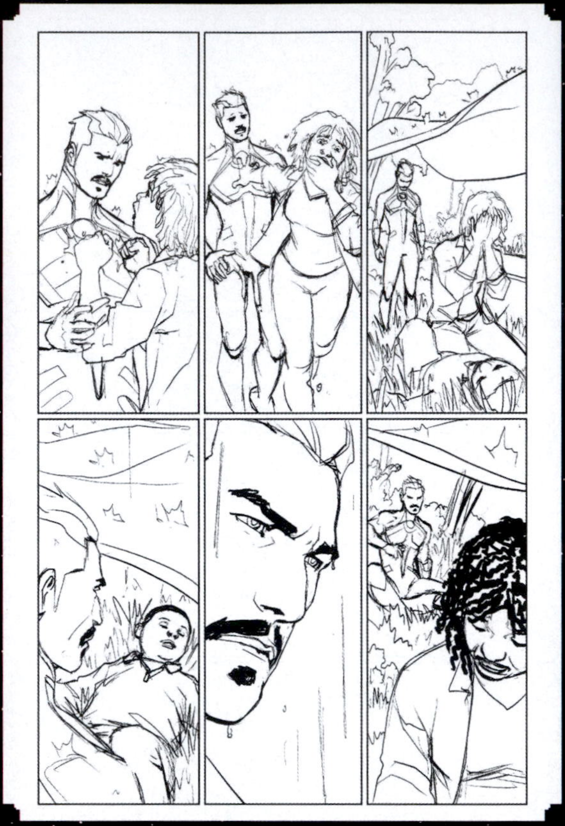
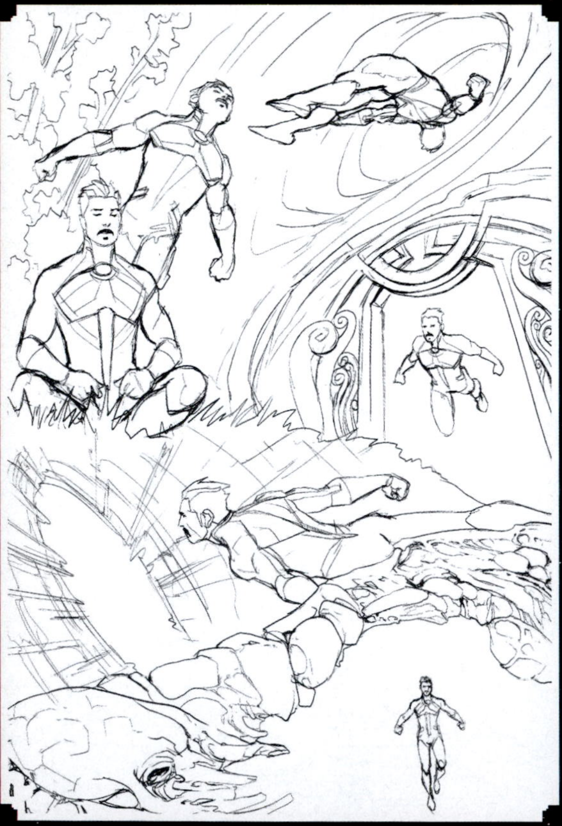
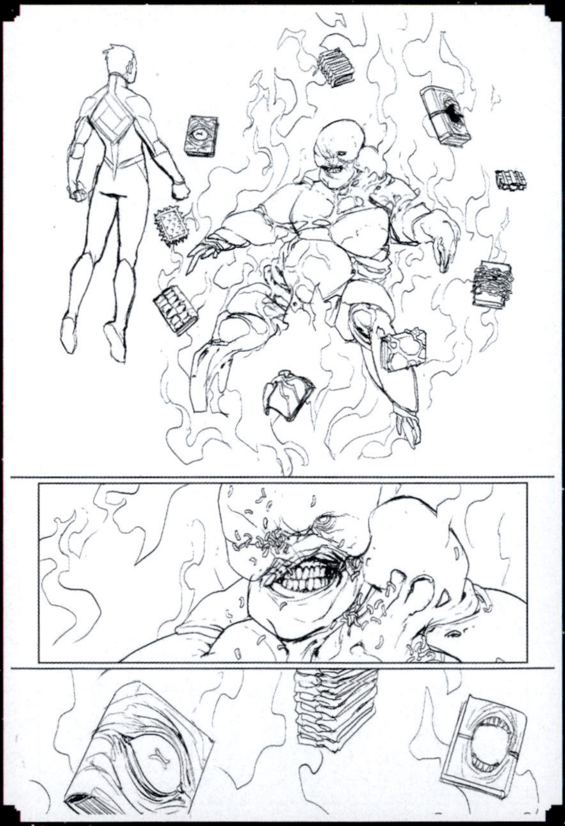

#1-9, PAGES 5-8 LAYOUTS BY

Jesús Saiz

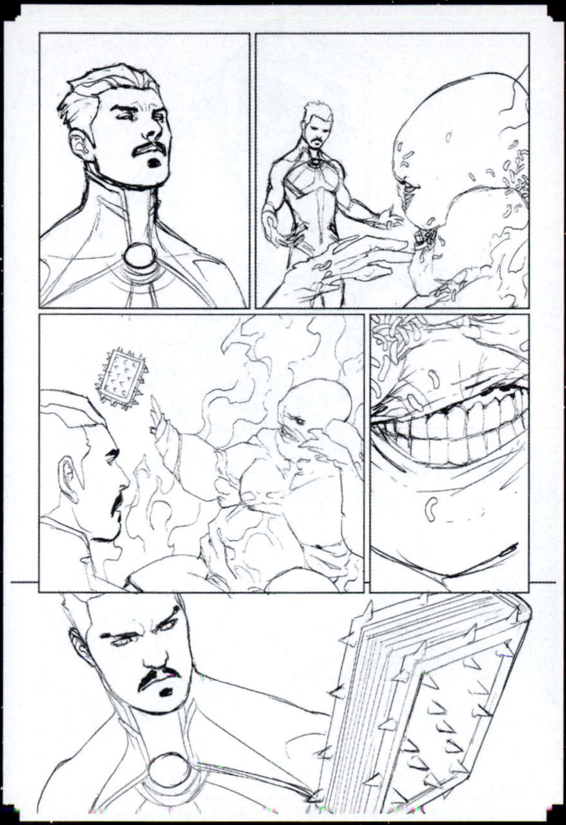

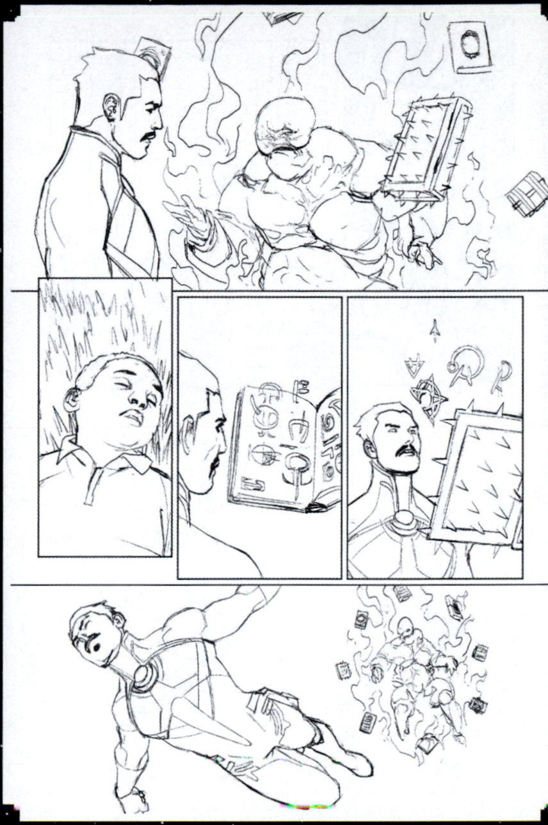

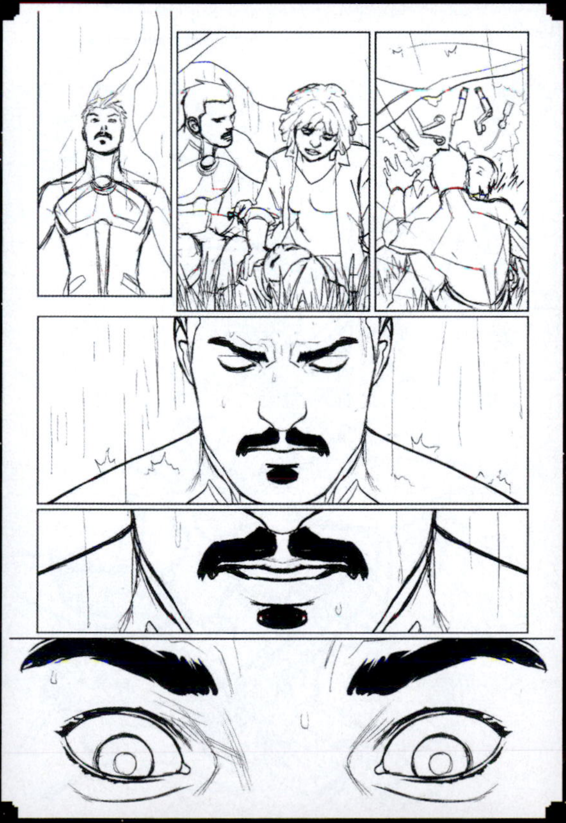

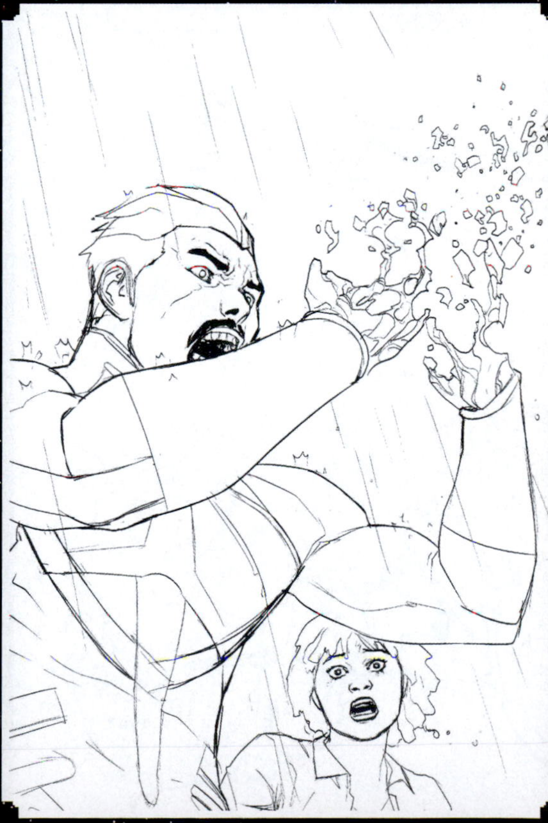

#19, PAGES 9-12 LAYOUTS BY

Jesús Saiz

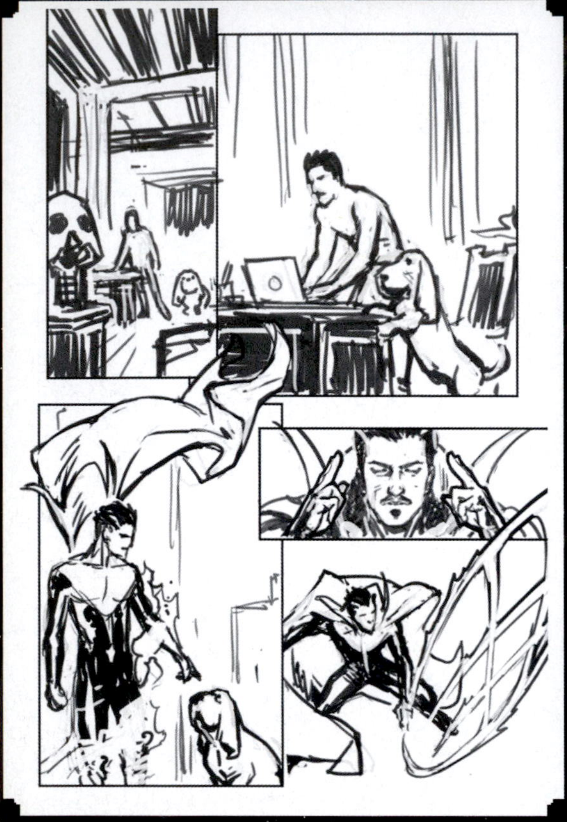
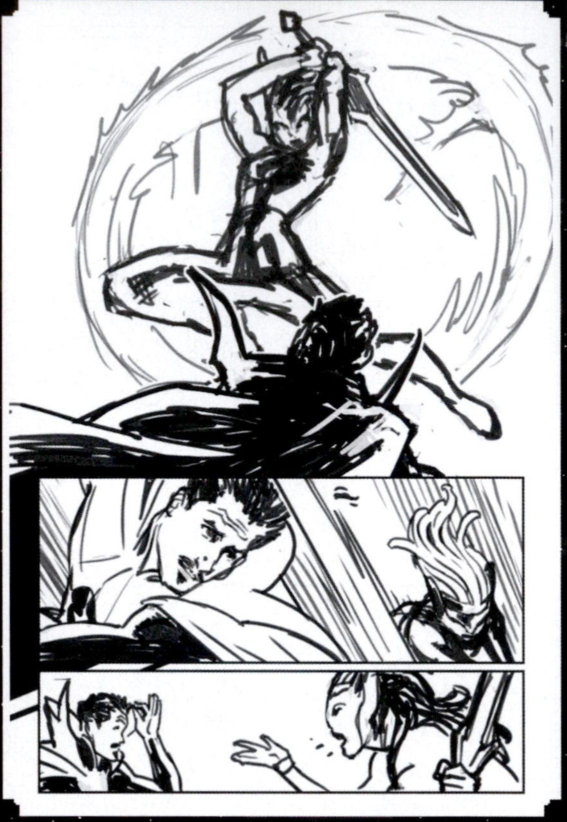
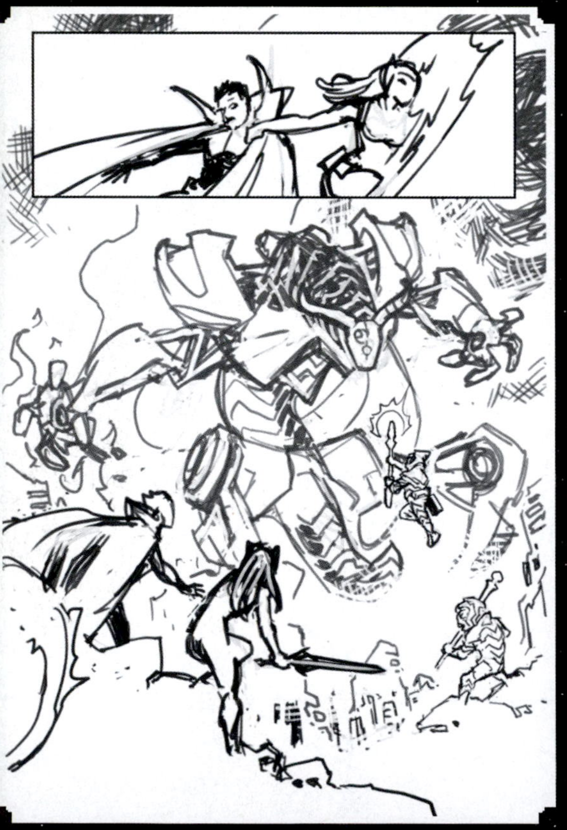
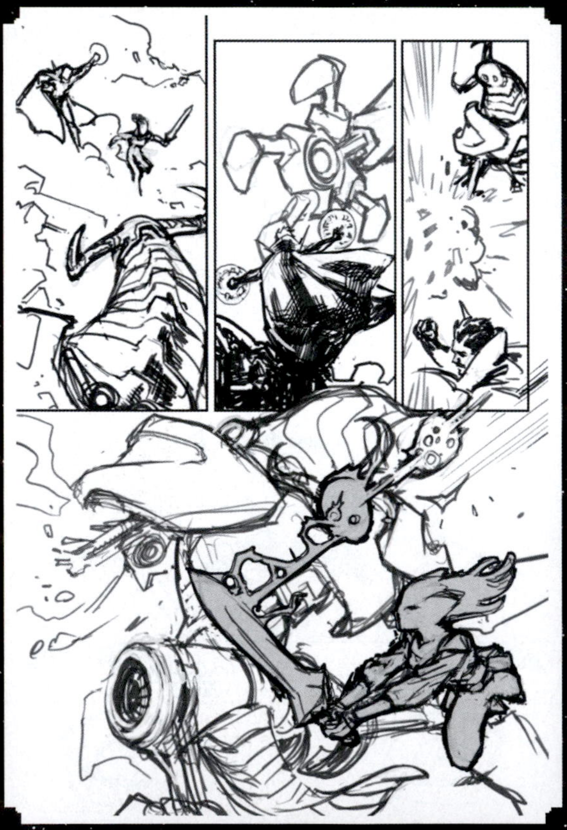

#20, PAGES 6-9 LAYOUTS BY

Javier Pina

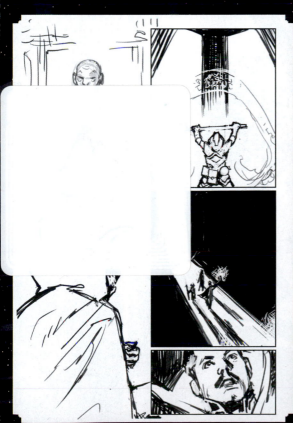

#20, PAGES 10-13 LAYOUTS BY

Javier Pina

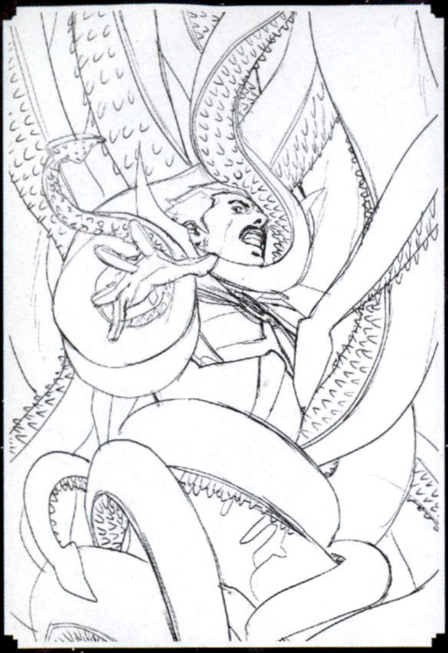

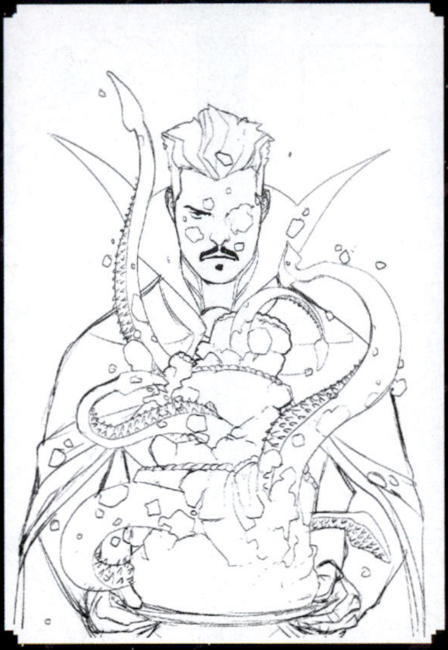

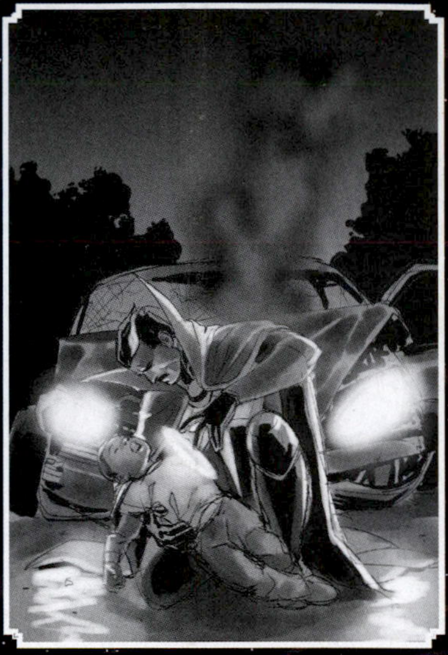

#18 AND #19 COVER SKETCHES BY

Jesús Saiz

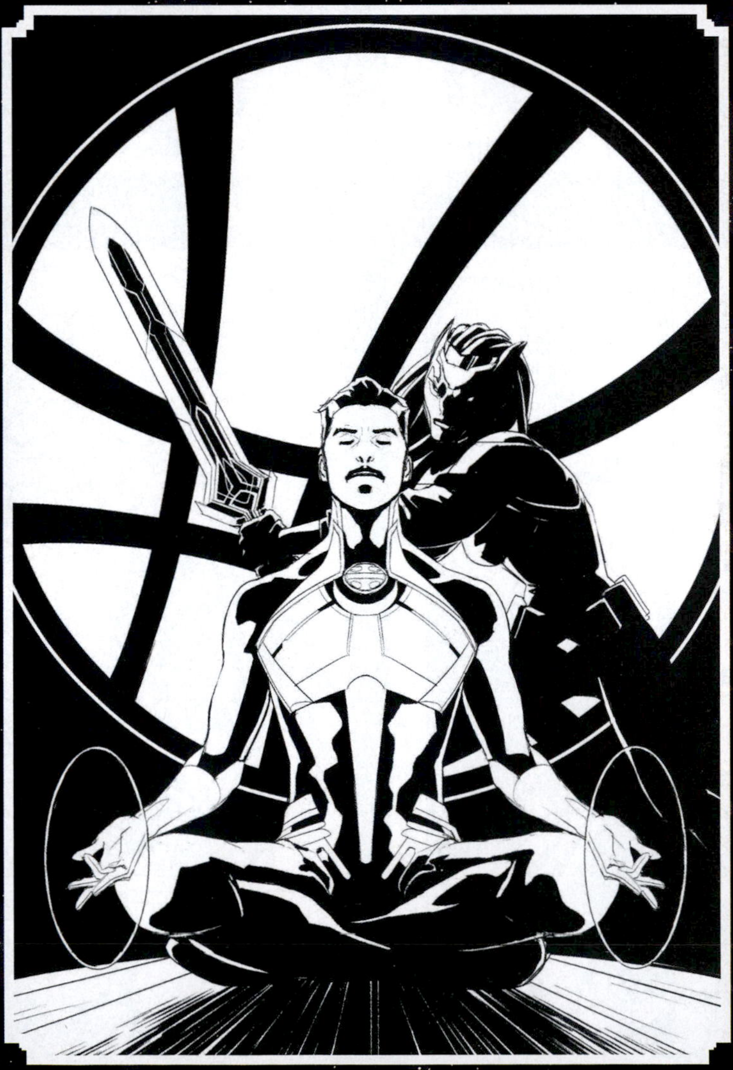

#20 COVER INKS BY

Jesús Saiz